BROTHERS

IN

ARMS

PETER DUFFY

BROTHERS

The True Story of Three Men

IN

Who Defied the Nazis, Saved 1,200 Jews,

ARMS

and Built a Village in the Forest

Published by Century in 2003

1 3 5 7 9 10 8 6 4 2

The author extends his grateful acknowledgment to YIVO Institute for Jewish
Research for permission to quote from the Yiddish-language autobiography
written by Tuvia Bielski, and to the University of Chicago Press for permission to
quote from *Forests: The Shadow of Civilization*, by Robert Pogue Harrison

First published in the USA in 2003 by HarperCollins, New York

The Random House Group Limited
20 Vauxhall Bridge Road, London SW1V 2SA

Random House Australia (Pty) Limited
20 Alfred Street, Milsons Point, Sydney,
New South Wales 2061, Australia

Random House New Zealand Limited
18 Poland Road, Glenfield
Auckland 10, New Zealand

Random House South Africa (Pty) Limited
Endulini, 5a Jubilee Road, Parktown 2193, South Africa

The Random House Group Limited Reg. No. 954009

www.randomhouse.co.uk

A CIP catalogue record for this book
is available from the British Library

Papers used by Random House are
natural, recyclable products made from wood grown in
sustainable forests. The manufacturing processes conform to
the environmental regulations of the country of origin

ISBN 0 7126 7696 1

Printed and bound in Great Britain by
Mackays of Chatham plc, Chatham, Kent

To my mother and my father

"There was something familiar about the forest, and in the worst case we could escape among the trees."

—Tuvia Bielski,
from an unpublished memoir, 1955

". . . [T]he forests were foris, 'outside.' In them lived the outcasts, the mad, the lovers, brigands, hermits, saints, lepers, the maquis, fugitives, misfits, the persecuted, wild men. Where else could they go? Outside of the law and human society one was in the forest. But the forest's asylum was unspeakable. One could not remain human in the forest; one could only rise above or sink below the human level."

—Robert Pogue Harrison,
from "Forests: The Shadow of
Civilization," 1992

"Compared to the ghettos, it felt like heaven. In the woods, we were free. That's all I can tell you. We had freedom."

—Charles Bedzow

PROLOGUE

"I will be famous when I'm dead."
—Tuvia Bielski

THREE MEN, BROTHERS, saved as many Jews during World War II as Oskar Schindler, and organized a military force that killed hundreds of enemy soldiers, nearly as many as did the fighters of the Warsaw ghetto uprising. Their names were Tuvia, Asael, and Zus Bielski; and to the twelve hundred Jews who walked out of the Belorussian forests in July 1944, and to the several generations of offspring of those survivors, these men were legend, revered as heroes. But outside this core group, the men behind the largest and most successful Jewish fighting and rescue force of the war have gone almost entirely uncelebrated; in the sixty years since, only a few books have detailed their achievements and hardly a plaque bears their names.

I stumbled upon this story while conducting a random online search. A stray reference to "Forest Jews" stirred my curiosity and led me down a path that would consume me for three years to come—a path that gave me a remarkable opportunity to gather the firsthand stories of Holocaust survivors, in a few cases just months and even weeks before they died.

And so, after dozens of interviews during which I heard stories about life in the forests of current-day western Belarus, where the Bielskis' stand against the Germans resulted in the creation of a village with makeshift workshops and primitive dwellings, I found myself, on June 27, 2001, standing at the edge of the largest of these forests. Guided by an elderly Polish woman named Leokadia Lankovich, I had a chance to imagine what it must have been like.

But nothing about the Naliboki Puscha—*puscha* is a word common to the Polish, Russian, Belorussian, and Ukrainian languages that means "dense forest"—indicated that it had been host to anything out of the ordinary. It looked like any forest in any country. Yet some of the most extraordinary acts of wartime courage and ingenuity occurred among these pine and fir trees.

The Bielski group contained an astonishing eight hundred Jews when it reached these woods in the summer of 1943. More than a year earlier, the brothers had established a forest base, populated by several relatives, in the woods near the Bielski family homestead. The oldest and wisest of the three, Tuvia, had insisted that the group be open to all Jews, no matter whether they were young or old, healthy or sick, soldier or invalid. "I would rather save one old Jewish woman," he would say, "than kill ten German soldiers." Slowly more people arrived, often rescued from the ghettos by Bielski fighters, until the unit was a huge collection of escapees moving from forest to forest one step ahead of the Germans.

In August 1943, Hitler sent his most ferocious and lawless troops into this *puscha*, with the intent to kill every member of the Bielski group. In a desperate bid for survival, the brothers led all eight hundred members through miles of *puscha* swamps as gunfire whistled past their heads and shouts of enemy soldiers filled their ears. They finally reached an isolated island in the very heart of the great forest, where they lived, in silence and without food, until the Nazis gave up their hunt. Not a single person was lost. It was an escape of breathtaking audacity.

Afterward, the three brothers identified a secure, dry spot in the *puscha*, where they directed the construction of a miniature city. It had living quarters; workshops for tailors, shoemakers, seamstresses, and carpenters; a large herd of cows and horses; a school for sixty children; a main street and a central square; a musical and dramatic theater; and a tannery that doubled as a synagogue. To the weary Jews who had narrowly escaped death by fleeing ghettos and labor camps, it was like a vision from another world, an astonishing place where Jews lived in freedom in the heart of Nazi-dominated Europe.

Ms. Lankovich, a squat Polish woman with an infectious laugh and a tendency for nonstop chatter, promised to show me to the exact location of the Jewish village. After we bumped along a road leading into the heart of the woods, she ordered the driver to stop his Russian military-style jeep. "This was the area," she said, hopping from the vehicle and pointing to the trees surrounding the truck.

Despite her age, Ms. Lankovich, as if energized by memory, began walking through the thick foliage so quickly it was difficult to keep up. "Here was one of the spots where they had a shelter," said Ms. Lankovich, pointing at a small pit filled with rainwater. It looked no different from any other hole in the woods. But Ms. Lankovich was insistent.

She pushed branches from her face as she moved forward, stopping momentarily to pick berries and point out evidence of more Bielski living quarters. And she kept talking. "When I would come to the camp, I couldn't just walk around wherever I wanted. The guards stopped me. I would tell them that I wanted to see a friend of mine named Sulia. Then they sent somebody and Sulia would come and take me into the camp.

"It was beautiful," she said. "It was like Minsk."

I tried to picture how these woods had looked more than half a century ago. What was it like in the bustling kitchen, which was watched over, I had been told, by a blunt man with a perpetually bloody apron who frenetically stirred a series of pots with a long wooden spoon? What did people talk about in the living quarters, the earthen dugouts covered with wooden roofs that were often occupied by people from the same village or who worked in the same profession? How did the gunsmith, whose pounding hammer could be heard all day long, manage to repair nearly destroyed rifles recovered from the countryside? After so many years of continuous growth of vegetation, it was hard to spot evidence of the brothers' base.

Similarly, the brothers themselves seemed to disappear after the war. Asael joined the Red Army and was killed fighting Nazis in East Prussia just seven months after leaving the forest. Tuvia and Zus moved to Israel, where they worked a variety of manual jobs. By the middle of the 1950s, both were living in a middle-class neighborhood of Brooklyn, New York, raising families with wives they had met while commanding their forest troops. Zus was more successful, eventually owning a small trucking and taxi company, while Tuvia, the great commander who rode a white horse, had a harder time of it. He drove a delivery truck and struggled to keep food on the table for his family. Tuvia passed away in 1987, Zus in 1995. They were forgotten men, average immigrant Americans trying to provide a solid future for their children.

In search of their fast-disappearing tale, I sought out each of the brothers' widows, proud guardians of their husbands' memories, and the fourth brother, Aron (Bielski) Bell, who was a plucky, twelve-year-old forest scout during the war years. I interviewed more than fifty survivors from the brothers' camps and mined every document, memoir, and photograph I could find that pertained to the forest experience. I spoke with gentile partisans and peasants, some of them allies of the brothers, some of them enemies. I discovered a book-length manuscript written by Tuvia Bielski, never translated into English and unknown to even his family.

It was stirring journey that turned me from a dispassionate outsider to someone with a deep personal connection to this community, its history, and its membership. So much so that, as the great survivors finally met their inevitable ends, I felt great sadness, not because they were important sources but because I had come to know them as friends.

And so I felt honored, and a bit undeserving, as I stood in the huge *puscha* at the site of the Bielski brothers' greatest triumph, one of the most sacred spots of World War II—a place not of Jewish death but of Jewish life. When I closed my eyes and listened to the voices of the survivors, I could almost see the place that so many of them came to call Jerusalem.

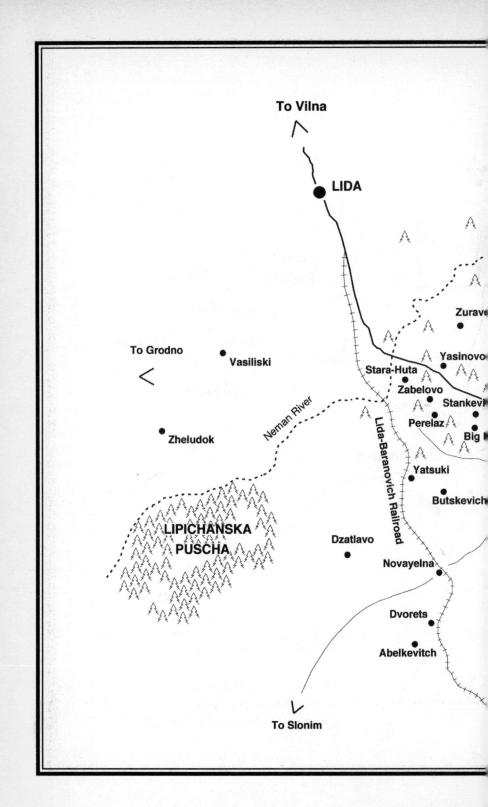

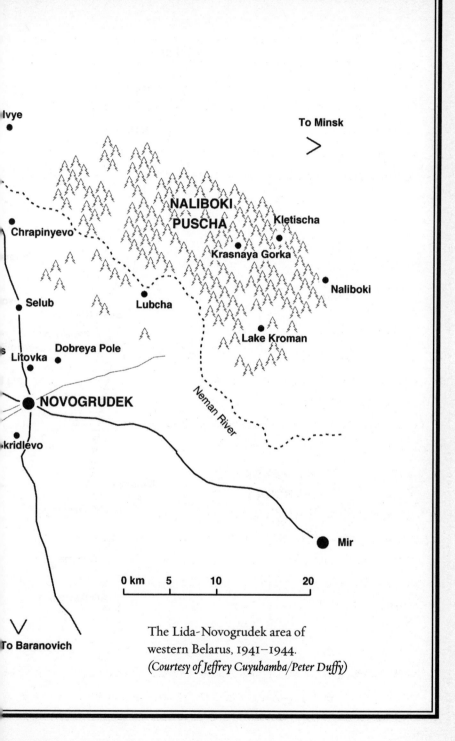

Ivye

To Minsk

NALIBOKI
PUSCHA

Kletischa

Chrapinyevo

Krasnaya Gorka

Naliboki

Selub

Lubcha

Lake Kroman

Litovka

Dobreya Pole

Neman River

NOVOGRUDEK

kridlevo

Mir

0 km   5   10   20

To Baranovich

The Lida-Novogrudek area of
western Belarus, 1941–1944.
(Courtesy of Jeffrey Cuyubamba/Peter Duffy)

BROTHERS

IN

ARMS

ONE

FROM THE TSAR TO THE FÜHRER

IN THE LATER YEARS of the 1800s, Elisheva and Zusya Bielski, the grandparents of Tuvia, Asael, and Zus, settled on a plot of farmland in the tiny village of Stankevich in the Belorussian region of tsarist Russia. It was less a village than a collection of a dozen or so wooden homes on the crest of a hill in one of the poorest, most backward corners of Europe. The Bielski home stood separate from the main section of the community, positioned down the slope and on the other side of a small lake fed by a river. And outsiders they were: The Bielskis were the only Jews in town.

The family's property, leased to them by a hard-luck Polish nobleman with a fondness for drinking and gambling, had a water-powered mill and two stables. Soon after arriving in the village in a horse-drawn cart, Zusya and his youngest son, David, started a business turning grains into flours and cereals.

Elisheva and Zusya's other children were married and living in cities, as were most of the Jews residing within the pale of settlement, the huge swath of territory from the Baltic to the Black Sea, where the tsar had ordered all Jews to live. They were subject to a startling number of discriminatory and ever-changing decrees within this large ghetto, forced to pay all manner of onerous taxes, prevented from speaking their native Yiddish language in public, and forbidden from serving in even minor civil-service posts. Tsarist restrictions also made it hard for Jews to live in rural areas, but Elisheva and Zusya were long accustomed to working the land away from population centers.

Not long after the family arrived in Stankevich, the tsar issued another string of anti-Jewish decrees, including one that made it illegal for Jews to buy, sell, manage, or lease rural property. The aging couple was greatly distressed by the order, worried that they would soon be expelled from their home.

But with the resilience that was necessary for a Jew to survive under the tsar, David came up with a way to keep the family in Stankevich. He negotiated a deal with one of the neighbors, a Polish man named Kushel, transferring the property's deed into the gentile's name. The man agreed that his involvement in Bielski affairs would remain in name only, and the arrangement enabled the Bielski family to stay in business. But the stress of the situation added to the miseries of Elisheva, who was suffering from a succession of ailments. David arranged for his mother to see several doctors, but to no avail. She died in a hospital in Vilna, the Lithuanian capital to the north.

By the turn of the century, young David was ready to start a family of his own. He married Beyle Mendelavich, the daughter of a shopkeeper from nearby Petrevich, and he settled into a miller's life, content to follow the path of his aging father, who was himself content to watch the arrival of a new generation. By the time old Zusya died in 1912, Beyle had produced four children—Velvel, Tuvia, Taibe, and Asael—and had another on the way. In honor of David's father, the next child, a son, was named Zusya and was known variously as Zusya, Zissel, or Zus.

The children were born into a simple peasant life long before the arrival of electricity or running water in a Belarus region that had for centuries been dominated by its larger neighbors of Russia, Poland, and Lithuania. It was a world of primitive wooden homes topped with roofs of straw, where a peasant's most valued possession was his horse and four-wheeled wooden cart. As the years passed, the family acquired farm animals of every variety, including a few horses, several cows, and some sheep; all the food they ate was produced by their own labor. The parents had their own room, while the children shared the remaining space, sleeping several in the same bed, or, in the summer, tired after a long day of work, on straw in the barn.

The extent of the children's education varied, but most didn't get very far in religious or secular schools. David at times would hire a teacher to come to the house. At other times, a child was sent to live with a relative in Novogrudek, the nearest city with a sizable Jewish population, to be educated in its local schools. The closest synagogue was also located in the city, a fifteen-kilometer trip that took three hours by horse and cart, making it difficult for the family to regularly attend services. Instead, a private home served as their house of worship. On the Sabbath and high holy days, the Bielskis visited the home of the Dziencielski family, who lived two kilometers through a path in the woods in the village of Big Izvah. Like the Bielskis, the Dziencielskis operated a mill and were the only Jews in their town.

David would sometimes lead the congregation in prayer, using a Torah scroll that was kept in the Dziencielski house. He didn't have much in the way of education, but he had a melodious voice and a strong grasp of the holy texts.

The children learned the local languages—Belorussian, Russian, and Polish—with a fluency that often eluded most Belorussian Jews who dwelled in Jewish neighborhoods in the cities. David's business required the family to come into constant contact with its neighbors, Orthodox Christian Belorussians and Catholic Poles. Fully aware that he was an isolated Jew living through a time when anti-Jewish violence was a fact of life, he developed a conciliatory nature that sought peace over confrontation.

When officials from the tsarist government arrived and announced that they suspected the family of managing the land in violation of the tsar's order, David and Beyle offered them a seat at their table. The couple plied the officials with food and liquor, until they stumbled out of the house after drinking themselves into a stupor. The tsar's men didn't file a report. When bandits came demanding money or goods, the couple treated them with similar kindness, bringing out a special batch of vodka.

David Bielski was not a fighter.

During the first year of World War I, when the children were still small—too young to be drafted into the imperial army—the German army launched its forces against the Russian empire. It was an auspicious beginning to a tumultuous six years for the people of the Bielskis' district. The invading army, like so many armies before it, took the shortest route to the Russian capital, directly through the heart of Belarus. The region around Stankevich was transformed into an occupation zone during the summer offensive of 1915.

The Germans were less harsh to the Jewish population than the Romanovs had been. The Russian ruler, now Nicholas II, had ordered the expulsion of some half-million Jews from his lands because he doubted their loyalty. The occupiers offered a more temperate style of leadership, repealing anti-Jewish measures and even issuing a proclamation of friendship.

Not far from the Bielski home, a group of German soldiers turned a large abandoned house into a military outpost. Barely ten years old, young Tuvia showed little interest in his schooling; instead he befriended the men and was soon wandering over every day. Warming to the youngster, the Germans gave him cigarettes for his father and occasionally offered him a piece of venison. "I didn't ask if this was kosher or non-kosher," he said. "This was war." His visits lasted for two years, long enough for him to gain a firm grasp of the German language.

The Great War brought disruption and hardship to the entire Russian empire on a massive scale. Industrial workers barely survived on pitiful wages, soldiers deserted in the face of the bloody fighting, and peasants could scarcely feed themselves. The winter of 1916, one of the harshest in Russian history, added to the general misery. Yet because of the old mill, the Bielski family was able to ride out the deprivations. Customers still required their grain to be ground into flour or their rye to be churned into meal. Often the peasants paid with the only thing they had: grain or rye or corn. No matter what happened, the Bielskis would always be able to eat.

The hardships of the sprawling empire eventually led to civil unrest, vaulting the country into greater turmoil. In February 1917, the tsar abdicated and a provisional government, which promised democratic reforms, was established. But it didn't do much better than its predecessor. On October 25 (November 7 on the modern calendar), the Bolsheviks, led by forty-seven-year-old political agitator Vladimir I. Ulyanov, who took the name Lenin, overthrew the tottering provisional government. Lenin set about establishing his long-sought-after dictatorship of the proletariat.

Unable to devote much energy to the fight with the Germans, the Bolsheviks sued for peace. In the Treaty of Brest-Litovsk, signed on March 3, 1918, Lenin ceded Belarus to a newly established, German-controlled Polish government. But political leaders in Minsk ignored the treaty and on March 25, 1918, quickly declared a "free and independent state." For the first time in history a nation bore the name Belarus. But the country existed just long enough, it seems, for its leaders to pose for photographs. When the allies vanquished Germany later in the year, Lenin ignored both the treaty and Belarus's declaration of independence. The country was incorporated into the fledgling Soviet Union in January 1919.

Not so fast, said the Poles, who were building an independent state out of the wreckage of war after more than a hundred years of nonexistence.

"Drunk with the new wine of liberty"—in the words of one statesman—the Poles wanted Belarus, along with Lithuania, Galicia, and the Ukraine, to bolster the country's eastern borders, all lands that in previous centuries had been part of Poland. Belarus had long been home to a wealthy Polish landlord class, the estate-owning nobility of the poor country, and they wanted their dominion restored.

Led by Marshal Jozef Pilsudski, who'd spent the end of the Great War in a German prison because he refused to pledge loyalty to the kaiser, Polish troops marched into Belarus and parts of

Lithuania in 1919 and early 1920. They had little difficulty occupying the region, largely because much of the Red Army was busy fighting a civil war farther to the east. The Poles took Minsk, Belarus's capital, in August 1919.

The Polish-Soviet War was fought across territories with large populations of Jews. Most remained neutral, which angered the Poles, and they responded with anti-Semitic attacks in several cities. The Bielski family also tried to avoid taking sides, even as battles raged around their village of Stankevich. The Bolsheviks commandeered a horse and cart owned by the family. Determined not to let the property be lost, Tuvia, then a young teenager, worked for six weeks as a Polish translator with the Russians, before returning home to Stankevich with the family's horse and cart.

With success in the north, Pilsudski's legions, as they were called, marched south, taking Kiev in the Ukraine in May 1920. But the Red Army, now victorious in the civil war, marshaled its forces and launched a counterattack. Held by the Poles for less than a month, Kiev was retaken by the onrushing Bolsheviks, who within six weeks had pushed all the way to the gates of Warsaw. Lenin was impatient to spread revolution and introduce communism to Central Europe. But Pilsudski wasn't finished yet. His resurgent troops attacked the Red Army from the south, inflicting enough damage to force Lenin to the negotiation table, in a triumph that the Poles came to call "the miracle on the Vistula."

After many months of negotiation, the Treaty of Riga was signed on March 18, 1921. The agreement gave the western portion of Belarus, including the small village where the Bielskis lived, to the newly instituted Second Republic of Poland.

It was a strange time, during which Stankevich felt a long way from the tumult. Telegraph connections between even major cities were hard to establish, and newspapers that reached the country-side were cut up and used as cigarette paper. The Bielskis were iso-lated, but what did they need to know? The new rulers, like the old rulers, were bound to regard them with callousness and suspicion.

During these years of war, David Bielski was able to end his "partnership" with his Polish neighbor Kushel and put the property in his own name. He expanded his business with the help of his wife and children, and he traveled to the regional cities of Novo-grudek and Lida, thirty kilometers to the northwest, to deliver goods to customers. The peasant neighbors were impressed with his industry, and many of them came to regard the family as well off. It wasn't as though the family was actually wealthy—its luxu-ries were few—but they were considerably better off than the dirt-poor folk of their environs.

"We had a small mill in our village, but it wasn't like theirs," said Maria Nestor, a Belorussian woman who was born in 1911 and grew up near Stankevich. "They had a real mill, and it was very popular."

Beyle Bielski, a hearty woman who was more blunt and out-going than her husband, continued to produce children at a steady pace. Four more were born between 1912 and 1921, three boys, one of whom died soon after birth, and a girl, the couple's second.

The older children had reached their teenage years. The eldest, Velvel, was proving to be a serious-minded young man interested in his studies, while Tuvia, born in 1906, was revealing a more adventurous and combative nature. Unlike his father, he wasn't willing to shrug off the slights of rough peasants who liked nothing better than to torment those who revealed weakness.

After some local farmers stole a portion of Bielski hay, a determined Tuvia confronted the men about the theft. "Run home," a peasant said, "or I'll give you a beating."

The teenager walked back to the house—"I was alone and didn't want to make a scene"—and told Velvel about the man's threat. His older brother just shrugged. But Tuvia's two younger brothers, Asael, two years his junior, and Zus, six years younger, were incensed by the story, and the three resolved to settle the score.

They armed themselves with scythes and walked toward the enemies of the family. Following a heated exchange, one of the brothers swung at a peasant with the scythe's blade. The blow missed, in part because it so intimidated the man that he turned tail and fled, followed quickly by his friends.

Later, when a peasant who rented a part of the family's field was also discovered to be expropriating Bielski hay, Tuvia again set out to rectify the situation. Armed again with a scythe, the teenager approached the thief, who was similarly armed, and four of the man's friends. "Get away from here or I'll kill you," the peasant screamed.

Tuvia ignored the threat and knocked him to the ground, where he pummeled him with his fists.

The peasant's four pals laughed aloud at the sight of their beaten friend. "A young Jew has done away with a scoundrel who the whole village was afraid of," said one of them.

From that day forward, the Bielski hay was safe. Tuvia now had a reputation for ferocity—and the first glimmer of what he would later call "Jewish pride" had revealed itself.

The new government of the Bielskis' region wasn't particularly kind to its Jewish residents, with institutional anti-Semitism remaining a fact of life. There was punitive taxation and restrictions on professional service. A strict quota system limited the entry of most Jews into Polish universities, and the ones who did make it were forced to sit on so-called ghetto benches in lecture halls. (Many of them stood in protest instead.) Jewish craftsmen, who made up most of the country's artisans, were forced to pass a discriminatory Polish-language competency test, even though Yiddish was their primary and often only language.

But in some ways life was better than with the tsar. Jewish political, cultural, religious, and educational organizations were allowed greater freedoms than under the despot. And they flourished in Novogrudek, called Navaredok by its Jewish residents, which had been home to a Jewish community since the sixteenth century.

The Jewish population weathered countless trials over its long history, including an effort in the mid-1500s by the Lithuanian king, then the ruler of the country, to have its Jewish Novogrudekers herded into a ghetto. They were also subject to the whims of the successive waves of invading armies—after the outbreak of the Russian-Polish war in 1655, Novogrudek was occupied and reoccupied by each army twice over the course of four years, and each was only too happy to maraud and pillage.

By the eighteenth century, during a period of Polish rule, the poverty of the Jewish population was worsened by efforts of local officials to prevent them from participating in the city's economic life. The arrival of the tsar in 1795 brought further trials. Still, the community grew in size and served as the base for several highly respected rabbinical figures. Among them was Rabbi Yechiel Michel Epstein, an author of texts on Jewish law, considered one of Russia's greatest rabbis. Wearing his satin coat and broad-brimmed hat trimmed with fur, Rabbi Epstein exuded the stately grace of a monarch as he departed his synagogue after Sabbath services followed by the members of his congregation. "My heart would swell with pride whenever I beheld him," a contemporary wrote.

In 1896, Rabbi Joseph Yozel Horowitz, one of the leaders of an Orthodox movement that placed an emphasis on ethical behavior, opened a yeshiva in Novogrudek. Reb Yozel, as he was known, developed what's known as the "Navaredok school" of the Musar Movement. Along with devoted study of texts, his pupils were instructed to place themselves in uncomfortable public situations—to walk among well-dressed people in rags, to board a train without any money for fare, to act oddly during a street-corner conversation—in an attempt to develop a serene ability to ignore ridicule. If they could lose their attachments to vanity and pride, he felt, they would be in a better position to advocate more forcefully for their vision of Judaism.

Reb Yozel's students were so dedicated that they could be heard chanting the sacred texts until the early hours of the morning.

By the time the Bielski children were visiting the city a decade or so later, more than half of its population and a majority of Novogrudek's tradesmen, craftsmen, and shop owners were Jewish. Their businesses were located around the marketplace, the cobblestone square in the center of the city, on one of its highest points, not far from the ruins of a centuries-old castle, Novogrudek's most recognizable landmark. (The seven-towered structure had withstood raids from Teutonic knights and Tatars throughout its history, but invading Swedes mostly destroyed it in 1706.) During market days, held on Monday and Thursday,

Jews and gentiles from throughout the region trekked up the several roads that lead from all directions to the marketplace to buy
and sell a rich assortment of goods.

"The farmers used to bring their butter, potatoes, flour, vegetables, and fruits," said Sonya Oshman, a native of the city.
"Whatever the ground would give. It was a plain gathering of people. Homemakers and farmers. Mostly you saw the women,
because it was during the day and the men would be off working."

"As kids we loved it," said Morris Schuster, who was also born
in Novogrudek. "It was a beautiful thing. The foods were so natural—raspberries, strawberries, and blackberries. They picked them
in the forest. Nothing was artificial. Oh, the butter! The bread!"

Most of the city's homes were dank, single-story structures
illuminated by candles or oil lamps and heated during cold winter nights by large wood-burning stoves. Residents obtained
water from wells placed throughout the town, often delivered by
a water carrier with a sturdy back. The lack of indoor plumbing
meant that outhouses were a necessary feature of every family's
property.

When the Poles resumed their rule in 1921, the city boasted
several synagogues, most located just off the marketplace in what
was known as Synagogue Square. Butchers, tailors, cobblers, and
small businessmen each had their own shul and adjoining house
of study. The largest was the Old Synagogue, which could hold
several hundred people, although it offered services only on the
Sabbath. The building, also known as the Cold Synagogue
because it was unheated, was believed to be frequented by ghosts.
Children were afraid to pass by at night. Each morning the cus-
todian would knock on the door three times before announcing
in a loud voice, "Go to your rest, you dead ones!"

The new government's tolerance of Jewish expression was a boon to Zionism, the increasingly influential movement that advocated Jewish return to the Land of Israel. The local Zionists were split into several factions, many of which had affiliated youth groups. There were also a confusing assortment of religious parties, some of which opposed Zionism, and secular parties, some of which saw socialism as a better path to Jewish well-being.

The new freedoms led to the establishment of secular Jewish school systems, which quickly sprang up throughout the expanse of Poland. In Novogrudek, the most popular was the Tarbut school, which specialized in Zionist teaching conducted in Hebrew, the sacred tongue then being transformed into an everyday language. Many young Jews also attended the Polish public schools, which, unlike the Jewish secular and religious schools, did not charge tuition. A smaller group attended the exclusive public secondary school, which was named for Novogrudek's most esteemed son, the great Polish poet Adam Mickiewicz, and where students wore neat black uniforms with badges on the right sleeves.

The greater freedoms, however, didn't translate into a higher standard of living. When Polish authorities lessened travel restrictions in the early 1920s, foreigners were given the opportunity to visit the city and many were shocked by the poverty they encountered. Native Novogrudekers living in faraway places resolved to help. Novogrudek-born Alexander Harkavy, a New York writer and linguist who translated *Don Quixote* and other works of classic literature into Yiddish, organized an effort through the Novogrudeker Synagogue on the Lower East Side of Manhattan, which served four thousand expatriated Novogrudek Jews. He urged donations for the "unfortunate, impoverished, persecuted, and oppressed" of their native city. In the end, more than $40,000 was raised, which helped establish a number of institutions in the city, including an orphanage, a soup kitchen, and a library.

The city of some ten thousand residents was also populated with Poles, who constituted the ruling, land-owning class (many of them had moved into the area in a government-initiated attempt to increase the Polish population), working-class Belorussians, and a few hundred Muslim Tatars. Despite the sizable gentile population, Novogrudek was a bustling center of Jewish life in the 1920s and 1930s, indeed throughout much of its history. As one former resident remembered it, everything was quiet on the Sabbath. Even the gentiles knew not to disturb the holy day.

Following the advent of the Polish state, Beyle gave birth to two more children, Yakov in 1924 and Aron in 1930, making a total of twelve, eleven of whom survived. The older children, when not occupied with duties at the mill, took advantage of the new opportunities in the city, where they were regarded as poor country folk by the comparatively better off city Jews. Zus attended the Tarbut school for five years and also sat in on a few gatherings of Betar, the youth group affiliated with the militant branch of the Zionist movement. Tuvia joined the Mizrachi organization, which was composed of religiously observant Zionists, and briefly considered leaving the country for Palestine. But when one of the Mizrachi members spotted him smoking a cigarette on the Sabbath, he was asked to stop attending meetings.

Indeed, despite a fierce pride in their Jewish identity, most of the children developed a less than reverential attitude toward religious observance. David and Beyle kept a kosher home, but the boys would often hide bacon in the stable and munch on it when the parents weren't around. One of David's older brothers, an ultra-Orthodox Jew, was aghast at how hard it was to distinguish the Bielskis from the peasant neighbors. "Give me one of the children and I'll make a real Jew out of him," he said. So David offered him one of the younger boys. The child, who was named Joshua, traveled with his uncle to Novogrudek, where he was given a thorough religious upbringing and sent to the finest rabbinical institutions. By the age of twenty-two, he was a rabbi.

In 1927, Tuvia, now twenty-one years old, over six feet tall, with dark good looks, was also ready to escape, eager to discover something of the world beyond the little village where he was born. He was drafted into the Polish Army and assigned to Warsaw, the cosmopolitan center of Polish life, where he served as a member of the 30th Infantry Battalion. Within six months he was performing so well, he was assigned to train new recruits.

In Warsaw, he also got a firsthand taste of the sort of anti-Semitism that he'd escaped in Stankevich. When he asked a cook if he could have a schmeer of chicken fat for his bread, the man responded: "Get out of here, you scabby Jew." Without a moment's thought, Tuvia grabbed the man with his right hand and pummeled him with his left. He shoved him against a table and grabbed a large knife—which, despite his anger, he refrained from using. Instead, he picked up a chair and smashed it across the cook's face.

After two weeks in the hospital, the cook was foolhardy enough to bait his attacker again. "Remember, Jew," he said, "I will catch you and I will kill you."

"If you give me such a warning again," Tuvia responded, "I will bury you alive, not dead."

The incident was subject to a thorough investigation. In explaining himself to a superior officer, Tuvia described his pride in serving in the army and defending his country. The cook's insult was directed not only at him, he said deftly, but at the Polish Army itself. "I am prepared to protect the honor of my uniform." No action was taken.

After two years of otherwise uneventful service, he returned home with the rank of corporal. He bided his time for a while before deciding to settle down. With the help of a matchmaker, he found a wife named Rivke and moved from Stankevich to the town of Subotniki, some fifty kilometers to the north. "Was she pretty? I will not lie," Tuvia said. "She was not too pretty." But her family ran a large, successful store, the biggest in the town, and Tuvia suddenly was a prominent businessman. Love was never part of the equation. "I was thinking about my own life," he admitted.

Like his army service, his marriage afforded him a chance to taste a wider world. He often traveled to Vilna, the great Jewish center regarded as the Jerusalem of Lithuania, to conduct business for the store. On one trip he bought a radio, the first in his town. The couple, regularly joined by their neighbors, listened to broadcasts from Moscow, Berlin, and Warsaw. Tuvia was a regular reader of several newspapers, in a variety of languages, and an engaging storyteller who used tales from Jewish scripture to illustrate current dilemmas. The handsome son of a humble miller— some called him the "Clark Gable of the Bielskis"—was developing an easy charisma, a curious mind, and a sophistication that belied his backwoods beginnings. He also had a sagelike air about him, a sense that he possessed deep wells of wisdom and thought deeply about the dilemmas of life. Anyone who met him invariably felt that he was bound for something greater than operating a store in a rural backwater.

By the early and middle 1930s, life back in Stankevich was changing. The Bielski family was doing well enough to hire a maid for the house and a man to help out at the mill. The mill worker was named Adolph Stishok, a blond-haired and -bearded Belorussian who over time picked up enough Yiddish to speak with his employers in their native language.

Tuvia was gone. Asael, the quiet brother who was two years younger than Tuvia, had a full hand in the business, which had expanded to include two additional mills in nearby villages; and his brash younger brother Zus, four years his junior, aided the day-to-day operations.

Their father, David, slowed into what today might be called semiretirement, and the villagers remember him walking with the aid of a cane. The other children were charting different courses for their lives. Velvel and another brother moved to America. One sister spent much of the year in school in Vilna. The younger children remained at home. They grew up in a household very different from that of their older siblings, particularly with the practical Asael taking on more of a leadership role in the family. He became something of a father figure to the kids, especially Aron, who was more than twenty years younger. When the boy ran away from school, he received a stern dose of discipline not from his father but from his older brother. Asael even acted in David's stead with the older children. When his sister Taibe announced her intention to marry a member of the Dziencielski family, the clan from nearby Big Izvah that had been the Bielskis' closest Jewish neighbors for decades, he negotiated the dowry with the groom's father.

To Aron, Asael was the father of the house—the one who took care of the fields, tended the farm animals, and hired the summer help. He was dedicated to his family in all ways.

Asael, whose thick black eyebrows anchored a broad forehead, also took responsibility for maintaining the family's finances, with an eye toward taking over the mill from his father. Without any bookkeeping education, he sought help from a teenage Dziencielski girl, Haya, who was whip-smart, politically active, and loquacious. While they worked together on matters of deficits and expenditures, Asael developed a crush on the girl, who was six years younger than he. But Haya was educated and sophisticated—indeed, she was a radical for her time, attracted by the ideas of the outlawed Communist Party—and Asael was, after all, a simple farmer.

"He fell in love with me but I was interested in someone else," said Haya, a dark-haired teen who was the youngest of eleven children. "There was a man in Novogrudek who was much more intelligent than Asael and he was a different class of person. I couldn't care less for Asael at the time. We grew up together, and I didn't think of him that way."

It wasn't as though he didn't have other options. Popular among the local girls, Asael was always eager to join in the local dances, where entertainment was sometimes provided by the Bielskis' hired hand, Adolph Stishok, a gifted accordion player. The gentile villagers remember that despite his reserved manner Asael was a spirited dancer who enjoyed having a good time. To the consternation of his parents, he had no compunction about having romantic flings with gentile girls.

If Asael was warmhearted and dedicated, Zus was flamboyant and pugnacious. He had a booming, low-pitched voice, a riotous laugh, and a strong singing voice, a legacy from his father, which he liked to employ after a few drinks. But, unlike his father, he was a fighter—when challenged, he threw punches first and asked questions later.

Tuvia's absence meant that Asael and Zus, who despite differences in temperament were close, were elevated to the position of principal defenders of the homestead. They saw the world in black and white terms—they were unwaveringly loyal to those who were their friends and unforgiving to those who were their enemies. Like their older brother, the two had no problem mixing it up with those who would trouble the family.

Once, a villager who had lent the family money arrived at the Bielski home half-drunk, demanding to be repaid. "If you don't give me the money now," he said to David, "I'll cut you to pieces." Zus, still in his teens, bounded in from the next room and grabbed the man, who was a renowned, and much older, troublemaker from Big Izvah. Only David's intervention prevented a fistfight. In another incident, Zus was arrested for punching a man who insulted him with an anti-Jewish slur in a grocery store. He compounded the trouble by threatening the arresting officer, saying, "If I hit you, you'll shit in your pants." The result was two weeks in jail, which he said wasn't too bad, because he played cards with others inmates all day.

Another man involved in a dispute with David threatened to damage the section of the mill that regulated the amount of water needed to turn the wheel. As he headed for the structure carrying an axe, Asael snuck up behind him and shoved him into the current, which pushed the man downstream. "No harm was done," said Aron, "except that he remembered until the end of his days never to start up with the Bielskis."

Gradually their reputation preceded them: Zus and Asael—

and by extension all the Bielskis—were not to be trifled with. "I grew up with gangsters," Zus later said. "I knew no better than them. If somebody attacks you, you hit back." There were even unfounded rumors that Asael and Zus had a killed a man.

As the 1930s wore on, the country's political stability fell on hard times. The increasingly authoritarian Polish government held rigged elections and suppressed political opposition. The Great Depression worsened the already woeful state of Poland's standard of living, which helped fuel an increase in political extremism. By the late 1930s, anti-Semitic attacks were on the rise. Nationalistic Poles periodically made appearances in the streets of Novogrudek, shouting slogans about deporting all Jews or urging a boycott of their businesses. Prior to Passover in 1939, a rumor went around the city that a pogrom was to be unleashed. Roving gangs did make an appearance, but the local police prevented any violence.

Things looked no better beyond Poland's boundaries. To the west, Hitler's Nazi Germany was consolidating its power and plotting world domination. To the east, the Soviet Union had devolved into a full-fledged dictatorship under the iron fist of Joseph Stalin, who had spent the previous decade ordering the imprisonment, torture, and execution of all manner of opponents (real and imagined) of the state. Although both leaders were wary of each other—Hitler regarded the defeat of Marxist Russia as one of his chief aims; Stalin loathed Nazi fascism and its tyrannical leader—they entered into a nonaggression pact in August 1939, a few months after Hitler had taken Czechoslovakia. Hitler wanted to keep Stalin from siding with his enemies, and the Soviet leader hoped to prevent a German invasion of his country.

Seven days after the pact was signed, on September 1, 1939, the Nazis—assured now that the Soviet Union would remain out of the fight—invaded the western portion of Poland, easily defeating the Polish army. The invasion led to declarations of war from Great Britain and France, making the brief battle for Poland the first skirmish of World War II. Then one million Soviet troops invaded Poland from the east, moving into the western portions of Belarus and the Ukraine, grabbing lands they had lost in the Polish-Soviet War of 1919–20. In the short operation, the Soviet Union snatched up 200,000 square kilometers of new territory and 13.5 million additional citizens, while losing only about seven hundred soldiers. Among the new residents of the USSR was the Bielski family of Stankevich.

In Novogrudek, the Jewish residents flocked into the streets to gaze at the Red Army's military hardware. "It was probably two weeks—day and night—that the Russians marched through our town," said Jack Kagan, a young boy at the time. "I had never seen so many tanks marching through Novogrudek. We thought they were so strong and that it would be impossible for them ever to retreat." In villages across Belarus, many Jews welcomed the troops with flowers, kisses, and applause, happy to be rid of their Polish tormentors.

The joy was short-lived. Following the troops were Communist Party officials who delivered lusty speeches about the glories of the Soviet state and then set about reorganizing the society in a manner similar to the Russian model. The politically suspect Zionist organizations were disbanded and the speaking of the Hebrew language was forbidden. The schools were shuttered and transformed into Russian institutions staffed by party ideologues. Komsomol (Young Communist League) chapters sprung up, filling young minds with stories about the greatness of Stalin.

More forbiddingly, agents of the NKVD, the secret service agency that was the forerunner of the KGB, began targeting those who were regarded as enemies of the new regime, with Poles being a particular target of ire. Jewish business owners were branded speculators, and their shops were looted. Zionists were harassed and arrested. Some were exiled to Siberia. The exercise of religion, although not banned outright, was greatly constrained. Several of the Novogrudek's synagogues ceased to hold services. The Old Synagogue that had once swarmed with ghosts was turned into a grain warehouse.

"I remember we were very happy that the Russians liberated us from the anti-Semitic government of Poland, and we were happy that the Germans didn't occupy our area of Belarus," said Charles Bedzow from Lida, a city to the northeast of Novogrudek, which also boasted a rich Jewish history. "But when the Russians came in, right away they took away my father's business. As a young fellow, I was then forced to go to a Russian school, instead of the Tarbut. The Russians forced my father to work for them. He was sweeping the floors because he was a capitalist, a bourgeois. He worked in his own store as a laborer. It was very hard for him."

Although they weren't as hated as the business owners, Jewish craftsmen—tailors, blacksmiths, shoemakers, hat makers, carpenters—also felt the wrath of the new government. They were forced to join cooperatives and received fixed (and none too princely) salaries. The economy of the region was shattered by the changes, and shortages of food forced everyone to stand in lines for hours to receive the meager amounts provided by the government.

Tuvia, who was still living in Subotniki with his wife, understood that as a businessman he was a potential target of the
NKVD secret service. After liquidating the business he helped
run with his wife, he left his Rivke—with whom he was no longer
getting along and who refused to leave her family—and fled to
nearby Lida.

The great utility of the Bielski family business protected the
mill from the zeal of Soviet ideology. Asael remained at the mill
and was even appointed chairman of an administrative council
set up by the new regime for Stankevich and surrounding villages.
It was a post he'd never have been able to hold under a Polish
government and he quite enjoyed this new level of prestige. Zus,
who also held a position on the council, was soon given a job with
a consumers' cooperative in Novogrudek. There he met a woman
named Cila, and they were married.

Now thirty-three, Tuvia rented a room in Lida and found a
job as an assistant bookkeeper, even though he had little idea
how to do the work. The head bookkeeper taught him the basics
and he stayed on the job for a year. Then he got a similar job at
another Lida business. He kept his head low and tried to stay out
of the sights of the NKVD.

"He was living in a room in my girlfriend's house and the
minute I saw him I went crazy," said Lilka Tiktin, then a shy, doe-
eyed girl who was barely a teenager. "I went nuts. Absolutely
nuts. I thought that he was the most handsome man in the world.
It was love at first sight. I immediately thought there was no
other man like him. But our difference in age was large.

"He was so kind to us. My mother had passed away and I was
anxious for kindness. He paid attention when nobody else did.
He took my girlfriend and me to Russian movies, love stories. He

would bring us candies and chocolates. Sometimes I would climb a ladder and look in the window in his room. I used to look to see if he was there, if he was sleeping. I was crazed."

The girl was much too young to attract Tuvia's romantic interest. But on a business trip, he met a woman his own age who did catch his fancy. Her name was Sonia Warshavsky and she was tall and blond, a beautiful woman with a quick wit to match Tuvia's. Others saw in her a haughtiness, even an arrogance, but Tuvia wasn't concerned. He was thoroughly smitten. As it turned out, Sonia was related—though not by blood—to the young Tiktin girl. After learning that Lilka often visited Tuvia, Sonia asked the girl to carry notes to him and keep an eye on his activities. Lilka didn't object. She was in favor of anything that allowed her to see more of this dashing man.

Tuvia's relationship with Sonia gave him an excuse to obtain a divorce from his cast-off wife in Subotniki, with whom he had had no children. He wasted no time in starting a life with Sonia. The tensions of the time prevented an official marriage ceremony, but from this time forward, Tuvia always referred to Sonia as his wife.

The war was slowly inching closer. Air raid drills were conducted in the bigger towns, and military planes flew overhead every day. In Novogrudek, a makeshift hospital was established for Red Army soldiers who were injured during the Soviet Union's 1940 winter invasion of Finland, giving the locals a first glance at war casualties.

Throughout the winter of 1940, refugees from the Nazi-occupied sections of Poland streamed into the region, many bearing tales of Nazi atrocities. One of the Bielski children, Abraham, who was a year older than Zus, married a woman who had fled from Warsaw. She told the family about Germans treating

Jews "worse than dogs," as Zus would later recall. "We believed very, very little," he said. The government-controlled media told nothing of what was happening to the west because, after all, Nazi Germany was an ally of the Soviet Union. "My mother used to tell us not to listen to those stories about German crimes," said Sulia Rubin, then a teenager living in Novogrudek. "She told us the Germans were intelligent, cultured people and they would never do such things."

By early 1941, both Zus and Asael were drafted into the Red Army. Zus's posting was more than a hundred kilometers to the east, near the town of Tykocin, which was not far from the border of German-controlled Poland. Asael was closer to home, stationed to the north of Stankevich, while the Bielski parents stayed at the mill to care for the eleven-year-old Aron and seventeen-year-old Yakov, a smart teenager who had grown into a committed Zionist eager to make *aliyah*—to immigrate to Palestine. Thirty-year-old Abraham and his wife moved to Novogrudek.

Then, on June 22, 1941, the Nazis launched a surprise attack against the Soviet Union, suddenly turning the tables on its former ally. It was one of the most ferocious days in the history of warfare. As historian Alan Clark wrote, "In terms of numbers of men, weight of ammunition, length of front, the desperate crescendo of the fighting, there will never be another day like 22 June 1941." More than three million men spread across a thousand-mile frontier and, supported by air fleets, thoroughly surprised the Red Army. The war was on.

TWO

JUNE 1941 –
DECEMBER 1941

Tuvia Bielski was sound asleep in his Lida home when the ear-splitting roar of a motor jolted him from his slumber. The thirty-five-year-old rushed to the window, where he looked with shock upon burning buildings and people desperately running for shelter. "The fear and panic was unbelievable, and there was catastrophe in the air, a sense of doom," he later wrote. Within a few hours, he heard over Moscow radio that the Germans had bombed the major cities of the region.

He was immediately called up for mobilization duty and assigned to help sign up other recruits. By midday, dozens of Luftwaffe planes swooped into Lida, dropping incendiary bombs that ignited large swathes of the city's wooden architecture. Entire blocks went up in seconds. Tuvia's commander ordered the recruits to retreat to a nearby forest, but they were soon met with a second pass of German fighter planes, this time targeting the woodlands.

It was pandemonium; not even the commander knew the right course of action. "Comrades, it's every man for himself," he said. "Get going!" For most of the men—Tuvia included—this was license to secure the safety of their families.

Tuvia rushed back to Lida to find his house ablaze. Sonia was safe, however, so they retrieved what possessions they could and joined the thousands of people speedily abandoning the city. The couple found an isolated spot along the Lida River, where they stashed their belongings and disappeared from sight. Before dawn the next morning, another wave of Luftwaffe bombers rained its cargo on the town.

By now, Red Army soldiers and Soviet officials, unprepared for the lightning-fast attack, were retreating through the area. They headed east in large, haphazard columns, followed by trucks piled high with goods. In the vacuum caused by the bombings, the sentiments of some Poles became quickly evident as they taunted the Jewish population, perhaps in resentment for warmly greeting the Soviets in 1939. "Hey, little Jews, where are your great tank divisions? Judgment Day is coming."

The couple set off for Stankevich to be with Tuvia's parents, "to share their fate with them." Tuvia felt he would be safest in the village of his birth. The journey took several days and required Tuvia to pass himself off as a gentile farmer to a German officer and then, to a Soviet official, as a Red Army soldier sep-arated from his unit.

Zus was more than a hundred kilometers away in Tykocin when the attack arrived from the west. He was finishing a midnight shift guarding an airfield he and fellow soldiers had been building in the weeks before the attack. Three planes—two German and one Russian—appeared in the sky and engaged in a brief dogfight. Over the next two hours, more than twenty German planes bombed the barracks and the airfield, leaving it badly damaged.

The soldiers were ordered to retreat eastward to the city of Bialystok, where they would be provided with weapons and supplies. After they marched for several hours, the orders were reversed and they were told to return to Tykocin. Zus noticed hordes of retreating Red Army soldiers and wondered why his group was moving toward the enemy. Before he could get an answer, the orders changed again: back to Bialystok.

They soon came within sight of the city and Zus saw that it was burning out of control. In an instant, Luftwaffe planes dived in the direction of his unit and everyone dashed toward the woods in search of cover. Huddled in a thicket, Zus heard the earthshaking sound of cannon fire. Could it be from Soviet anti-aircraft guns? he wondered. Or had German ground troops already reached this far into the country?

Once the attack subsided, the soldiers regrouped and moved quickly through Bialystok—where friendly locals gave them cigarettes and canned goods. After a long, tiring march, they found a place to camp, fifteen kilometers to the east of the city. Provided with a fresh batch of weapons, the men engaged in a few disorganized skirmishes with the enemy, who indeed had advanced into the region. But without any clear orders from a central command, Zus's platoon was fighting blind.

Exasperated, Zus and a few of his fellow soldiers shed their military uniforms, donned civilian clothing, and pretended to be Poles. They knew a Russian combatant discovered by the Germans would have a harder time of it than a Polish civilian, even though Germany had declared war against both countries.

Sure enough, they were spotted by a German officer, who asked who they were.

"We were prisoners of the Russians," Zus said.

"What did you do?" the German asked.

"Forced labor," he responded.

The officer waved them along. "Go home," he said.

A few moments later, they noticed four Jewish soldiers who hadn't shed their uniforms. Another group of Germans forced these men to their knees and shot them at close range.

Later in the journey, Zus approached a group of Russian soldiers, thinking he and his men might join up with them. A Soviet lieutenant demanded information about their backgrounds.

"I am a Jew," Zus said, which he knew was better than saying he was Polish.

The lieutenant was skeptical, thinking he might be a Nazi collaborator trying to sneak into the country—"We shoot Jews like these," he warned—and called over a Jewish member of his unit, who spoke with Zus in Yiddish, confirming his identity. Once again, Zus's quick thinking had provided safe passage.

Finally reaching Novogrudek, Zus found his wife, Cila, and discovered that his home had been destroyed in the bombing. Bedraggled and hungry, he promptly set out alone for Stankevich to see his parents, while Cila, who was eight months pregnant, stayed with relatives in the city.

The ever-protective Asael, whose unit also disintegrated into chaos following the attack, had a much shorter journey to Stankevich and he was already at the mill. So were plenty of other relatives. Too many, in fact, to fit into the house, and the family's stables were used to handle the overflow. But Stankevich wouldn't remain a safe haven for long. By July 1, a Wehrmacht unit arrived at the Bielski property, and a German officer barged into the house.

"Who are all the people in the house?" he demanded in Polish.

"This is David Bielski and his family, the proprietors of the house, of the fields, and the mill," said Tuvia. "We are staying indoors because of the war."

The German noticed that Tuvia wasn't dressed in the simple manner of a country peasant. "Who are you?"

"I am from Lida," Tuvia responded. "But I returned here when the city was bombed. I came back to my father."

"What did you do in Lida?"

"I was a bookkeeper, an assistant bookkeeper," Tuvia said.

Meanwhile, the military unit was setting up tents on the farmland and turning the barn into a makeshift headquarters. The German announced that anyone who didn't live permanently at the mill had fifteen minutes to pack up and leave. Those who disobeyed would be shot.

The Bielski parents were devastated by the turn of events, and a worried Beyle sobbed for the fate of her children. The two were so broken up that Tuvia grew worried about their state of mind. Mrs. Bielski urged her sons to leave and protect what she called their Jewish honor. "Go away as far as possible," she said.

In search of safety, Tuvia and his thirty-year-old brother Abraham ventured on horse and cart into the city of Novogrudek, where Tuvia thought they might find lodging with a friend. The two arrived to discover Germans marching through the streets of the bombed city, which Tuvia didn't think had been hit as hard as Lida. The windows of a friend's home had been knocked out during the bombardment, but it was habitable. "Move in if you like," he told the brothers. "And don't worry about the rent."

Just then a Polish man who had been recruited by the Germans to serve in a militia—he was wearing a white armband to

denote his position—approached and told the two Bielskis to
report for work at a building in the center of town. When Tuvia
said he wasn't a resident of Novogrudek, the Pole sputtered that
he would be shot if he didn't obey the order.

At an administration building formerly occupied by Soviet
government officials, the brothers and a group of fifty other Jews
were told to transfer pieces of furniture to another building and
to throw portraits of Soviet leaders into a bonfire. As they completed the work, a smattering of Poles gathered to congratulate
the supervising Nazi officer, thanking him for "freeing us from
the Jewish yoke."

"Under our regime you will only see Jews on the silver
screen," the German told them. "These are Hitler's orders and
we will settle accounts with them."

Encouraged by the Germans, the Poles began taunting and
beating the Jewish workers, using wooden sticks and leather belts
to complete the task. Both brothers were beaten. Tuvia burned
with rage, but he didn't respond. At the end of the day, the group
was arranged in rows and ordered to march to the next job site.
One of the workers was told to lead the marchers carrying a
small bush—meant to mock the dignity of the procession—while
the Germans and Poles continued to taunt and strike the men.

Tuvia and Abraham slipped away under the cover of darkness, found their horse and cart, and headed back to Stankevich.
When I meet you again, Tuvia thought, *I will do so with a weapon in my
hand.*

The two arrived at the mill to discover the Germans had
moved on. Tuvia decided it was best to hide in the forest surrounding the house. Zus and Asael had already made the same
decision; they too were living in the woods. The circumstances of

the brothers' lives had changed radically in the two weeks since the invasion, and they had to decide how to respond to the new reality.

The radio in the family home was broadcasting reports indicating how the Soviet government wanted people like the Bielski brothers to react. "In areas occupied by the enemy," Stalin said in an address on July 3, "guerrilla units, mounted and on foot, must be formed. Diversionist groups must be organized to combat enemy troops, to foment guerilla warfare everywhere, blow up bridges and roads, damage telephone and telegraph lines, set fire to forests, depots, and trains. In occupied territories, conditions must be made unbearable for the enemy and all his collaborators. They must be pursued and annihilated wherever they are, and all their measures must be brought to naught."

Never averse to risk, Zus boldly returned to Novogrudek to check on his wife. Disguising himself as a gentile peasant, he slipped into the city and found his way to her residence. The German military was now in full control of the city's administration, and Zus learned that it had imposed regulations to control the Jewish population. In the first days of the occupation, Nazi officials sought out prominent Jews to serve on the Judenrat (Jewish Council). Its members would be responsible for communicating orders of the German rulers to the Jewish community and ensuring, under the penalty of death, that the demands were followed to the letter. The council and a Jewish police force to aid in the Judenrat's work were formed after the Germans had beaten and killed many of the initial enlistees. It was obvious that this occupation would be nothing like the more benign rule of the German Army of World War I.

A number of anti-Jewish measures were enacted. Jews were ordered to wear a yellow Star of David on the front and back of their clothing. They were forbidden to walk on the sidewalk. They were prohibited from speaking to or doing business with gentiles. They were placed under a strict curfew. And men and women from young teenagers to senior citizens were ordered to report each morning for forced labor duty.

The workers performed the most menial jobs while enduring the most galling of humiliations. Several men were ordered to strip to their underwear and use their clothing to clean German vehicles, while drunken Nazis beat them with sticks and blamed them for starting the war. A smaller group was commanded to sweep the city streets with their hands during a heavy rainstorm. One man was tied with an electrical cord and lowered into a well to retrieve some tools that had fallen to the bottom.

The Germans were aided in their work by a police force made up of Belorussians and Poles who had volunteered for duty. The locals were particularly helpful in pointing out those Jews who were trying to evade the new laws.

Safely hidden with his wife, Zus was able to avoid the brutalities of the authorities, but on July 26, the Sabbath, he witnessed a stunning example of how the Nazis intended to govern. While walking near the city's center, he caught sight of several people fleeing the marketplace. He walked toward the square, where he saw a group of Jews—many of them doctors, lawyers, and other professionals—standing in five rows surrounded by local policemen and German soldiers. The men were bedraggled and confused, obviously the recipients of severe beatings. Nearby, German musicians were playing orchestral music, identified by at least one witness as upbeat Strauss waltzes.

A car pulled up carrying a Nazi officer. He disembarked, drew his pistol, and fired into the air. The assembled soldiers then opened fire on the first row of ten Jews, who slumped to the ground. The action was repeated and repeated again. Just before the final shots rang out, Zus watched as a boy in the last row turned to his father and mouthed the words, "Father, they are killing us." Fifty-two bodies were lying lifeless in the ancient square when the shooting stopped.

A contingent of Jewish teenage girls was told to load the bodies into horse-drawn carts. One of the girls, Rae Kushner, glimpsed the lifeless faces hanging over the sides of the carts, recognizing many of them. The girls were instructed to scrub the blood from the cobblestones while the murderers celebrated. "The Germans had a ball," Kushner said. "They were dancing in the square."

The perpetrators of the atrocity were likely members of one of the bands of killers that the Nazi high command had unleashed to follow the Wehrmacht into the Soviet Union. Four Einsatzgruppen (action groups) made up of personnel from various strands of Heinrich Himmler's feared SS (Shutzshaffel, or elite guard) organization—including the SD or Sicherheitsdienst (security service), Orpo or Ordnungspolizei (order police), Gestapo (secret state police), Waffen-SS (armed SS), and Kripo or Kriminalpolizei (criminal police)—had begun conducting slaughters in the days following the invasion. Officially targeted were Communist officials, Polish intellectuals, and partisan fighters, but mostly it was Jewish civilians who were executed.

Six days earlier, a slaughter of Jewish community leaders occurred in the city of Mir, forty-five kilometers to the southeast, and nine days before that, a similar killing was conducted in Slonim, fifty-five kilometers to the southwest.

Zus had now witnessed two shocking acts committed against Jews—the first being the execution of the four Jewish soldiers during his retreat from his Red Army posting—and he had little doubt that the Nazis were dedicated to the destruction of his people. When a member of the Judenrat demanded that he join a work detail of 250 Jews, he refused to comply and urged the man to do the same.

Later, a young cousin of the Bielski brothers told Zus that two local policeman had come looking for him. Clearly it was unsafe for him there. He decided to return to Stankevich, while his wife, unable to travel because of her pregnancy, remained in the city, a decision that he said was difficult to make. On the way out of town, he avoided the notice of a pro-Nazi local whom he spotted walking the nearly deserted streets. Further down the road, a ten-year-old Pole confronted him. "You're an unwanted Jew and you're not supposed to be on the sidewalk!" the boy yelled.

Zus smacked the "little toad," as he called him, and resumed his journey to his parents' home in Stankevich. It was evening by the time he arrived. Approaching with caution, he looked through a window and saw that the place had been ransacked. Inside, he found his mother sitting alone, in terror. She said that the Nazi-allied police had done the damage. But there was more: His father had been taken into custody.

Tuvia had since made the return journey northwest to Lida with his wife, Sonia, who was eager to be near her family. He discovered that Lida, like Novogrudek, had been occupied by the German military soon after the initial bombardment, and the same litany of anti-Jewish measures had been issued to a sizable community. A Judenrat had been formed with a schoolteacher at its head, and forced laborers were assigned to clear rubble from a city that was nearly destroyed by Luftwaffe bombs. Among the duties of the workers was picking through the remains of Lida's grandest synagogue.

As happened in Novogrudek, a death squad arrived in town to eliminate members of the Jewish intelligentsia. Several personnel from Einsatzkommando 9 (commando unit 9) of the larger Einsatzgruppe B were dispatched to Lida soon after the Wehrmacht took control of the city on June 27. Led by Dr. Alfred Filbert, an SS veteran who held a doctorate in law and spoke fluent English and French, the main body of the commando unit reached the town of Varina on July 1. From there, Filbert sent a Teilkommando (partial commando unit) of between fifteen and twenty men, an amalgam of SS, Gestapo, Kripo, and SD officers, to Lida, where it arrived in several trucks on the morning of July 5.

Some three hundred Jews were hauled from their homes and led to a school building to be interrogated by Teilkommando members. Skilled workers and craftsmen, numbering a little over two hundred individuals, were released, while about ninety with higher educations were escorted to a location outside the city. In groups of five, the Jews were ordered to stand facing large craters created by fallen bombs. Teilkommando marksmen then shot them from the rear. Since most of the bodies didn't fall into the pits, the next group of five was forced to toss the corpses into the bomb craters before lining up for their own deaths.

On the following day, July 6, a German named Dr. Andreas Hanslmeir, who was present during the action, wrote a letter to his wife back home. "Yesterday afternoon I was witness to an experience that I will not be able to forget," he wrote. "Execution of people. I don't wish to write more about it."

The killings were a blow to the Jewish community, but many felt that the remainder of the population would be safe. Sonia went to Lida to be with her relatives, while Tuvia decided to stay in a nearby village, at the home of a young man, Arkady Kissal, whose life he had saved fifteen years earlier. Then ten years old, Arkady fell into a river not far from one of the Bielskis' mills. Fully clothed, Tuvia jumped into the water, grabbed the drowning boy by the hair, and dragged him to shore. Now the Kissal family greeted him as a savior and showed him to a warm bed. And he slept, for an entire day.

Tuvia had learned all he needed to know about the Germans during his visit to Novogrudek. He vowed that he would never again be subject to their cruelties.

From gentile contacts he obtained false papers, one identifying him as a Belorussian, another as a former Polish Army officer named Andzoi. He grew a moustache and began supporting himself by felling trees and cutting firewood.

Back in Stankevich, David Bielski was released from jail the morning after his arrest. He walked the few kilometers from the police station to the mill, and described to his wife how the officers had beaten him. But they weren't interested in him, he told her. They were looking for Zus and Asael.

Several local men who had joined the Nazi-allied police were launching a campaign to catch the two brothers, he said. The men had told the Germans how they had held positions in the Soviet administration and even brought up the old accusation about the two murdering a villager. It seemed that any local with a grudge against the family went to the anti-Semitic authorities, who were only too happy to harass isolated Jews.

One of the policemen leading the effort was the Stankevich resident Vatya Kushel, a descendant of the Pole who had helped David Bielski maintain control of the mill after the tsar forbade Jews to own rural property. Kushel had urged the German authorities to arrest a Belorussian woman who had served in the Soviet administration with Zus and Asael. The brothers had heard that he had personally executed the woman and her sister. Now the former family friend was turning his sights on the Bielskis.

David gave his sons a simple message: Stay in the woods. This war won't last forever.

Zus and Asael now had the difficult task of finding shelter while being hunted by people who knew the area as well as they did.

Some evenings they would stop by the family home's back door to get some food from their mother, while they camped out in the wooded area closest to the home. At other times, the two, usually separately, would stay with friendly gentiles who had been loyal customers of the mill or whose daughters had once attracted their interest. They also made a point of seeking out families with sons serving in the Red Army, farmers who would likely be receptive to the services of men with sturdy backs. And they wouldn't enter a home without a clear idea of how to escape back into the woods.

Once Zus was eating a meal of fresh meat, bread, and peas with a peasant family when he noticed a squad of policemen nearing the house. The owner suggested he hide in the pantry. The police knocked on the door, but in this case they weren't interested in Zus. They were attracted by the smell of the food. As the men sat down to eat, Zus slipped through the back window and disappeared into the forest.

Asael spent a week working as a builder in a nearby village. But even with his unassuming manner he was noticed and reported to the police. He left town before he could be caught.

The swift-footed, eleven-year-old Aron, who knew the pathways through the forests even better than his older brothers, served as a messenger between Zus, Asael, and his parents, moving between the mill and their hideouts like a secret agent. Even he didn't know quite how he found his brothers. It was almost a matter of instinct—he would walk to a spot in the forest where he thought they might be and simply wait for one or both of them to walk by. More often than not, a brother showed up.

Asael and Zus successfully avoided capture for several weeks. Frustrated, the policemen focused their attention on the family members they were able to find. Abraham, more delicate than his older brothers, had remained at home with Aron and seventeen-year-old Yakov, who was suffering from a foot injury, and he became a target of the terror campaign.

After several mounted policemen surrounded the homestead, Abraham tried to escape by running into the fields, dodging bullets as he sprinted. The officers caught up to him, pushed a revolver to his throat, and dragged him back to the house. But he refused to divulge any information about his brothers. A short while later, he was arrested and taken to the police station. There, he was beaten so badly that when he returned home he was confined to bed.

David was also subject to more beatings. A Belorussian policeman, a man who had known the family for years, shoved the slow-moving patriarch against a wall and struck him in the ribs with the barrel of his rifle. Young Aron watched in horror as his father doubled over in pain, several of his ribs broken.

Then a squad of Germans and policemen arrived at the mill, dragged both Abraham and Yakov from their beds, and took them to the police station in Novogrudek, a considerable distance from the station nearest the Bielski home.

Fearing the worst, Mrs. Bielski immediately began working to secure their release. She collected signatures from important gentiles, who vouched for the innocence of her boys. She arranged for food to be sent to them, although it was confiscated before they could eat it.

She traveled to Novogrudek and other towns with Aron and visited relatives, Judenrat officals, anyone who might be able to help. During one trip to the city, Aron walked on the sidewalk (he wasn't wearing the yellow Star of David) while Mrs. Bielski, as was required by the Nazis' racial laws, remained in the street. The young boy spied the Stankevich policeman Vatya Kushel farther up the road. He watched as the Pole called over a couple of German soldiers and pointed in Aron's direction.

The Germans rushed up, grabbed him, and took him to the police station, where he caught a brief glimpse of one of his brothers. Taken outside by a crew of German soldiers, Aron was told to dig a hole with his bare hands. While he set to work, the soldiers manipulated their rifles, and the jarring sounds reverberated in the young boy's ears. "Tell us where your brothers are or we are going to kill you," they said.

He dug and dug until the hole was big enough to hold his body. The Germans told him to lie down in the makeshift grave and then asked him again where Zus and Asael could be found. But he said nothing. Not a word.

Finally, they picked him out of the hole and dragged him into the station. "Run home," a German barked at him.

Although Mrs. Bielski's campaign to free her sons was showing no signs of success, she wasn't about to give up. Hearing that the prison warden was susceptible to bribes, she brought him anything she could find in the house—a pillow, kitchen utensils, work boots. But he wasn't interested in merchandise. He wanted gold. She sold household items and scraped together some money. Not enough, she was told.

Weeks passed and still nothing worked. The brothers' fates were sealed: Abraham and Yakov were later killed while trying to escape during a transfer to another prison in October.

Tuvia, who remained hidden mostly in the area around Lida, was stunned when he learned of the deaths of his brothers. He couldn't conceive what these young men could've done to deserve such a cruel death.

With these thoughts nagging at his mind, he moved from place to place, relying on a constellation of gentile acquaintances he had known from his years of living in Subotniki, Lida, and Stankevich. Since the police were actively searching for Zus and Asael, he felt comfortable enough to occasionally travel back to the mill and check on his parents. But the visits were always fleeting.

He, too, had had occasion to come face to face with the invaders. He was saved by his ability to pass himself off as a Christian. His appearance wasn't recognizable as typically Jewish, and he spoke the gentile languages without an accent.

Once he walked into a village that was full of German soldiers, who caught sight of him before he had a chance to flee. Feigning nonchalance, he strolled down the main street, feeling the heat of their gazes. But his heart froze. He walked into the house of a Belorussian friend and discovered two Germans sitting at the man's table, drinking glasses of milk. The friend quickly greeted Tuvia in Belorussian and introduced him to the visitors as a neighbor.

"How are things going at the front?" Tuvia asked the Germans, after joining the group at the table.

"The supreme commander has ordered the army to capture Moscow within fourteen days," one of the soldiers said.

Tuvia remarked how happy everyone was that the Germans were putting an end to Russian communism.

The Germans finished eating and left the house. Tuvia's relieved friend begged him to leave, fearing that they would be both killed.

Another time Tuvia knocked on the door of a gentile's house and heard a voice speaking in German. "Come in," the voice called out. In a cold sweat, he walked inside to find four German officers and four local women sitting down to a meal. In German, Tuvia wished them a good meal.

"Is this your brother?" a German asked one of the women.

"Yes," she responded.

After Tuvia took off his coat and hung it on the wall next to the Germans' weapons, one of the Nazis offered him a glass of cognac, which he accepted, and they all commenced to toast his "sister." Sitting down, Tuvia joined the meal and the conversation.

In German, he told them how he remembered their countrymen from the Great War. He then asked how things were progressing at the front.

"Our cannons are shelling Moscow," one of them replied. "Our aircraft are bombing the capital. The city is burning. Victory is assured, Russia is kaput."

"Good!" Tuvia said.

As the talk progressed and the alcohol flowed, Tuvia decided to touch on the subject of Jews. "Why are the Germans hounding the Jews?" he asked. "Couldn't you use them to produce goods for the military?"

The response was full of anti-Semitic bile about Jewish speculators and profiteers controlling German industry. The man claimed that British Prime Minister Winston Churchill was Jewish and that he had grossly manipulated prices at a coffee plantation he owned in India. "Was it possible to let such a speculator remain alive?" the German asked.

Then the man made a toast to the death of the Jews. "The earth burned under my feet," Tuvia said. After thirty more minutes of such surreal conversation, he shook hands with everyone at the table and escaped what he called "a den of vipers."

Yet Tuvia had managed to remain calm and self-assured during this and similar encounters. It was becoming clear that he possessed remarkable gifts of control, cunning, and self-possession not found in the average man.

The arrival of autumn brought a change in the Nazi administration in Novogrudek. The Wehrmacht rulers were replaced by a civil administration, which was populated by loyal Nazis, "men of the party," whom Hitler entrusted with overseeing his new territory. The members of the regional commissariat (RC) were easily identifiable in their honey-colored uniforms and swastika armbands, which inspired German soldiers and civilians to call them "golden pheasants."

Sweeping into town one October day was the regional commissar (Gebietskommissar) of RC Novogrudek, Wilhelm Traub.

He was the new top Nazi for the area, the man who would be responsible for the governance of the city and the surrounding district. For the next two and a half years, Traub would preside over a reign of terror of almost unimaginable ferocity.

A thirty-one-year-old of medium build, with a long Roman nose and dark blond hair, he was born in the region near Stuttgart. He completed secondary school in Cannstadt and took a few math and science courses at a polytechnic college in Stuttgart. But he was too busy with his military work to focus on schooling. He was twenty-two years old when he joined the Sturmabteilung (SA, or storm troopers), Hitler's internal terror squad, where he served until 1937, the year he was admitted into the SS. By the time he was assigned to Novogrudek, he was an SS-Sturmbannführer (major) who had served at a number of posts in the SD, the SS's intelligence branch.

He reached the city with his wife, Svea Wierss, who, he boasted on an application for marriage filed on September 12, 1940, "is known personally to the Reichsführer" Adolf Hitler. "The marriage," he added, "has already been personally approved by the Reichsführer."

An arrogant man with almost unlimited power, Traub surveyed his domain and set about implementing his vision of total control. He installed pro-Nazi mayors in the rural towns and set up offices to coordinate such activities as agricultural output, taxation, and forestry services. He established a penal court system and organized German gendarmerie posts in the city and outlying towns, which were staffed by personnel from Nazi police formations and local volunteers.

Taking advantage of the age-old tensions in the city, Traub encouraged conflict between Polish and Belorussian leaders who were hoping to convince the new rulers to grant privileges to their people. Then he and his men turned their attention to the Jewish community.

"One of the first major goals of the German measures must be to separate the Jews from the rest of the population rigorously," this according to guidelines issued to RC officials like Traub on September 3, 1941. "Generosity toward Jews is to be stopped immediately. Creation of ghettos is to be attempted . . . in Belarus this will be facilitated by the presence of more or less closed Jewish settlements. The labor forces . . . are to be employed under guard in productive, largely physical work (road building, railway construction, canal building, agriculture, etc.). Jewish skilled craftsmen, artisans and home manufacturers (in production units) can continue to ply their accustomed trades. . . ."

The man on Traub's staff responsible for the Jewish population—the Judenreferent—was an SS officer named Wilhelm Reuter. He was about thirty years old, tall and bulky, with chestnut-brown hair and eyeglasses. He also arrived in town with his wife. The two would ride their horses every morning before breakfast, a leisurely jaunt before diving into the day's work.

Some Jews were hopeful that the new administration would make their lives better. The Wehrmacht rulers had been simple military men. The RC officials were of higher rank and, surely, greater sophistication. It didn't take long for those hopes to be dashed. One of the first acts of the new rulers was to execute the entire Judenrat, accusing them of insubordination. They then restocked the council with Jews of their own choosing. The daily routine of harassment and random killing remained a fixture of life. People began noticing that sick Jews never returned from visits to the hospital.

Rumors also spread through the community about mass executions of Jews in other cities. With the eastward movement of the Wehrmacht finally slowing after months of victories, many of the mobile Einsatzgruppen personnel following on its heels were assigned to offices throughout the occupied zones, from which they would launch subsequent anti-Jewish actions in cooperation with local police, RC staff members, and German gendarmerie. The units were aided by the addition of thousands of SS personnel newly assigned to the Soviet Union.

The office closest to Novogrudek and Lida was an SD outpost established in Baranovich in the fall 1941, and it would soon consist of fifteen members of the Waffen-SS, a smattering of Kripo, SD, and Gestapo officials, and teams of Lithuanian and Latvian auxiliaries.

In November, a story circulated among the Novogrudek Jews about a killing in Slonim. The action took place on the fourteenth of the month, and was conducted by a contingent from the SD office in Baranovich aided by Nazi and Nazi-allied officials in the city. The regional commissar of the RC Slonim, Gerhard Erren, crowed that the slaughter had rid his jurisdiction of eight thousand "unnecessary hungry mouths." A rumor was also heard about a massacre in Mir. It occurred on November 9, and was perpetrated by a company of Wehrmacht soldiers and local police, apparently without the help of the seasoned killers of the SS. More than fifteen hundred Jews were killed.

The details, of course, were unknown to Novogrudek's residents, and, in the absence of hard proof, many found the tales hard to believe. Sure, they will kill some Jews, people said, but all the Jews? It makes no sense. They need us to work. Besides, other, more hopeful rumors were being heard during those months. Learning that the German drive into Russia had slowed, many speculated that the Soviets would soon arrive to liberate the city. Some religious Jews said they detected signs that the Messiah would appear and liberate the Jews from German enslavement.

The stories of the hardships in the city even reached the hiding places of Zus and Asael Bielski. Zus was racked with concern for his wife, Cila, who he learned had given birth to a baby girl. He was forced to contemplate the future of his firstborn child while sleeping on hay in strangers' stables, hiding from people who wanted him dead.

Although it was clearly unsafe for Jews in the city, the two brothers hoped that the Jews of the villages—David, Beyle, and Aron Bielski, and the members of the Dziencielski family who were still in Big Izvah—would somehow remain exempt from Nazi brutalities. They also hoped that they could continue this kind of transient existence during the cold of the Belorussian winter.

Back home, young Aron did his best to comfort his stricken parents. His mother was inconsolable over her lost boys. His father, still suffering from the beatings given to him by the police, was confined almost completely to his bed. The work of the mill continued—it was their livelihood, after all—and their longtime mill worker Adolph Stishok performed much of the labor unthreatened by the new authorities.

Then, on a day in early December, at about three o'clock in the afternoon as a light snow was falling, Aron heard the sound of an engine as he was walking between the mill and the stable. Turning, he saw that a German truck had stopped on the bridge leading to the family's property. Several Nazi soldiers and local policemen jumped from the vehicle and marched purposefully toward the house.

Aron dropped the load he was carrying, ran into the woods, and watched the scene unfold from behind a tree.

Responding to the commands of the soldiers, Beyle appeared from the house with Stishok, and the two helped David onto the back of the truck. Beyle joined her husband on the vehicle. She turned to Stishok and asked him if he would go into the house and get her a pair of galoshes.

"Where you are going you don't need any galoshes," he responded.

As the truck pulled away, Aron realized instantly what had happened. He ran off to find Asael and Zus, who he knew were staying at a gentile's home nearby. Zus, standing near the door, noticed a figure coming toward them far off in the distance. As it moved closer, he realized it was his little brother, anxious to give them news. Asael looked up from the food he was eating.

"Our parents were taken away in a truck," Aron said.

His two older brothers glanced at each other, but they didn't say a word.

The two quickly canvassed friendly neighbors and learned that the Nazis were not through rounding up the Jews of the countryside. Finished with Stankevich, the Nazis were now headed for the village of Big Izvah. That meant they were bound for the Dziencielski family, the only Jews in the settlement of about fifty homes. Staying with the family was the brothers' oldest sister, Taibe, who had married Abraham Dziencielski. The couple now had a baby girl.

"We needed to act," Zus later said.

Shortly after midnight, the brothers woke up the family and told them to pack their belongings. Everyone in the house—from Taibe's baby to the elderly Dziencielski parents—was gathered up, and the group headed for the forest. They walked most of the night, stopping every now and again so Taibe could feed the baby, before finding a place to camp beside a stream. Huddling by a campfire, they rode out the frigid evening, terrified for the future.

"Don't worry," the brothers reassured them. "We will turn to our friends, who will surely offer shelter."

In Novogrudek, public notices were posted all over the town, signed by Regional Commissar Traub, instructing Jews not to return for work the following morning. A chill ran through the Jewish population, especially since they had been hearing rumors about gentiles digging large pits on the outskirts of town. It was clear to many that a mass killing was planned. Wehrmacht soldiers blocked all the roads leading out of the city and the many Jews who tried to flee were shot.

On the evening of Friday, December 5, Nazi officials, along with local police and Judenrat members, went from house to house, ordering Jewish men, women, and children to report to the courthouse, which was actually a complex of buildings, or to a school run by an order of Catholic nuns, the Sisters of the Holy Family of Nazareth. Each person was allowed to bring a small piece of luggage. For most of the day, as a wet snow fell, some six thousand Jews gathered on the courthouse grounds before being allowed to enter the buildings late in the evening. A much smaller number were taken into the Catholic school.

Raya Kaplinski, who was nineteen years old, didn't report to the courthouse as ordered. Instead, she hid with several of her relatives in a tiny room in the family home. Another family with a small child found a place to hide in the building's cellar. Several Germans were alerted to their presence when the child began to cry. "Come out or else we will shoot you all!" the Germans shouted.

Kaplinski and her family did as they were ordered. "A German hit my uncle in the head with a blackjack and my uncle gave such a scream that I thought he had been killed," she said. "We were all pale and frightened."

The group was sent to the courthouse, where thousands were crammed into rooms that could barely contain them all. Few people were able to sleep that horrible evening. They could hear the Germans outside talking among themselves, smoking cigarettes, and urinating against the walls.

On Sunday, December 7, the day the Japanese bombed Pearl Harbor, pulling the United States into the war, a hundred Jews were taken from the courthouse and forced to dismantle a fence that surrounded the marketplace. They were told to carry its pieces to a run-down neighborhood, containing about forty houses, known as Pereshika. Mounted Wehrmacht soldiers and local policemen prodded the workers with iron rods, rifle butts, and wooden sticks. If someone fell down, he was executed on the spot, and the survivors were forced to carry the dead body to a burial site. Dawn was breaking by the time the group returned to the courthouse, exhausted by the abuse and weeping for the dead.

On Monday morning, members of the RC, including Reuter and Traub, along with SS officers and Lithuanian and Latvian commandos, arrived at the courthouse. They stormed into the building and demanded that the head of each family speak to a waiting SS official. "What is your profession?" the Nazi would ask. "How many children do you have?" Then the German, with a flick of his gloved hand, would direct each member of the family to stand either on the right or on the left. Skilled workers went mostly to the right. Nearly everyone else went to the left and was taken to idling trucks.

"Just like that, we were in two groups and people started to scream and cry," said Sonya Oshman, then a teenager. "The Nazis would say, 'Don't cry. We're only going to separate you for a while. We're going to give you homes. You'll have everything. Don't worry. The women and children will be taken care of.' And that's how they did it. The trucks were waiting near the courthouse."

In groups of fifty of so, people from the contingent on the left and from the nuns' school were loaded onto trucks and driven a few kilometers southwest of town to the small outlying area of Skridlevo. After the vehicles passed the military barracks, which had been built by the Russians, they took a right turn off the road and traveled a winding, slightly downhill path through the woods, bouncing in the ruts as they went. After reaching a small clearing, the Jews were ordered off the truck, where they were insulted and beaten by the soldiers.

With the temperatures hovering far below zero, the Jews were then directed to remove their clothing and stand facing two forty-by-three-meter graves that had been dug days before. The shooters then machine-gunned them to death. The action was repeated throughout the day, as trucks returned to the courthouse to pick up additional victims. As the sun set on that black Monday, more than four thousand Jews had been murdered. Among those lying dead in the ditches were David and Beyle Bielski, Cila Bielski, and her baby girl.

A woman who somehow escaped being killed crawled out of a pit late that evening and made her way back to the courthouse. Paralyzed by terror, she was unable to speak that first night, but the following day she told of the horrible scenes she had witnessed. Jews also learned details of the slaughter from a Belorussian policeman, who described how a barber attacked an SS officer with a razor before several Nazis beat the man to death with their rifle butts.

Back at the courthouse, those who were spared—numbering some fifteen hundred people—were marched to the Pereshika section of the city that had been enclosed by the marketplace fence. Curious locals gathered to watch the grim procession to what would now be known as the Novogrudek ghetto. Most showed either no emotion or outright disdain. One overcome gentile removed his hat as the group passed by out of respect for their suffering.

After spending that first evening in the woods, Asael and Zus, both of whom had recently obtained pistols, searched for safe homes for the Dziencielski relatives they had saved from Big Izvah. The more vulnerable of the group—the older relatives and Taibe's baby—were to be placed first. There was no problem finding spots for the aged members. It was tougher locating a place for a baby, whose cries would easily attract the neighbors' attention. The brothers were turned down a few times before finding a Polish couple receptive to the idea. The couple was won over by the sight of the child, who bore a striking resemblance to a child of theirs that had died.

A plan was devised whereby the Bielskis would leave the baby at the couple's back window late one night, with a note pinned to her clothing, bearing a Christian name. After finding the child, the family would notify the authorities, who would then be told of their decision to keep the doorstep surprise. It was an act the Polish couple hoped would inoculate them against any charges that they were harboring a Jew.

Bundled up in blankets, baby Lola was placed behind the home late one cold evening. Within a few minutes, as some of her wrappings came loose, she burst into tears. That's good, thought everyone hiding at the edge of the forest, because it will hasten the arrival of the couple. But minutes passed and no one came. Increasingly anguished by the sounds, Taibe had to be restrained from running toward her baby, whose cries were growing weaker. Then the man appeared. He called to his wife, whose shouts of joy attracted a crowd of neighbors.

The following day the local police chief arrived to see the child. Like the Polish couple, he was captivated when he gazed into the beautiful baby's dark eyes.

"I want to adopt her," he announced.

The woman refused. "The Lord has sent *me* this child," she said. "I am childless and she is mine!"

The police chief relented and gave his permission for the baby to stay in the home. Within a few weeks, the Jewish Lola was baptized into the Catholic faith.

After the most vulnerable members were placed in safe homes, the brothers found spots for the rest of the group. They promised to periodically check up on everyone and move people to new locations if the situation grew dangerous. Asael showed particular concern for Haya Dziencielski, now twenty-three years old and still an object of his affections. After she complained of a cough, he traveled many kilometers, at great risk, to find a pharmacist who could provide medicine for her.

Once everyone was safely hidden, Zus and Asael were left to contemplate the horrible events of Novogrudek. Their parents were now gone, murdered in a vicious manner that could hardly be more at odds with the quiet lives they had led. Zus's wife was also lost, killed along with a toddler who would forever remain unknown to the man who had fathered her. The brothers knew that the war had changed them irrevocably.

But these tough and resilient men were loath to admit any weakness to those they were protecting, and they succeeded in keeping their sufferings private. The one emotion they expressed without qualm was anger. Throughout their lives, they had responded to any attack by attacking back with greater force. Their initial instinct was to launch a counteraction against the killers and their helpers. But both men knew that their pistols were little use against an enemy of this magnitude. They couldn't jeopardize the safety of the people whom they were committed to watch over. Any action would have to wait.

Stationed farther to the north, Tuvia had learned from peasant friends that a policeman beat each of his parents before throwing them into the ditch where they were filled with bullets. As it had with his brothers, his despair quickly turned into fury. But he was also nagged by his conscience. Why had he left his mother and father to face the killers alone? Why didn't he do more to save them? And what would he do now?

THREE

DECEMBER 1941–
JUNE 1942

BY THE WINTER OF 1941, the war wasn't going well for Stalin. The Germans were pummeling Leningrad, which was nearly cut off from the outside world, and the desperate populace was slowly starving to death. Hitler hoped the relentless shelling of the city would result in its complete destruction. Moscow was also buckling under the German war machine, and Stalin polled his commanders to determine if it was possible to hold the capital. The losses suffered by the Red Army during the first six months of the war were devastating—more than 2.5 million soldiers were dead and 3.5 million had been taken prisoner. The führer was itching to drink tea in the Kremlin.

It would be the latest in a long line of conquests. Hitler's army had taken France, the Netherlands, Belgium, and Luxembourg in the spring and early summer of 1940, by which time Italy, led by its dictator Benito Mussolini, had entered the war on the side of Germany. After the victories in Europe—the Nazi flag now flew from Norway to the Pyrenees—Hitler turned his sights on Great Britain. Throughout the summer and fall, Luftwaffe warplanes dropped tons of bombs upon British population cen-

ters as German generals prepared to launch a land invasion. Led
by a combative and eloquent Winston Churchill, the Royal Air
Force put up a spirited defense, shooting down twice as many
German aircraft as they lost. By September 1940, Hitler
scrapped his plans for taking the country and shifted his atten-
tions to the Soviet Union.

Operation Barbarossa, as the attack on the huge landmass
was code-named, represented a major escalation in the Nazi war
against the Jews. The four Einsatzgruppen killing units, initially
staffed by just under three thousand Nazi personnel, murdered
hundreds of thousands of unarmed Jews during a killing spree
unequaled in the annals of history. Before any of the major concentration camps were operational, the killers traveled in four
motorized columns, which were often split up into smaller commando and partial commando units, and used pistols, rifles, and
machine guns to complete their gruesome tasks. Native people
assigned to auxiliary units ably assisted the German murderers.
As historian French L. MacLean wrote, "The locals spoke the
language, knew the terrain, and could convince neighbor to
betray neighbor."

On September 29 and 30, more than thirty-three thousand
Jews were shot to death by a commando unit of Einsatzgruppe
C at Babi Yar outside of Kiev, Ukraine, in one of the largest
massacres in the history of World War II. On October 23, more
than nineteen thousand Jews were shot near Odessa, Ukraine;
and on November 20, upward of thirty thousand were massacred in a forest outside Riga, Latvia. By the middle of November, the commander of Einsatzgruppe B, a former criminologist
and author of detective stories named Arthur Nebe, reported
that his men had killed 45,467 people since the start of the inva-

of Zionism. After Rabbi Reines's death in 1918, his son-in-law Rabbi Aron Rabinowitz replaced him as the city's most prominent rabbi, and he was still serving when the Nazis marched into town.

Like Novogrudek, Lida had always been a district city, containing all the important governmental entities for the surrounding towns and villages. The Germans also made it the seat of a regional commissariat.

Tuvia arrived in a city where power had recently been transferred from the military to a Nazi civil administration headed by Regional Commissar Hermann Hanweg, a thirty-four-year-old Nazi Party member since 1928, who had a bald spot and was known to favor Russian fur coats. Like Wilhelm Traub, his counterpart in Novogrudek, Hanweg had established a ferociously anti-Semitic system of governance.

The Jewish population had already become familiar with two of Hanweg's sadistic assistants. One was Leopold Windisch, the twenty-nine-year-old deputy regional commissar and Judenreferent, a slight, dark-blond Nazi diehard. He joined the Hitler Youth when he was fourteen, spent time in prison in the early 1930s for his Nazi police activities, and became an enthusiastic member of the SA storm troopers. His prewar superiors regarded him as a "fresh, steadfast National Socialist" whose "versatility and talent in cultural areas made him capable of leading larger groups."

As the Judenreferent, Windisch established workshops staffed by Jewish craftsmen that would provide goods for the war. He organized an effort to register every resident of Jewish extraction on a master list, noting each person's name, occupation, and address. But his work day consisted mostly of instilling terror in the population. With the help of German gendarmes, he conducted investigations of anyone he regarded as an opponent of the Nazis, and oversaw a series of group executions of anywhere from five to twenty people.

The other principal agent of Jewish misery was the thirty-four-year-old Rudolf Werner, the RC official responsible for economics and industry matters. Like Windisch, he had been involved in Nazi political activities since his teens. For sport, he took sleigh rides around Lida armed with a shotgun and a horsewhip, which he used to taunt Jews busy with their forced labor assignments.

He was most remembered for his ferocious German shepherd, named Donner (Thunder), which he trained to attack when he said the words "seize, Donner, Jew." Werner would roar with laughter as the dog tore at a Jew's clothing or bit into his buttocks. At least once, Werner killed a man who dared to defend himself against an attack. Another time, a laborer who had trouble lifting a barrel of turpentine was so badly mauled that he died from his injuries.

Shortly after arriving in the city where these men held sway, Tuvia reached the home where Sonia and her relations from the Tiktin family were staying and found that most of them were reluctant to abandon the city. He wouldn't hear a word of protest from his wife, whom he simply ordered to leave with him. But the other relations couldn't be convinced to budge. Sonia's sister's husband, Alter Tiktin, said he didn't want his wife, Regina; daughter, Lilka; and stepson, Grisha, to take the risk. "Why try and be smarter than the others?" he said. "There is no other way. After all, thousands of Jews are here with us. What will happen to everybody will happen to us."

Tuvia left the home in a state of frustration, and he sought to warn others about what he thought the future held. He spoke to members of the Bedzow family, whom he had known for many years, and told them that even a winter in the forest would be preferable to living under these monsters. But they weren't ready to follow. Neither were several merchants whom he spoke with. "Do you think they won't be able to find us in the woods?" one of the men wondered.

The decision to flee was by no means an easy one. Few knew the countryside as well as Tuvia, and few could, like him, pass themselves off as gentiles and thus avoid the suspicions of peasants. "There were ways to escape if you wanted to," said one man. "But you would freeze to death in winter. And there was no guarantee that people would let you into their house. Some escaped and then they would come back because they didn't know where to go." In addition, the full extent of the Nazis' intentions wasn't known. Unlike Novogrudek, Lida hadn't yet experienced a mass killing. Perhaps they would be spared.

On his way out of the ghetto, Tuvia was noticed by a passing man, who called out in a loud voice, "Bielski, Tuvia, wait a minute!" The louder the man shouted, the faster Tuvia walked, until he and his wife had cleared the city limits. Two kilometers to the west, he visited a wealthy Pole he was acquainted with, named Wilmont, who welcomed the couple into his home and agreed to shelter them. Sonia took on a position as his household seamstress, and she easily fit into the family's routine. The Pole proved helpful in another way: He gave Tuvia a pistol, a Belgian Browning, and four bullets.

Now I have a gun, he thought. Perhaps I can find some allies and contribute something, however insignificant, toward ending Nazi rule. He had heard radio broadcasts that repeatedly urged all citizens behind the front lines to fight the invaders. He had even heard stories about fledgling bands of partisan fighters, who were making strikes against the enemy.

The search for compatriots led him to seek out a Belorussian friend named Misha Rodzhetsky, a communist whose family was a regular customer of the Bielski mill and who had helped Tuvia find work in Lida during the 1939–41 Soviet occupation. Hearing the man was in hiding, Tuvia canvassed the peasants and found him on a farm owned by a mutual friend.

Tuvia greatly respected Misha's intelligence and was eager to hear his thoughts on armed struggle. Misha was receptive to the idea. The two decided they would recruit some fighting men and find a military radio to give them a sense of the situation at the front. But the further they planned the operation, the better both of them understood the difficulty of operating a group together—i.e., a Jew with a gentile. Tuvia noticed how a peasant who treated Misha cordially would treat him with contempt, and he wondered how Misha and his comrades would react toward him in a time of crisis.

Tuvia voiced his concerns and the two friends agreed the plan would not work. They parted amicably.

Tuvia then trekked back toward Lida, crossing over the Neman River, the "Father River" of Belorussian lore that flows underneath the road that leads from Novogrudek to Lida and marks the halfway point between the two cities. In a forest not far from the river, he stumbled across three Soviet soldiers, men who had been separated from their units after the German invasion.

Equipped with just a single rifle, the three were eager to find more weapons. Tuvia mentioned his pistol and suggested that they all team up to secure more weapons. The soldiers liked the plan. But the men's true feelings about Jews surfaced after they had imbibed too much alcohol one evening. One of them pulled a knife on Tuvia, shouting something about his "Jewish snout." Tuvia reached for his Browning, which he later learned was inoperable, and pushed it against the man's temple.

The fight was broken up before anyone was hurt, but Tuvia understood with striking clarity that he couldn't depend on men of this sort. *If this is the way my allies treat me,* he thought, *what can I expect from my enemies?* He knew he must join with those he could trust.

That meant one thing: He had to reunite with his brothers. If he was to accomplish anything, he realized they would accomplish it together.

He set out toward Stankevich with the idea of forming a fighting force of Bielskis. On a cold evening in late February or early March of 1942, he was walking along a forest path when he heard his name shouted from behind a tree. After hesitating a moment, he realized to his relief that it was Asael, Zus, and little Aron. They had taken cover when they spied the lone walker approaching in the darkness.

As the three older brothers greeted each other, Aron felt an overwhelming sense of safety. *Now we can't be touched,* he thought. *Nothing can hurt us when my brothers are united.*

But the three weren't yet convinced of their own invincibility. For one thing, Zus and Asael had become increasingly worried about the safety of the hidden relatives. The Germans and their police helpers had made explicit what they would do to those who harbored Jews: They would kill them. Plastered throughout the rural areas were posters signed by Novogrudek's Regional Commissar Wilhelm Traub ordering the capture of "persons without stars [recognition badge of the Jews] but who by their appearance are recognizable as Jews." The message was sinking in: Asael and Zus were noticing an increased reluctance of even those who were friends to support them with food and shelter.

Things weren't helped when a selfless Polish farmer named Kot, a man who was housing a few Bielski relatives, looked out his window one morning and noticed a group of local police surrounding his house. In seconds, they forced their way into the dwelling, struck the elderly farmer with the butt of a revolver, and demanded to know where the Bielski brothers were hiding.

"They were here," admitted Kot. "But they left."

"Why did you shelter them?" the police demanded.

"They are armed," Kot responded. "They come and take what they want."

During a search of the house, the officers discovered the Jewish fugitives—including the elderly Dziencielski parents—whom Kot quickly identified as his relatives. They also found Mrs. Dziencielski's set of false teeth, which she used to place in a glass of water beside her bed each evening. "Are these the teeth of a Jew?" the policeman shouted, apparently thinking that only Jews could afford the luxury of false teeth. "Perhaps a Bielski?"

Claiming ignorance, Mr. Kot was arrested and taken to the local police station. Viciously beaten and tortured, he died from his injuries.

The three brothers knew that incidents of this sort would make it hard for them to rely on increasingly skittish peasants. As Tuvia had learned in his encounter with the three Soviet soldiers, the brothers knew they had to operate from a position of strength. Only this way could they ensure their survival.

So, it was simple: They had to find weapons. But how? Nothing was more valuable in this war than guns. With no money and few possessions to barter, their chances didn't look good.

They needed a bit of good fortune, and it arrived in the hulking form of two Russian partisans. Tuvia and Zus stumbled across the pair after spending an evening sleeping in a peasant's barn; the proprietor's wife had fed them in the morning but begged them to leave after their stomachs were full.

The partisans, who were armed, were walking along the river that leads out of Stankevich, accompanied by a small boy who was known to the Bielski brothers. The boy shouted when he caught sight of Tuvia and Zus, and the partisans and their small assistant walked toward the wary brothers.

The partisans greeted them warmly and announced, "We're looking for ammunition for our rifles."

If they need ammunition and we need weapons, Tuvia thought, *perhaps we can help each other.*

"I have an idea," he told them.

Having visited a friendly peasant who had offered some ammunition to the men, the brothers suggested a plan that would've been impossible to complete without the partisans' firepower: an attack on a notorious local policeman named Kuzmitsky who they knew was stocked with arms.

The Russians, who liked the idea of punishing a Nazi collaborator, heartily agreed.

While two of the partisans waited outside, Zus rushed into Kuzmitsky's kitchen, where the family was sitting down to a meal. "Nobody move!" he cried as he shoved a pistol into Kuzmitsky's face. Startled, the policeman tried to grab for a weapon that was leaning against the wall. Before he could reach it, the partisans leaped into the house to restrain him. The four then collected the weapons stashed in the house and marched Kuzmitsky into the forest to be interrogated by the partisans' commander.

His name was Vladimir Ugriumov, but this former Red Army soldier from Georgia was known by his nom de guerre "Gromov." He was thrilled to hear of the action against Kuzmitsky and congratulated the brothers on the success of their attack.

After the policeman was taken deeper into the forest by one of Gromov's men, the commander turned to the brothers and told them how he began his life as a partisan. He had been trapped in the area when his unit became dispersed during the first days of the Nazi invasion. He then joined with a few other former soldiers—many of them, like him, from outside of the region—and started waging minor strikes against the occupiers. They had recently completed a few successful actions, including a raid on a police outpost that had netted prisoners and weapons.

"We have plenty of weapons, but not a lot of ammunition," Gromov said.

Tuvia was impressed. He broached the idea of he and his brothers participating in joint actions with Gromov and his men.

But Gromov was unwilling to share responsibility for Bielski's women and young people. He suggested that the brothers form their own group. "It's obvious you know what you're doing," he said.

"We need guns," said Tuvia.

No problem, Gromov replied. He told them partisan protocol dictated that Kuzmitsky's weapon now belonged to the man who had stripped him of it: Zus. To show his good will for the brothers' assistance, he offered them several working rifles, one defective one, and a bit of ammunition—a huge bounty. "Good luck to you," Gromov said with a smile before disappearing into the woods with his men trailing behind him.

The weapons gave the brothers a surge of confidence, a belief that they were now partisans. The three visited their hidden male relatives—including teenage brothers Pinchas and Josef Boldo and brothers Shlomo and Abraham Dziencielski (Taibe's husband)—and offered each of them a rifle. They buried the broken rifle in the ground, planning to fix it at a later date.

Asael also visited Haya Dziencielski, the young woman on whom he'd had a crush since she helped him balance the books for the mill years ago. He presented her with a pistol. But he didn't give her the weapon simply so she could protect herself. It represented, rather, a declaration of his love for her.

Now thirty-four years old, Asael arrived at the peasant home where Haya and her parents were hiding late in the evening. With little fanfare, he turned to the Dziencielski couple and announced that he was seeking permission to marry Haya. Pleased to hear the news, Haya's father gave his consent. Asael then recited lines from the marriage ceremony in Hebrew—"Behold thou art consecrated unto me by this ring according to the Law of Moses and Israel"—and presented the young woman not with a ring but with a small handgun, a German Mauser of the sort used by the Nazis. The Polish peasants watched the entire scene, although they didn't understand a word of what was being said.

Since there was no opportunity for a formal ceremony conducted by a rabbi in the midst of this war, Haya's acceptance of Asael's offer would be viewed by everyone, particularly her parents, as the equivalent of a real wedding.

"When he gave me the pistol, I was already in love," Haya later said. She had grown enamored of his loyalty and quiet self-sacrifice in the service of his relatives. She also knew that she had a better chance of living to see the end of the war if she were side by side with a man of such strength.

The two then went into the barn and Asael showed Haya how to fire the pistol. But, as Haya would later recall it, she felt no surge of romantic love as she held the weapon. She was thinking that she could kill herself if the Germans ever captured her—she would be able to end her life before being forced to endure the indignities of the Nazi criminals. It was far from a wedding night of bliss.

Not much good fortune was penetrating the walls of the Novo-grudek ghetto during the spring of 1942. The Jews who had survived the December 8 massacre were squeezed into tiny living quarters in the city's Pereshika neighborhood, with up to twenty people living in a single room. The number of residents steadily increased as Jews from outlying villages and towns were transferred into the packed ghetto. The few thousand new residents were forced to find shelter in basements and attics, in sheds and stables.

Every morning the population was marched to work either at the courthouse—where skilled tradesmen like shoemakers, tailors, leatherworkers, and others toiled—or the barracks near Skridlevo, where the group of manual laborers met before being dispatched to job sites throughout the area. The barracks workers had to contend with a fearsome Nazi whom they called Hazza, because he resembled a dog by that name that used to roam the city before the war. He would stalk the workers from atop a horse, hitting the slower ones with a lead-tipped whip. The sight of him so horrified the laborers that production increased markedly whenever he was on duty.

Reuter, the Nazi Judenreferent, periodically gathered every-

one together and spoke about the importance of increasing pro-
ductivity. He would tell the ghetto Jews that their meager ration of
bread would be upped if they showed more dedication to their work.

Even if that had been true, the additional bits of food
wouldn't have had much effect. People were already dying of starvation, and every day bodies were buried in a nearby field. Some
people became adept at smuggling food, often obtained through
barter with gentiles, through the closely guarded ghetto gates.
But rarely did anyone get enough to eat.

A ray of hope was provided by rumors about the partisan
Gromov who had been so helpful to the brothers. It was said that
he would sneak into the city, visit a barber for a quick shave, and
then shout that the Red Army would soon arrive to vanquish the
German fascists. "Tell all the citizens that Gromov was here!" he
would yell. Frantic Nazis searched throughout the city for him,
but always came up empty—or so the stories went.

Inspired by these tales, young men plotted joining up with
the guerrillas. A group of ten, with guns painstakingly assembled
from spare parts, managed to make it past the borders of the
ghetto. They traveled through thirty kilometers of countryside,
across the eastern branch of the Neman River and into the huge
Naliboki Puscha, rumored to be a partisan enclave. Before long,
word arrived that the men had been killed in a German ambush.
Rumors also spread that Soviet partisans were opposed to letting
Jews join their groups and that they would shoot them, fearing
they were Germans spies.

The Judenrat, the Jewish council that was forced to oversee the
ghetto for the Nazis, did what it could to prevent ghetto escapes.
Warned by the Germans that the whole population would be
executed if any Jews went missing, the council members confis-

cated the boots of those they suspected of plotting a run for the forests. Sometimes they detained a would-be partisan for a night or two. But their actions were nothing compared to the punishment meted out by the Germans. An attractive girl who was captured trying to flee with a gentile was hanged from a tree, her body mutilated by soldiers, as a stark warning to all those who sought freedom.

As the months passed, many ghetto residents had a sense that the Germans were planning another slaughter. Some believed that if they followed the Germans' orders, they would be spared. Others tried to create hiding places, somewhere to stow away on the day the Germans arrived with their trucks.

In Lida, where the Jewish population was restricted to three separate neighborhoods, the horrors were also increasing throughout the early months of 1942.

Late in February, the Judenreferent Leopold Windisch, who was known to shoot Jews he discovered hiding something as trivial as a stick of butter, was given a greater opportunity to terrorize the Jews under his jurisdiction. He learned that a small group from the ghetto had been accused of robbing an Orthodox Christian priest. He confronted the Judenrat leadership and demanded that they turn over the thieves. After struggling with the decision, the Judenrat handed over six men.

During questioning, the men denied that they had any role in the crime. In fear for their lives—and angry that the Judenrat had given them up—the men proceeded to detail a long list of the wrongdoings of the Jewish council. They told the German that several Jews from Vilna were illegally hiding in the city after obtaining forged identity papers from the Judenrat.

Just after dawn on March 1, the entire Jewish population of

Lida was rounded up and taken to an area near the RC headquarters. The Germans shot anyone who resisted, and even
killed elderly and sickly Jews who had trouble keeping up the
pace. The gathering of several thousand people stood in the
square for several hours, certain that something dreadful was
about to happen.

Then everyone was instructed to pass through a specially
constructed gate ringed with local police and Nazi officers. One
of the thieves stood near the gate and pointed out the people
from Vilna, who were yanked from the line. Several were shot on
the spot, while an additional thirty or forty were imprisoned in
the Lida jail, where they were soon executed.

A week later, the leaders of the Judenrat were arrested, and
an angry Windisch presided over an investigation into their role
in the affair of the Vilna Jews. The verdict was never in doubt. At
least seven men were tortured and then killed. Kalman Licht-
man, who had been the Judenrat chairman, had his eyes gouged
out. His face was so disfigured his friends were forced to identify
him by his clothing.

The murders shook the population, who had regarded the
Judenrat leaders as protectors. But many residents clung to the
hope that if they proved themselves useful to the Germans they
could avoid death. An idea was proposed to establish expanded
workshops, which the new Judenrat officials hoped would show
the Germans how committed they were to the war effort.
Windisch's boss, Regional Commissar Hermann Hanweg, liked
the idea when it was presented to him, and a number of shops
were allowed to open.

Jewish leaders did everything they could to employ people in
the workshops, thinking that it would save their lives. As many as

a thousand people ended up working as tinsmiths, dressmakers, bookbinders, toy builders, electricians, and carpenters. But the humiliations didn't stop. When spring arrived, many sensed more trouble was coming. "The ground was burning under our feet," said one man. The number of random executions was increasing. At least eighty Jews who worked at a warehouse for confiscated goods were shot for no discernible reason.

In early May, Windisch ordered a Judenrat official to prepare a new list of all able-bodied Jews. Then a contingent from the SD outpost in Baranovich, along with squads of German gendarmes and Lithuanian and Latvian auxiliaries, were seen moving into town. On the evening of May 7, gentile villagers were dispatched to dig three large trenches on the northeast outskirts of town, which they did by enlarging bomb craters.

In the predawn hours of May 8, the commandos, in teams of ten to twelve men, surrounded the Jewish sections of the city and demanded that everyone come outside to have their papers examined. The soldiers didn't wait long before storming in and forcibly driving everyone out. Many people were pushed into the street in their nightgowns and pajamas. Residents from each of the city's three Jewish sections were then marched to central locations, where, as during the December action in Novogrudek, they were instructed to present themselves to a waiting German. Anyone who lagged behind was shot.

After speaking with the German, the Jews were told to gather either on the left or on the right. Young skilled workers and their families were generally directed toward the group on the left, which would be unharmed, while nearly everyone else was pointed toward the gathering on the right, bound for the execution trenches.

Windisch, assisted by a Polish interpreter, supervised a portion of the selections and often sent able-bodied workers with work permits to the right. He even reprimanded his commanding officer, Hermann Hanweg, for allowing too many Jews to be spared. "I demand that you send all Jews right!" he told him.

Rabbi Aron Rabinowitz paced feverishly, reciting the Shema Yisrael (Hear, O Israel)—a summary of the creed of Judaism recited through the centuries by Jewish martyrs—and screaming to the sky, "Jews are being killed in Your name!"

Those marked for death were lined up and marched to the edge of the city.

One man fled the procession as it neared the execution ditches. "A member of the guard ran after me and kicked me to the ground," he later said at a war crimes trial. "He then shot at me a number of times with a machine pistol. . . . Two shots hit the back of my head. I lay, covered in blood, and pretended to be dead. In reality, I was so shocked and weak I couldn't have stood up. I lay in this site, about a hundred meters from the execution place. In the course of the day, I briefly looked up and toward the executions now and then.

"I saw that the Jews were forced to disrobe a short distance from the execution site and then walk over boards that had been laid over the graves. Then they were shot with fixed machine guns. . . . I saw Windisch and Hanweg at the execution site. I do not know if [Rudolf] Werner was there or if he shot at fleeing Jews. I did see how Windisch shot a child that had been thrown in the air by a Lithuanian or Latvian. . . ."

Of a total of three trenches, one was reserved for children, many of whom had been torn from the hands of their parents just before they were killed. The gunmen, numbering about a hundred men, mostly Lithuanians and Latvians, swilled alcohol during pauses in the barrage, and witnesses recall that they were visibly intoxicated.

By five P.M. that evening some fifty-five hundred Jews had been killed, more than half of the approximately eight thousand Jews who were living in the city. The drunken execution squad returned to Lida, where a special meal was prepared for them at a canteen. They were given additional supplies of alcohol, and most of the group remained until past midnight.

Windisch and Werner, along with six members of the SD from Baranovich, enjoyed what a witness described as a "cozy get-together" in one of the rooms of the regional commissariat headquarters. They drank liquor deep into the evening and listened as an Austrian-born man who took part in the slaughter played a violin with what the witness described as "noticeable" virtuosity.

On the following day, the same RC officials and execution commandos traveled to nearby Zheludok, where the process was repeated, killing at least eleven hundred Jews. Eighty-two skilled workers were spared. On May 10, the executioners went to Vasiliski and organized the deaths of eighteen hundred more Jews. About two hundred Jews were allowed to live. In Voronovo, on May 11, about two thousand Jews were killed. "We, the noble German race and our führer, will not rest until we do away with you," Windisch told the small group of Voronovo survivors. "In the meantime, Jews, the select few among you are still alive. If you disobey our laws and rules, not a trace of you will remain." On May 12, in Ivye, twenty-three hundred Jews were killed. After the executions were completed, Windisch watched as a Jewish burial squad covered the graves with calcium oxide (quicklime) and dirt. "Quick, quick, away with the Jewish shit!" he shouted.

When Tuvia learned about the Lida killings, he sped north, to the home where his wife, Sonia, remained hidden. He found a gentile emissary to carry a letter to the Tiktin family members, all of whom had survived the attack. "You must get out now because there will be another slaughter," he wrote. "I can't guarantee that we won't face hardship in the woods, but at least we have a chance to live. Leave immediately." He included directions to his hiding spot.

As before, Alter Tiktin was reluctant. All the surviving Jews from Lida—and from the four other towns where massacres were conducted—had been herded into a single section of the city, enclosed by barbed fence. But after a few weeks of continued humiliation, he realized that Tuvia was speaking the truth. There was no future in the Lida ghetto.

Late one evening in June, Alter woke up his wife, Regina; stepson, Grisha; and daughter, Lilka, and told them all to keep quiet and follow him out of the overcrowded home where they were living. The four slowly made their way through the deserted ghetto streets until they neared an exterior fence. Everyone dropped to their stomachs and slowly crawled toward it. Fearful of alerting the vicious guard dogs that periodically patrolled the perimeter, the Tiktins barely breathed as they slid under the cold wire meshing.

They continued to crawl until they made it across a field and into a wooded area. Then they followed the directions to the home where Tuvia's wife, Sonia, was sheltered. Once there, they rested for a time before Tuvia led everyone on the long journey back toward Stankevich. As they walked, Tuvia explained that he and his brothers, now sufficiently armed, had relocated seventeen relatives from various peasant homes into the forest. Everyone was now together.

Traveling most of the night, Tuvia, Sonia, and the four Tiktins made it to a small forest camp, which the former ghetto inhabitants looked upon with a mixture of relief and surprise. Several people were sitting around a small campfire, over which two chickens and a pot of broth were cooking. The oldest of the Bielski relatives, Aron Dziencielski, Haya's father, was serving as the cook.

"Is all this food kosher?" Tuvia joked, knowing that it surely wasn't.

"Oh, yes," Mr. Dziencielski replied with a laugh. "That's my responsibility."

After a pleasant meal, the members of the fledgling forest community shared a warm chat and slowly drifted off to sleep.

FOUR

JUNE 1942 –
OCTOBER 1942

IN THE EARLY days of May 1942, at about the time the Germans were conducting the mass killing in Lida, the brothers decided to move their relatives into a small forest near Stankevich. For Tuvia, Asael, and Zus, it was an easy call. They had lived within meters of the woodlands all their lives and each had spent parts of the first months of the war sleeping among the trees. For the others, the decision seemed more perilous: As hard as it had been living in haylofts and underneath floorboards, these circumstances were nothing compared to weathering the elements of the wild.

But the brothers weren't interested in debate or in putting the idea to a vote. Simply, there was no way they could watch over a group that was living in a series of near- and far-flung homes. The addition of the guns from Gromov meant they could provide protection for the women and elderly, and the warming spring breezes meant they could sleep outside without freezing to death. The time to head to the woods was now. "There was something familiar about the forest, and in the worst case we could escape among the trees," Tuvia later wrote.

So they ventured into a world of pine, oak, and fir trees, of occasional patches of wild mushrooms, of scattered bushes of blackberries and blueberries. They slept under quasi-tents made from blankets propped up by tree branches and assigned an armed guard to protect the bare-bones encampment from intruders.

The most pressing challenge was finding enough food to feed a community, which, with the addition of the Lida escapees, now included more than twenty members. Before, the peasants who sheltered the fugitives provided them with all the food they needed. Now, finding and collecting food would become a full-time occupation of the brothers and their armed cohorts. The Bielski family had many allies, friends from before the war, but how long would they remain allies? The peasants had heard about the mass killings and they knew the Germans were deadly serious about their plans for the Jews. And if the brothers used their guns to intimidate nearby villagers—and sometimes there was no other way to procure a chicken or some potatoes—they risked inspiring the farmers to run to the Germans.

With the group so vulnerable to attack, the brothers sought to create the impression that they were a large and ruthless collection of fighters, the kind of men who would deal harshly with anyone who denied them supplies or informed on them to the authorities. Asael and Zus already had a reputation for roughness, but the three wanted the Bielski name to strike terror in the hearts of villagers. It was the only way they felt they could survive.

They accomplished this by sending those without guns on missions equipped with long sticks, which in the dim moonlight looked like rifles. They wore ammunition belts bulging with already used bullets. They sang rousing martial songs at the top of their lungs in Russian while circling repeatedly through a village. Zus, the most confrontational brother, resorted to more explicit threats. On several occasions, he took a peasant's son from his home, led him out of sight, and fired a shot into the air. Then he returned to the house and announced to the farmer and his family, "We've killed one son. Now let's kill another." The grief-stricken man invariably offered weapons or food.

The addition of weapons was vitally important to the safety of the group, but Tuvia increasingly felt the need to add more people. "Tuvia understood the war better than anyone else," said Pinchas Boldo, a relative of the Dziencielski family who was part of the early contingent. "Everyone thought it would be just a few weeks before it would be over, but Tuvia understood that this could drag on for years and that we had a better chance of surviving if we had a big group." Asael and Zus were inclined to keep the unit small, but they respected their older brother's instinct.

As the weeks passed, they discussed recruiting new members. Ever since the mass slaughters, the ghettos had been ringed with fences and guards. The brothers desperately needed to find someone who could carry a message to the Jews of the Novogrudek ghetto, encouraging them to escape and take up with the Bielskis.

They decided to pay a visit to a longtime Belorussian friend of the family, Konstantin Koslovsky.

Konstantin, known as Kostya or Kostik, was a quiet, unprepossessing man who made his living traveling the countryside in a horse and cart selling cheap merchandise—someone who was barely noticed by his neighbors as he went about his business. He lived just outside the village of Makrets, a kilometer or two up the road from Stankevich; he and his brothers had known the

Bielski family from childhood. Indeed, the Koslovsky boys spent so much time with their Jewish neighbors that they picked up a working knowledge of the Yiddish language. Zus joked that Konstantin could speak the language better than he could.

In temperament, the Bielski and Koslovsky brothers couldn't have been more different. The Bielskis cut a battalion-wide swath even before the war—romancing the local women, getting into trouble with the police—while the Koslovskys were content to live in quiet isolation. "We were all boring compared with the Bielskis," said Irina Koslovsky, Konstantin's niece. As such, the Koslovskys were perfect for the stealth missions the Bielskis had in mind.

By the time of the war, Konstantin and his five children—his wife had died in 1939, in childbirth—were living on a homestead a short distance from a home shared by his brothers Mikhail and Alexander and their families. The structures were on the edge of the forest, far enough off the main Novogrudek-Lida road that passing vehicles couldn't see them. Nor could the nearest neighbors, who lived over a gently sloping hill in Makrets. A fourth brother, Ivan, worked for the local police, allied with the Nazis, in Novogrudek.

Konstatin was thrilled to see the Bielskis and quickly offered everyone a glass of *samogonka* or "self made," the vodka moonshine that is the Coca-Cola of the Belorussian countryside.

"My heart told me you would be coming," Konstantin said in Yiddish.

He then described the stories he had been hearing about the Bielski brothers. "It is said that you are robbing people," he said. "And that your sister Taibe Dziencielski and the women are taking part in it all." Konstantin reported that according to his brother Ivan, the Germans had also heard the rumors—and that the Germans were trying to recruit people to catch the Jewish hoodlums.

Always wary, even of his friends, Tuvia wondered aloud about Konstantin's loyalties. "How do we know you aren't siding with the Germans?" he asked. Konstantin responded solemnly, telling about all that had happened to the Jews in the last year. Tears rose in his eyes at his powerlessness to stop the killings. "My relationship with your family hasn't changed," he said. "And I will do whatever I can to aid you."

"What about Ivan?" Tuvia asked. "Isn't he working for the Nazis?"

Konstantin told Tuvia that his Nazi-allied brother Ivan had grown to loathe the invaders and might be willing to aid in the brothers' search for weapons and supplies.

Reassured, Tuvia asked Konstantin to get word to his cousin Yehuda Bielski, who was imprisoned in the Novogrudek ghetto. He then took out a piece of paper and scrawled a letter, which he then entrusted to his longtime friend.

> *Dear Yehuda,*
>
> *We are hiding in the forest and we do not plan to submit to the Germans. Bring your wife, a few good men and we will build something together. Please do not hesitate. I hope to see you soon in the forest.*
>
> *Your cousin, Tuvia*

But had the brothers acted quickly enough? The Germans of Novogrudek were busy planning the city's second major slaughter for early August 1942. Many of the ghetto inmates had been feeling the portents of tragedy all summer, as the SS murderers and their allies committed several large-scale Jewish killings in the region. As always, the warning signs loomed larger day by day.

In the first days of August, the Germans abruptly executed Novogrudek's entire twelve-man Judenrat.

Then, on August 6, the Nazi officials escorted a few hundred Jews from the ghetto to the courthouse complex, where they had been employed in a number of skilled trade workshops. A few hundred other Jews, manual laborers without any particular skills, were taken from the ghetto to a location in the southern section of the city, the military barracks, where they usually gathered each morning before being taken out for their work assignments.

A few thousand Jews remained behind in the ghetto.

That evening, the Jews taken to the courthouse and the barracks weren't permitted to return to the ghetto as they normally would have after a day of work. This only added to the panic of the large population locked down in the ghetto. Many attempted to flee, and perhaps as many as 150 people, including a large number of children, slipped through fences and snuck across town to the courthouse. Its occupants, everyone felt, had a better chance of remaining alive. Parents scrambled to find hiding places for their children within the complex of buildings, fearing that the Germans would regard them as useless and therefore expendable.

On the following morning at four A.M., the Nazi commandos and their collaborators herded everyone from the ghetto out in the street. "Lie down!" one of the Germans shouted. For several hours, everyone was stretched face down on the ground. Soldiers stalked among the gathering, occasionally choosing someone for a random execution.

Then the entire group was loaded onto trucks and taken to a small village just north of the city called Litovka. Unlike during the December 8 massacre, the Germans didn't bother trying to disguise their crime by driving the vehicles deep into the forest. The execution pits had been dug no more than a few meters from the road. In the manner of the previous slaughters, the Jews were taken off the trucks, forced to line up in front of the pits, and then shot to death. By the end of the day, some three thousand Jews—the estimates range from a thousand to five thousand—had been killed, their bodies covered with layers of chemical agents like quicklime and bucketloads of sand.

Afterward, the commandos arrived in force at the courthouse and began searching for the hidden children. "They took my little sister," said Lea Berkovsky. "I wanted to run after her, but my mother said to me, 'Don't do anything. They are just bringing the kids to the ghetto.'"

A group of foreign auxiliaries scoured the property, savagely throwing any children they found onto the pavement below. When one of the searchers had trouble opening a rusty lock in the basement, he ordered a Jewish handyman, Shmuel Oppenheim, to do the work for him. After fumbling with the lock, Oppenheim shook his head. "It's too rusty," he said. "Impossible to open." The soldier moved on and Oppenheim let out a sigh of relief. Behind the door, as he knew full well, were several children.

The next day, the survivors, roughly twelve hundred split evenly between the group in the courthouse and the group in the military barracks, were ordered to resume their labors. At nightfall, the courthouse workers were instructed to remain in the complex, now ringed with barbed wire and surrounded by extra guards. It had become Novogrudek's second ghetto.

The manual laborers, after a few days of living in the barracks, were marched to the original ghetto in the Pereshika neighborhood, now an empty, ghostly place. The houses were ransacked and their windows and doors were flung open. The streets were full of bloodstained clothing; German officers poked through the refuse. The Nazi Judenreferent Reuter stood near the ghetto entrance and told the laborers to gather in a central area. "From this moment on," he said, "there is no longer a Jewish community here. Here we have a Jewish work camp and those who work well will continue to live. But any illegal activity will mean instant death."

In the aftermath of the city's second major massacre, some Jews, especially the skilled workers in the courthouse ghetto, talented artisans whom the Germans needed for the war effort, felt they were safe from further harm. Many of the manual laborers in the first ghetto in Pereshika felt far less safe. They feared it was only a matter of time before they were all dead.

A few days after the August 7 massacre, Konstantin Koslovsky reached Novogrudek's Pereshika ghetto and delivered Tuvia's letter to Yehuda Bielski, encouraging him to escape as soon as possible and walk to the twelve-kilometer marker on the road toward Lida. He was then to turn left off the road and toward the forest, where after a short distance he would find Konstantin's home. Further instructions would await his arrival.

Yehuda, the son of one of David Bielski's brothers, had been contemplating leaving for some time. He had heard from Jewish workers transferred to Novogrudek from a small city called Dzatlavo that Jewish partisan groups were operating in the Lipichanska Puscha, a forest many kilometers to the west. He thought about making the journey himself but was discouraged when he learned that a few likeminded ghetto escapees had been killed by anti-Semitic Russian partisans while making the trip.

But when Yehuda received the note from his cousin, he didn't think twice.

He gathered together a group of friends (including his wife, Ida) and discussed the idea of heading for the Bielski brothers' refuge. One of them, a twenty-four-year-old former barber named Pesach Friedberg, voiced worries that gnawed at anyone who thought about fleeing: What about the Jewish police, whose officers continued to stop escapes. And what if escape results in the deaths of those who remain behind? Is it worth the risk?

But the recent massacres in Novogrudek had resulted in the killing of more than seven thousand Jews. Most of the remaining Jews, and most certainly those living in the ghetto of manual laborers, were clearly marked for the execution ditches. We are going to die anyway, Pesach finally concluded; why not die on our own terms? The group decided to leave for the forest one night in the middle of August.

In the days that followed, Pesach studied the movements of the ghetto guards. He watched how the Belorussian and Polish collaborators walked around the perimeter of the small ghetto once every few minutes, leaving sections of it unguarded for short periods of time. He also saw how the few German guards remained near the entrance of the ghetto and rarely made detailed checks of its circumference.

And so, on a dark night after the local guards made their regular pass, the group of eight or nine broke three fence boards and crawled through a large hole. Suddenly, they noticed that one of the guards had turned around and was walking back toward them along the exterior fence. The fugitives froze in the darkness. At the last instant, the guard turned back and resumed walking with his comrades.

"A miracle," Pesach later said.

The group crawled across an open field and reached a small section of woods, then began walking to Koslovsky's house, using back routes for most of the journey. Since they periodically lost their way, the trip took most of the night. When they finally arrived, Yehuda walked to the Koslovsky house, while the others hid nearby in the woods.

Konstantin greeted the tired wanderer warmly and told him that he had just missed the Bielski brothers. "Don't worry," Konstantin said. "They come by often. They will be here again soon."

When Yehuda told the Belorussian about the others hiding nearby, Konstantin offered a can of milk and a loaf of bread for the group.

Yehuda returned to the woods and placed the food on the forest floor. It wasn't much, but it tasted like a bountiful feast. They chatted the night away, anticipating the new life they were embarking on.

The following morning, one of the escapees awoke in a panic. "Hurry, get up," he shouted. "The workers are waiting, it's time to go!" The drowsy group burst into laughter. "Now there are no more work details," Yehuda said with a smile. "There are no Germans and there is no ghetto. We are in the forest!" But as they wiped the sleep from their eyes, they could hear the sounds of the peasant wagons clattering along the nearby road. *The Germans use that same road,* Yehuda thought. *We may have escaped from the ghetto, but we aren't safe.*

A short time later, the group held its collective breath at the sounds of someone approaching through the woods. It was Konstantin himself, bringing a breakfast of *samogonka,* bread, and sausage. As he left, he counseled vigilance. "Be careful," Konstantin said. "The forest has ears."

In the patch of forest near Konstantin's house the men waited for the Bielski brothers. They watched as German vehicles passed on the road during the day and occasionally sprayed small-arms fire into the woods. They noticed how quiet descended during the evenings, when few patrols ventured out in the isolated countryside. They grew more and more restless.

A few days later the Bielski brothers finally reached Koslovsky's house. They marched the new recruits through the woods for several kilometers to a newly created camp location, just southwest of the village of Butskevich. Their arrival marked a turning point in the evolution of the brothers' organization: It now included Jews who weren't close relatives.

Tuvia, Asael, and Zus were then faced with a fresh dilemma: How many more Jews would they be able, and willing, to accept? They knew that if a stream of people traveled from the ghetto to the forest, the likelihood of being discovered would greatly increase. The Germans would simply follow the Jews into the woods and spring upon the location of the base (or upon Koslovsky's home). The probability of this was heightened by the fact that nearly all of the ghetto inmates were unfamiliar with the rural areas.

They also knew that if a large number of escapees arrived in the woods, a greater burden would be placed on the armed fighters, who would be responsible for finding ever more food. To procure additional amounts of food meant putting themselves into more dangerous situations and dealing with a larger circle of gentiles. Above all, the chances of enemies discovering the camp would increase.

The brothers had a major decision to make.

Initially, Asael and Zus felt that only young Jewish fighters—and few at that—should be admitted into the group. Both men were itching to fight the Nazi murderers, whose crimes against their family and their people angered them profoundly. They thought it would be wisest to operate much like the fleet-of-foot Soviet bands that were springing up in the region: Strike quickly and melt back into a small forest hideout.

Tuvia shook his head. Yes, he said, we must inflict damage on those who are dedicated to killing us. But we cannot turn away Jews who come to us for shelter.

Furthermore, Tuvia believed it wasn't enough to *allow* Jews to enter the camp. Since the massacres in Lida and surrounding towns and the two slaughters in Novogrudek, he knew the Germans had no intentions of sparing any Jewish lives. (The talk about "useful Jews" was all part of "bloodthirsty German tricks," he would later write.)

Soon after the arrival of the new members, a meeting was convened to discuss the group's expansion. After everyone had gathered together, Yehuda Bielski rose to speak.

"We have come here into the forest, my dear ones, not to eat and drink and enjoy ourselves," he said. "We have come here, every one of us, to stay alive." He then outlined a simple plan that pleased everyone: The goal is to find more weapons and strike at the invaders. "We must think only of one important thing: revenge and revenge again on the murderers," he said.

"We must choose a commander and we must give our unit a

name," he continued. "For the responsibility of commander, I nominate my cousin Tuvia Bielski."

Tuvia stood—tall, broad-shouldered, clearly prepared to assume the authority about to be bestowed upon him—and launched into an impassioned speech about the necessity of rescuing Jews.

"We cannot simply hide ourselves," he said. "We must do something for our people. We cannot sit in the bushes and wait until the wolf comes for us. We must send people to the ghetto to save Jews."

"You're crazy," said Aron Dziencielski, one of the eldest people there. "There are more than twenty of us and already there is almost nothing to eat. What will we eat if there are more?"

Tuvia wasn't interested in a debate. When Asael and Zus, who possessed a similar stubbornness, voiced acceptance of their older brother's plan, it carried the force of law.

Still, there were further murmurs of disapproval.

"We have lost our wives and our children and you want us to go into the ghetto to bring out strangers?" said one of the newcomers.

Pesach Friedberg, inspired by Tuvia's words, didn't wait for Tuvia to respond. "What a shame that I called on someone like you to go into the forest," he said. "I meant to call to the forest the kind of people who understood why they'd been chosen. Tuvia, your proposal was that we go into the ghetto. I will be the first one to go!"

Tuvia brushed aside Pesach's suggestion. "The first ones to go will be those who have refused to go," he said. "And if they do not do it, they do not have any place here with us. We don't want them here. If they don't have any sense, this will teach them sense."

Then, Tuvia discussed his rules of governance. Drawing on

his experiences in the Polish Army, he declared that the group would be arranged like a military organization. To survive, the unit would have to operate as a single, cohesive entity. Everyone would have to follow orders, whether or not they agreed with them. He had no patience for dissenters.

"Everyone must say, 'We will do and we will listen,'" he said, repeating a line from Exodus, spoken by the Children of Israel after Moses described the words and commandments of God. He plainly felt the unit, with its new goal of rescuing Jews, would be acting on the highest principles of his people.

If anyone could convince the weary lot to follow such a risky plan, it was Tuvia Bielski. He communicated an air of fearlessness that, coupled with the backing of his imposing brothers, helped nearly everyone have an instinctive confidence in his ability to lead. But he was more than simply a warrior. His aggressive certainty about his vision was tempered by a warm manner, an ability to put people at ease, to reassure them during times of trial.

His power of suasion was further enhanced by his almost mystical attachment to the Jewish people. He wasn't ashamed to say that he felt the hand of God directed the actions of the brothers Bielski.

His was a personality full of contradictions. After angrily castigating those who dared oppose him, Tuvia openly wept in front of the same men while speaking of the viciousness of the Nazi killers. He could be cruel and tender, charismatic and profane, intelligent and hotheaded. Above all, he was passionate and utterly determined.

Pesach Friedberg seconded Yehuda Bielski's nomination of Tuvia as the group's commander. Everyone voted with a show of hands, and the nomination was carried unanimously. Zus and

Asael consented to the arrangement, as Zus would later say, because they were taught to respect their older brother. But it was strikingly obvious to all that Tuvia, now thirty-six years old, was the natural leader among the brothers.

Thirty-four-year-old Asael was named second in command, and thirty-year-old Zus, the third in the hierarchy, was appointed to oversee intelligence gathering. Pesach Friedberg was given the chief-of-staff position, responsible for organizing the fighting men and preparing them for missions.

Tuvia suggested that the unit be named for Marshal Georgi Zhukov, who he knew from radio broadcasts was Stalin's supreme military commander. Without any official contact with a partisan command organization, the brothers didn't see themselves as members of the growing Soviet partisan movement so much as they recognized in the Communists opposing the Nazis the possibility of an alliance that might prove useful at some point down the road. The brothers never had any real affection for the teachings of the Communist Party or for the existence of the Soviet Union. It was an accident of war that they had to pass themselves off as staunch members of the state, which, of course, they were happy to do at a time when it was waging war against such a ferocious enemy of the Jewish people. Although the group was now dedicated to saving Jews, it would in all outward appearances be working for the victory of the Russian Motherland over the fascist invaders, as propaganda messages put it.

And so it began.

Men from the group led by Yehuda Bielski and Pesach Friedberg were sent back into Novogrudek to bring people to the woods. Word was already spreading in the manual workers' ghetto—news always traveled quickly in the ghettos—about the shelter that could be found with the Bielski brothers of Stanke-vich. Everyone was talking about the flight of the brothers' cousin and many were eager to follow the same path. They also heard about Konstantin Koslovsky, whose home, it was said, was serving as a way station for those forest-bound.

The debate about whether to risk escape was raging. With a clear destination now in mind, many were willing to take the chance. In the manual workers' ghetto, the escapees only had to make it past a single wooden fence and dodge the Belorussian and Polish guards.

Once-reluctant parents were urging their children to leave, and some Judenrat officials were willing to furtively aid fugitives. Others were discouraged by rumors that the Bielski brothers refused shelter to anyone not related to them or unwilling to give them money.

But in the latter days of August 1942, the exodus began. Two Bielski fighters snuck back into the ghetto and approached Sonia Boldo, a twenty-year-old woman who was related to the Dzien-cielskis, and offered to take her to the forest. Initially reluctant, she was urged to leave by her parents. "You have to go," they said. "It is better to die from German bullets in the forest than slowly perish in the ghetto." Thinking she would be able to retrieve her parents later, she decided to make the journey.

She urged her friend, Lea Berkovsky, who was eighteen years old, to come with her. The idea terrified her, and she declined.

"No, I can't do it. Not without my parents," Lea said. "You go."

Sonia became angry. "You have to come with me," she said. "I'm afraid, too, but it is our only chance."

When Lea's parents learned of the idea, they urged their

daughter to make the journey to save herself. Her mother sewed money in the shoulders of her coat. "This coat will cover you," her mother said. "You'll sleep with it and it will keep you warm."

On the day of escape, Sonia's father passed a bottle of liquor to the ghetto guards, who proceeded to get so drunk that they neglected their duties. That night Lea, Sonia, the two fighters, and a few others slipped through the fence, dodged the soused guards, and began a twelve-kilometer walk through the country-side to the Bielski camp in the Butskevich Forest.

Before entering the forest, the fighters whistled three times, in a signal to the perimeter guard.

Sonia Boldo and Lea Berkovsky then walked into the camp and were astonished by the sight. A fire was roaring and men were walking about with firearms. But the Germans were so close! How could this be?

"I was too frightened to look at them," Sonia Boldo later said. "I wasn't used to people like these. They had been in the forest for months and they looked rough and disheveled. They didn't look like townsfolk to us."

She spotted Haya Dziencielski, a friend from before the war. Haya excitedly related how she was engaged—in effect, married—to the strapping Asael Bielski, one of the commanders of the group. Sonia, not known for her subtlety, responded: "Is there another commander for me?"

Indeed, there was. Zus, who had lost his wife and baby girl in the December massacre, was the only brother unattached, although he was by no means shy with women. But when Sonia took one look at the hulking man with pistols strapped to his waist and liquor on his breath, she paused. She was a pampered rich girl who had attended the best schools and dreamed of enrolling at a university in Paris, a city she visited twice prior to the war. As she stood before this vision of rough-necked masculinity, she felt her dreams of sipping coffee in the cafés of Europe slipping away.

"Do you want a little vodka?" Zus asked.

"Yes," she said hesitantly, having never before tasted alcohol. She took a sip. "Do you want something else?" he asked.

"No. I just want to rest."

Zus took off his coat and placed it over the young woman, who quickly fell asleep.

Over the next several days, Zus pursued her, asking her repeatedly if she would be his girlfriend. Sonia was resistant. "I thought to myself, 'How can I go to this man? I don't know him and I don't love him.'"

It was also hard for her to think of her pleasure while her parents were still imprisoned in the ghetto. She decided to make a deal with Zus: Take my parents from the ghetto and I will agree to stay with you.

Once the escapes began, they were not easy to contain. More and more people from the manual workers' ghetto of Novogrudek arrived during the end of August and the beginning of September.

Some of them found their own way into the forest. A young man named Michael Lebowitz who had left Novogrudek with his three brothers and four other men traveled to the home of someone he had known before the war. He asked if there was any news about the Bielskis and was told they'd been in the village a few days before.

Another peasant then offered to take the men close to the

Jewish camp. Not willing to trust him completely, Lebowitz pulled out his gun and pressed it to the man's back as they walked. "We don't trust anybody," he explained.

After they traveled a kilometer into the woods, the peasant pulled out a pistol and fired a signal shot into the air. Then a second shot was heard off in the distance.

"Over there," the peasant said, pointing through the trees. "You see the little fire? There they are."

Another young Novogrudek man, Ike Bernstein, reached Konstantin Koslovsky's house even though he had no idea how to find it. He snuck through the ghetto fence late one evening and spent all night wandering with two of his friends. After they stumbled upon the home, the kindly Belorussian greeted them with a smile. "You guys are lucky," he said. "You are going to live."

He offered the three a hiding place in his hayloft, where they got little sleep after the tensions of the escape. On the following day, Koslovsky prepared a bath for his guests and served them a meal of bread and potatoes. Later that night, four armed men from the Bielski camp arrived and the seven journeyed to the forest base.

A young woman from Novogrudek, twenty-year-old Raya Kaplinski, who had failed to evade German capture in December 1941 by hiding in her home, decided to leave the ghetto after receiving a letter of invitation from a Bielski fighter. But by the time her group of eleven friends was ready to depart, the guards were increasing their watch over the ghetto fences. Still, they decided to risk it. The escapees passed through the hole in the fence, but were spotted by several local police and Germans sitting on a distant hill. The soldiers opened fire. They dashed through an open field, unharmed.

Eventually, they reached the Koslovsky homestead, where Pesach Friedberg and young Aron Bielski happened to be there to greet them.

"Friends, do not be afraid," Friedberg said. "You are now free—nobody will chase after you here."

On the way to the forest camp, a dog barked loudly, causing the escapees to cower in fear. The Bielski fighters laughed. "They can't do anything to you now," they said.

During these extraordinary few weeks the size of the group more than doubled. Among the escapees were Sonia Boldo's parents. Zus had fulfilled his promise to the woman who was now his girlfriend—and who eventually became his wife.

But many in the ghetto weren't interested in leaving. Some had lost loved ones in the massacres and felt so distraught that they saw little point in life. "What do we care about leaving the ghetto?" a man who had lost his daughter said. "If we are to die soon, why don't we just die here?" Others feared spending the winter in the forest. For some, the Germans made the decision: They clamped down on security after the Kaplinski group left, slowing down the number of escapes.

Not everyone felt the same admiration for the Bielskis.

In the waning days of August, the brothers' gentile contacts warned them that a group of Russians were seething over reports that members of the Bielski unit were stealing from peasants.

It was inevitable that such reports would surface. Tuvia had told his men to be careful, to avoid unduly antagonizing a group of people upon whom they depended. The rules were simple: Take only what is necessary for survival and leave everything else. But as Jews they knew that what they did would be judged differently from what the gentiles did. An angry peasant, incensed by the idea of giving up his food to a bunch of Jews, was sure to complain about the "thieves." (Some in the partisan movement conceded as much. In a document dated November 11, 1942, a Soviet official noted that the "population here [west of Novogrudek] doesn't like Jews. They only call them Yids. If a Jew calls at a house and asks for food, the peasant says that he has been robbed by the Jews. When a Russian comes together with a Jew, everything goes smoothly.")

The word was that these partisans wanted the Jewish group eliminated. The first serious threat to the existence of the unit came not from peasants or Germans, but from guerrilla fighters who were on the same side of the battle as the Bielskis. The brothers felt they couldn't afford a violent confrontation with the presumably well-armed partisans. After discussing the issue among themselves, they decided to see if they could reason with them.

Emissaries were sent, contact was made, and a meeting was set. Fully armed, the brothers embarked with some hesitance, fearing the possibility of a clash.

After arriving at the appointed farm, they were introduced to a young Russian named Viktor Panchenkov.

Just a few months shy of his twenty-first birthday, Viktor was considerably younger than the three Bielski brothers. Even so, he already had plenty of military experience. A graduate of a military academy, he had served during the Red Army's 1940 invasion of Finland. He was then promoted to lieutenant and put in command of a machine-gun battalion stationed along the Soviet Union's western border. His unit was overrun when the Nazis invaded in June 1941, although the surviving members fought on for several days. He retreated to the Novogrudek area, far from his hometown in the Smolensk region to the east, and disguised himself as a farm laborer.

After the winter of 1941–42, he joined with other stray soldiers and local men to form a partisan unit. By April, the group numbered thirty men. Like the Bielski brothers, the budding partisans had established a leadership hierarchy and adopted a name on their own. Viktor was voted commander and the group was christened Unit No. 96.

The serious young man was also strikingly handsome, and the local women were always chasing after him. Even half a century later, several women proudly claimed to have been his wartime girlfriend.

The sight of him didn't have the same intoxicating effect on Tuvia. Surrounded by several armed guards, Viktor looked poised for confrontation.

"Why does the local population call your people a Jewish gang?" Viktor asked, getting right to the point. "Why do you plunder?"

Tuvia replied that he was not the leader of a "Jewish gang" but the commander of the Marshal Zhukov partisan group. "If you are Soviet citizens, you should know that the motherland needs us to fight the common fight against the German fascists," he said. "The motherland doesn't distinguish between Jews and non-Jews, but only between loyal citizens and riffraff that cause trouble."

It was not an unwise position to take with Viktor, who by all accounts was a loyal Communist, a true believer in the mandates of the party. He had grown up in a region that had been controlled by the Soviets since 1917, and his father had been the chairman of a collective farm. He believed that in the workers' paradise anti-Semitism would be nonexistent. Still, he had reservations.

"But the peasants insist that you are robbers," he said.

Tuvia suggested that the only way to resolve the issue was to investigate the charges. The two then agreed that they would travel to the village where the complaints were coming from.

Several nights later, men from both groups arrived in the village of Negrimovo, and advanced on the house where Viktor said one of the accusers lived.

Tuvia knocked on the window and requested that the peasant bring him some food.

"I don't have anything," the man said. "The Yids robbed me. They took everything, even the tablecloth from the table."

A young woman chimed in, saying that the Yids deserve to be killed. "We can't hold out any longer," she said. "For our Russians, we would give it up. The Germans take things by force. But the Yids!?"

Viktor was outraged by what he heard. His anger increased when he entered the home and found it stocked with food and alcohol. He grabbed his gun and threatened to shoot the man.

But Tuvia interceded. After identifying himself as the commander of the Marshal Zhukov unit, he castigated the now trembling peasant for his lies, threatening to execute him if he ever repeated the slander. "As long as this war goes on," he said, "you must never distinguish between partisans. A person who carries a gun at night and comes asking for food, whether he is a Jew, a Pole, a Russian, a Belorussian, or a Gypsy, is a partisan. If you do not learn this lesson from me, you should know that the bullet would teach you."

Tuvia was repeating the party line, echoing the radio broadcasts from Moscow—which was a wise tactic in winning over Viktor. Tuvia and Viktor repeated the action at the homes of the other accusers, which served to clear the Bielskis of all charges.

The investigation warmed the relationship between Viktor and the Bielski brothers, and they agreed to combine their forces for a partisan action.

With the harvest upon them, silos and barns were bulging with grain, ready to be carted away to the city and back to Germany or to the troops on the front lines. Viktor and Tuvia devised a plan to set fire to the bounty and shoot at anyone who came to extinguish the flames.

The two divided their men into small units and assigned each to light the fires at precisely midnight on September 1, 1942. The plan worked brilliantly. The fires were set—destroying, in Tuvia's estimation, thousands of tons of wheat and lighting up the sky for miles around.

As the men celebrated from a distance, they noticed Red Army aircraft flying above them, apparently returning from bombing missions farther to the west. Then a strange and fortuitous thing occurred. The planes dropped bombs on the fires, adding considerably to the conflagration.

"We enjoyed a beautiful show," Viktor later wrote. "The bread of the fascists blazed everywhere and the Soviet airplanes droned overhead."

The bombing greatly enhanced prestige of the two partisan groups. They had grown so strong, the rumors went, that they were now in contact with Moscow. It was even said that the Nazi Regional Commissar Wilhelm Traub was taken aback by the action and feared a partisan invasion of Novogrudek. It was wonderful news for the Bielski brothers. What better way to convince the peasants of the importance of providing supplies to the Jewish partisans?

To Tuvia, it was a sign from God that he was on the right track.

The action with Viktor had gone so well that the two groups discussed the possibility of more joint operations. But the brothers and others in the forest were still wary of an alliance with gentiles.

Why would they remain loyal to us? What would prevent Victor's men, if they were ever captured, from pointing their finger at the Jews? Although Viktor seemed like a good man, his associates were different. Zus characterized them as "bandits and anti-Semites."

Viktor, ever a Communist idealist, stepped forward to assuage their fears. He spoke about how anti-Semitism was foreign to the Soviet way of thinking. Anyone who expressed hatred toward Jews was an enemy of the Soviet people, he said, and deserved nothing better than to be shot as a traitor. "I will gladly fire the weapon," he said.

Viktor was also a gifted military leader, as became apparent when the two groups joined together for another action.

The idea was to strike at Germans who were appropriating food from peasants, in an attempt to discourage them from taking supplies that they saw as property of the partisans. The two groups devised a plan to ambush a German supply convoy along the highway that ran southwest from Novogrudek to the village of Novoyelna.

The Bielski fighters, numbering perhaps a dozen men, situated themselves close to a spot in the road where the vehicles would be forced to slow down. The fighters from Viktor's group, some ten partisans, hid on the other side of the road, just to the rear of the Bielski men. A young girl from a nearby village was instructed to tell the partisans when a convoy small enough to attack was moving in their direction.

The men bided their time while large, well-protected lines of German vehicles passed by the bend in the road. Eventually, the young informant arrived with the news that two vehicles—a small car filled with Nazi officers and a truck loaded with goods—were fast on their way. The fighters crouched into position.

After an agonizing wait, the lead car suddenly appeared, and the partisans unleashed a barrage of gunfire. But the car was moving too quickly to be hit. The men had just enough time to adjust their aim before the second vehicle became visible. This time the volley of gunfire found its mark. The truck's tires were shot out and its driver was hit, which caused him to slump in his seat.

Several Germans and local police jumped out and fired their weapons at the partisans. But they quickly realized that they were outmatched and dashed in the opposite direction, toward the forest, leaving behind a few dead comrades. The partisan fighters descended upon the truck, overjoyed at the sight of such an abundance of guns and food. Before returning to the woods, they set the vehicle on fire.

"We took as much food and supplies as we could carry on our shoulders," Michael Lebowitz, one of the Bielski men, recalled. "Later the Germans came back to retrieve the dead men and search for the people who had done this to them. They grabbed a guy who was chopping wood. They thought they found Tuvia Bielski. But he wasn't a partisan. They took him back to Novogrudek and hanged him in the marketplace."

The two groups divided the spoils, which included a few

machine guns, some rifles, hundreds of rounds of ammunition, and barrels of fresh food. After moving the camp deeper into the forest to ensure its safety that evening, the Bielski group enjoyed a festive meal, a spirited celebration of its first victory over armed Germans.

The successes bred confidence within both groups. They swaggered a bit more as they strolled through the tiny villages west of Novogrudek.

But life was full of monumental struggles, to say the least. In early September some Bielski group members tried to observe Rosh Hashanah and, ten days later, Yom Kippur, the period of self-examination and repentance that marks the holiest time of the Jewish year. The intense emotions of the holidays brought back all the pain of the slaughters. The enormity of the losses was almost unbearable.

Rosh Hashanah, the Jewish New Year, is traditionally a time to reflect on all that had happened in the previous year, to measure how one has lived up to God's expectations. Alter Tiktin, Tuvia's brother-in-law, resolved to conduct services with prayer books that had been smuggled out of the ghetto—to defy the Germans and affirm his identity as a Jew.

Several people gathered near him as he stood next to a tree and began reading. Eventually he came to the powerful Unetaneh Tokef prayer, written in the eleventh century by Rabbi Amnon who was told by a Catholic bishop in Mainz, Germany, to renounce Judaism or suffer the amputation of all his limbs. When the rabbi refused, according to the legend, he recited the prayer as the torture was being administered, and he slowly died. As Alter Tiktin read the stirring lines—"Who will live and who will die? Who by water and who by fire, who by sword, who by beast, who by famine, who by storm, who by plague, who by strangulation?"—he was overcome by despair. He fainted. It was many minutes before he could be revived.

The fighters of the Bielski and Panchekov groups also experienced their first failure together. They had planned an attack on the German-controlled Yatsuki railroad station, a small, isolated outpost of the Lida-Baranovich railroad. Surrounded by forest and located not far from the Bielski camp, it was manned by some forty Germans and protected by three machine-gun nests.

Late on a cool autumn evening, three squads of men from both groups took up positions surrounding the station and waited until early morning before beginning the attack. The signal to fire was given at six A.M. Initially startled by the fusillade, the Germans recovered and launched a counterattack, which enabled their men to crawl into position in the nests.

With the partisans under steady machine-gun fire, a train neared the station and passed by under heavy protection. The attackers used the opportunity to retreat, unable to destroy the station or to even capture any enemy weapons. "We didn't take any trophies," said Zus. On the other hand, none of the partisans had been injured.

After the battle, the Germans deployed additional soldiers to protect the railway outpost. The new men dug a trench around the installation and encircled the area in barbed wire. They also cut down much of the nearby forest in an attempt to limit the ability of partisans to launch another surprise attack.

The brothers were consumed with worries about challenges that lay ahead. With winter rapidly approaching, they wondered how they would keep more than a hundred people from freezing to death. With peasants spreading rumors about a possible German offensive into the woods, they wondered how they could defend against a large incursion. And their thoughts returned to the ghettos, where Jews continued to suffer. They had to rescue people before another slaughter.

Still, they found it hard to contain the feeling that they had achieved something significant. In the two months since Tuvia sent the letter to his cousin in the ghetto, the first real act of the group's expansion, the unit had grown from a small family gathering to a Jewish fighting force that had delivered blows against the Nazis. The brothers were now spearheading an against-all-odds resistance against a fearsome enemy that was expending every resource to eliminate Jews. How could they not feel pride?

"It was satisfying in a larger sense, a real spiritual high point, that the world should know that there were still Jews alive and especially Jewish partisans," Tuvia later wrote of these days. "We wanted to persuade the anti-Semites who lived in opulence and luxury on the account of our suffering that Hitler's weak prophecy—that a Jew would become something only seen on the movie screen in the cinema—was an outrageous hoax."

FIVE

OCTOBER 1942 – FEBRUARY 1943

As THE COOL AIR of autumn arrived in 1942, the brutal war was raging throughout the world.

Hitler's Final Solution was moving forward at a ferocious pace. A large portion of the killing was now being done by gas chambers in concentration and death camps, a chilling innovation intended to increase the body count. In a single month from late July to late August 1942, more than 200,000 Jews were killed in the hell of Treblinka, nearly all of them from the huge Warsaw ghetto. Historian Martin Gilbert called it "the largest slaughter of a single community, Jewish or non-Jewish, in the Second World War." The same sort of thing was happening elsewhere. More than 145,000 Jews were murdered during approximately the same period in the Belzec Death Camp a few hundred kilometers south of Treblinka.

The work of the Einsatzgruppen killing units in the occupied Soviet Union had slowed, largely because they had already slaughtered a huge number of the region's Jews—more than a million, according to some estimates. But it still wasn't enough for the Nazi killers. German officials were calling for a faster pace in the killing operations, pushing for more deportations of Jews from Eastern and Western Europe to the killing centers and for the execution of the remaining Jews of the occupied Soviet Union.

Though the Red Army had heroically prevented the Nazis from capturing Moscow and Leningrad, it was still struggling against a relentless enemy. In the spring, Stalin ordered a number of counteroffensives, all of which failed, depleting an already exhausted force. The Soviet leader was showing himself a poor military commander. But by the summer of 1942, Hitler was feeling more confident. In July, the Germans set their sights on Stalingrad, the city on the Volga River some two thousand kilometers from Berlin.

The attack began at the end of August when a Luftwaffe force of six hundred planes rained bombs on the city, killing an estimated forty thousand residents. The Germans readied themselves for a quick victory, but the Red Army stood fast. The blistering attack, from both the air and the ground, continued throughout September, leveling the city's landscape and inflicting huge amounts of civilian and military casualties. The Nazis felt it wouldn't be long before they marched through the streets of the city named for the Soviet leader.

The Soviet Union's Western allies, Great Britain and the United States, were busy with their own efforts against the Axis powers, leaving them unavailable to attack the European mainland and open up a western front. In the fall of 1942, the Americans joined the British Army in North Africa, where it had been fighting against the Germans and Italians since 1940. In November, the British Eighth Army scored a triumphant victory against General Field Marshal Erwin Rommel's Afrika Corps at the second battle of El Alamein, Egypt. But the African campaign was far from over.

The Pacific war, too, was unresolved.

Following the surprise attack on Pearl Harbor, the Japanese, intending to quickly destroy the naval power of the Americans and the British, won a series of spectacular victories throughout the early part of 1942. They took Burma, Guam, the Philippines, Hong Kong, Malaya, and Singapore. Then, in June 1942, the Japanese Imperial Navy attacked a smaller American fleet at Midway Island. Aided by intelligence gained from breaking the Japanese code, the Americans sunk four of Japan's largest aircraft carriers, shot down some 250 aircraft, and killed more than 2,500 Japanese sailors. The United States lost 307 lives, more than 100 aircraft, and a single aircraft carrier (the *Yorktown*). In August, U.S. Marines landed on Guadalcanal. It soon became obvious that a mammoth effort would be required to subdue the Japanese and take the island.

For the Bielski brothers, the rapid expansion of their group in August and September meant a considerable transformation of its structure.

For one thing, the young men from the ghettos had to be organized into small squads to fulfill the principal objectives of the organization—retrieving food; participating in actions against Germans, local police, or collaborators; and rescuing Jews from imprisonment in the city.

The three brothers, who now rode atop horses they had obtained from peasants, were clearly in charge. Tuvia was grow-ing into his role as the leader and symbol of the group. "I would rather save one old Jewish woman than kill ten Nazi soldiers," he would say. Zus and Asael, far from idealistic visionaries, were happy to leave the orations to their older brother. Both would rather direct the troops.

Asael had developed into a particular favorite of the young fighters, exuding the sound judgment and natural confidence so vital to young men inexperienced in war. He was willing to literally lead them into dangerous situations, to be the first, for example, to enter a strange peasant's home. But he was easygoing, and the soldiers regarded him as a friend. They didn't feel they had to watch what they said around him. If Tuvia was respected and honored, Asael was loved.

The brassy and boisterous Zus was more showy than the introverted Asael, more prone to move about the camp with a bold swagger and more willing to castigate those who he felt weren't measuring up. He wore his pistol shoved visibly into a belt that he wore at a forty-five-degree angle, like a cocky frontier fighter eager for a battle. He had none of Tuvia's innate generosity or Asael's easy warmth. But no one was better at scouting the countryside, which he could march through blindfolded. A better comrade during an anxious retreat from an attack on a police outpost couldn't be imagined.

The overall leadership during these months was aided by the arrival from Novogrudek of Layzer Malbin, a stocky forty-one-year-old who had lost five relatives in the August 7, 1942, massacre, including two daughters, ages seven and eleven. A stutterer, he was far from verbose, but he was a paragon of order and discipline, someone Tuvia felt "didn't know the meaning of fear." Malbin, who was a former officer in the Polish Army, quickly rose to the top of the command structure, becoming chief of staff in place of Pesach Friedberg, who took the position of quartermaster, overseeing the storage and distribution of food and supplies. A strategic thinker with an understanding of military tactics, Malbin was perfectly suited to help prepare the fighting units for missions.

When new men arrived in the camp, however, it was Tuvia who outlined the group's mission.

Like trainee soldiers, they were told to line up for review. After everyone was in position, the three brothers would arrive, imposing figures in their long leather jackets and knee-high military boots. One man remembered Tuvia taking off his right glove and shaking hands with each of the men before turning to introduce his two younger brothers.

Then he spoke. "We need more people with rifles," Tuvia said. "More people will be coming from the ghettos and we have to be ready for them. Commander Viktor [Panchenkov] is a good man and will help us all he can. Enemies surround us. We have to fight together with Viktor's unit against the Germans."

The young soldiers, men of action, were the most valued members of this new community. They set its tone, striding about with confidence, drinking *samogonka* obtained from peasants, and speaking in coarse language. Not surprisingly, the forest felt at times like military barracks. "It was rough," said Sulia Rubin, who was eighteen years old when she arrived. "It was difficult to get accustomed to it, because it was completely different from a protected home and wonderful parents."

Inevitably, despite the hardships that everyone had lived through, romance blossomed in the forest. Couples stole away to search for a private spot, while the whisperers back in the camp gossiped about what was going on. Many of the women felt that they had a better chance of survival if they entered a relationship with a young fighter. But several of the unions proved longstanding, far deeper than the initial surge of attraction.

If the men of action were the most valued, the unarmed, who represented the majority, were the least esteemed—no matter what Tuvia had decreed about the importance of protecting the most endangered Jews. They were jeeringly referred to as *malbushim,* the Hebrew word for clothes, which communicated the sense that they were as useless to survival of the base as a pair of pants. People grumbled when the old and sick or the young and vulnerable arrived, said Lilka Tiktin, the teenage girl who had escaped from Lida ghetto with her father, stepmother, and stepbrother. "People said, 'We don't need them. We don't need them.'"

As the weather grew colder, the brothers had to devise a way to keep the group protected from the elements. They decided to create two small winter bases in adjacent forests near the old family homestead in Stankevich. Some of the group would be placed in a forest known as Perelaz, while the others were assigned to the Zabelovo Forest, a short walk away.

But it was clear that the group couldn't sleep on the ground or under blankets propped up by tree branches. They had to create insulated structures. Under the guidance of Yehuda Levin, a carpenter who had arrived in the camp at the end of August, construction was begun on four large earth-and-wood dugouts—two in Perelaz, two in Zabelovo—that would hold twenty to forty people each.

Using saws and axes obtained from peasants, the workers cut down trees and placed several wooden posts along the perimeter of a few-meters-deep hole. The spaces between the posts were filled with smaller pieces of wood to keep out the dirt. Then taller wooden posts were placed in a row along the middle of the hole to hold up the roof. The planks of wood that formed the flat surface of the roof were braced against these center posts on one side and against the ground on the other side. The surface of the roof was packed with dirt, branches, and vegetation to camouflage the structures.

The dugout's residents entered and exited via a small ladder located on one end. After stepping down onto the dirt floor, they saw two lines of wooden bunks, usually covered with straw "mattresses," on either side of a narrow hallway that led to the far end of the room. Not much light penetrated into the space, but burning strips of damp pine bark, which could smolder for hours, generated a dim glow. Although most of the dugouts were spacious enough to allow a person to stand upright in the middle passageway, the space was cramped. If a person turned over during the night, the entire row of sleepers had to turn over with him.

Once the shelters were built in Perelaz and Zabelovo, another dugout was built at a third location nearby. It served as a sort of hospital, although the group had few medical supplies. Pits were also dug to store potatoes and other perishable goods.

The brothers' enterprise was aided by its strengthening bond with the partisan Viktor Panchenkov.

The young Russian shared intelligence with Tuvia and consulted with him before going on military actions. The two also divided the nearby villages among them, and each agreed to lead food expeditions only into designated zones. But Panchenkov's most important assistance was his willingness to direct wandering Jews, many of whom had fled the ghettos without a clear idea of where to turn, to the Bielski camp. He would either accompany them to a spot where they could spy the location in the distance or he would deliver them to a friendly peasant who would show them the way. The assistance didn't always spring from kindness. It reflected his unwillingness to abide anyone who might disturb the peasants upon whom he depended. But with stories circulating about Soviet partisans arbitrarily killing Jews, Panchenkov's cooperation was a godsend.

The two groups also joined together for social occasions. Members of both units celebrated the anniversary of the Great October Revolution on November 7, 1942. They listened to patriotic radio broadcasts from Moscow, which, as always, urged all Soviet citizens to harass the German occupiers. On November 16, the date of Viktor's twenty-first birthday, they met again to sing partisan songs and stuff themselves with peasant food.

During these weeks of relative peace, the brothers were growing more confident about their ability to protect their people. They were also feeling that they might be able to remain in the woods of Zabelovo and Perelaz indefinitely.

They were wrong.

In the early days of December 1942, with the ground now covered in snow, the Germans launched a major offensive in the forest, beginning many kilometers to the west, in the Lipichanska Puscha, a stronghold of Soviet resistance fighters and home to Jewish partisan groups formed from escapees from the ghettos in Dzatlavo and other small cities.

Within days, the brothers were hearing harrowing tales of the carnage from Jews who had fled the fighting. They told how the Nazis were combing every inch of the forest, burning down homes and executing unarmed peasants; they described how the

Germans fired indiscriminate barrages of artillery and showed no mercy toward those who were captured. Among the dead were Dr. Yeheskel Atlas, a brave Jewish partisan leader who was posthumously awarded the Hero of the Soviet Union award, and Hirsch Kaplinski, a ghetto escapee who had formed a Jewish fighting group in the summer of 1942.

The ferocity of the attack led the brothers to put everyone on high-alert status. With the Bielski camps now containing more than a hundred Jews, evacuation plans were discussed and the fighters were drilled on how they would defend the bases.

But with the sound of the gunfire coming closer, the brothers decided it was time to move. They resolved to abandon the carefully constructed dugouts and head north toward what they hoped would be safer territory. The brothers had obtained horse-drawn carts from peasants, which helped to transport cookware and tools. The convoy set off through the forest pathways that the brothers knew so well.

Within a few days, they reached a forest outside the tiny village of Zuravelnik. Large fires were built and makeshift tents were constructed. Everyone wrapped himself in animal pelts and blankets and huddled before the flames.

But the brothers still worried about the possibility of enemy attack. They feared that police spies had followed them to the new location. When a suspicious woman was found wandering nearby—she claimed to be searching for mushrooms—they knew they had to move yet again. The procession resumed its trek to the north for a few more kilometers, this time stopping in a forest outside the little hamlet of Chrapinyevo.

It was a trying journey. But on the first evening, a few of the younger people grew comfortable enough to sing softly in front of the fire. One of the most popular songs that night was an old Gypsy song that speaks of "how the camp sleeps and the fire slowly dims while all around is silence."

"Come my dear, awaken me," a verse goes, "come and heal my distress. Always for you, my friend, I will wait. Always for you."

A few days later, some even quietly celebrated Hanukkah. The holiday commemorates the miracle of the oil that lasted eight days in the menorah of the Temple upon the victory of the Maccabees over the Hellenistic occupiers of Jerusalem and defilers of the Temple. After recounting the familiar tale, one of the men mentioned that he had heard that the Soviets were finally scoring victories in the East. Someone predicted that the Red Army would push the Nazis back to Berlin by Passover in the spring.

But such moments of optimism were few. Most were suffering terribly in the new location, especially since they no longer were able to sleep in the relative comfort of the wooden dugouts they had just abandoned. Some of the fighters, tired of the aggravation of supporting the unarmed and helpless *malbushim*, spoke about leaving to form their own units.

The most vocal dissenters were two brothers from Novogrudek—Aron and Mordechai Lubchansky—who loudly declared their intention to strike out on their own.

It was just the kind of agitation that Tuvia had warned against in August when the group was first formally organized. Asael and Zus wanted to attack the two, but Tuvia resolved to deal with the matter in a more measured way. He ordered everyone in the group to assemble in a sort of military formation. He then denounced "a certain anarchy" that had been initiated by the two Lubchansky brothers.

"Our aim, as I have already said, is to bring more Jews into our ranks and take them into our family with wide-open arms," he said. "We have proceeded on this holy mission with true sacrifice. And now we've received a 'reward' from the Lubchansky brothers. I ask the brothers themselves, 'Who was it who taught you to shoot? And from whom did you get your guns?'"

Then, without hesitation, he ordered the Lubchansky brothers and their allies to be expelled from the group—but not before their weapons had been confiscated. He gave them twenty-four hours to leave and threatened to have them shot if they delayed.

It was a clear signal to everyone how Tuvia intended to deal with those who challenged him. He felt that the group was strongest when it was united, and he wanted to halt any movement to split it into parts. He knew that his ideas had to be backed up with strength.

In this case, the Lubchanskys backed down. They recanted their denunciations and asked to be reinstated into the group. Tuvia agreed to let them stay, on the condition that the weapons be returned only after they proved their loyalty.

Within another week or two, the fear of a German attack subsided and the brothers decided that the danger had passed. They began sending small groups, escorted by armed fighters, back to the original wooden dugouts in the Perelaz and Zabelovo forests to the south.

The Bielski brothers remained behind to aid a group of Jews who had escaped from a small ghetto not far from Lida. But they weren't the only group members who didn't return to the secure bases. A small contingent of the unit's higher echelon (about twelve people in all) instead sought shelter in two peasant homes near Chrapinyevo, occupied by elderly Poles. It would turn out to be a tragic mistake

Tuvia's wife, Sonia, who was suffering badly from the cold, went into one house with her sister, Regina Tiktin, and Regina's son, Grisha Mites, all of whom had been removed from the Lida ghetto months earlier by Tuvia. A few armed fighters joined them. Zus's wife, also named Sonia, stayed in the other home with Haya, Asael's wife, and Israel Kotler, a ruthless fighter who was ironically nicknamed Salanter, after the far-from-ruthless founder of the Musar Movement, Rabbi Israel Salanter.

They couldn't have chosen worse places to hide. In the early afternoon of January 5, 1943, a troop of local police and Germans, dressed in long, white coats that camouflaged them against the snow, marched to the houses. They overtook the single guard that the Jewish partisans had posted on the road, killing him instantly, and made their way toward the tired, ill partisans.

Two Russian fighters who were traveling nearby saw what was unfolding and made their way to the house where Salanter and the wives of Zus and Asael were staying. "Get out now!" one of them said. "The Germans are coming!"

The three ran out of the house as quickly as they could, pushing through hip-deep snow. Suddenly Zus's wife, Sonia, dropped below the surface of the powder, apparently falling into a hole used to store potatoes.

"Haya, you go," she said to Asael's wife. "Tell my parents and Zus that I am finished."

Haya and Salanter refused to abandon her. They grabbed Sonia, at first by her hair and then by her arms, and yanked her out of the hole. The three then trudged toward the tree line, finally reaching the safety of the forest.

They were the lucky ones. The enemy soldiers lobbed a grenade through a window of the other home and opened fire on everyone who tried to escape. Everyone in the house was killed.

A few moments later, the Germans discovered Lev Vulkin, who had hid in the outhouse behind the main dwelling. He was taken from the scene and questioned about the whereabouts of the brothers' camp. When he refused to divulge any details, the young man was viciously tortured—Haya heard that his eyes were gouged out—and later hanged in the marketplace in Novogrudek.

Though Tuvia, Zus, and Asael were some distance away, they could hear the sounds of gunfire. The three galloped on horseback toward the homes. But they were too late. Both structures were fully engulfed and bodies were everywhere. "It was something indescribable," said Tuvia. All three men assumed their wives had been lost in the battle.

At least nine Jews were killed in the tragedy near Chrapinyevo, the first losses suffered by the Bielski unit in the six months since it had been officially formed. Three Poles who owned the houses, and who risked so much to harbor the Bielskis, were also killed.

That evening, a group of men from Chrapinyevo, who had been recruited by the local police commander, arrived to bury the bodies.

"About fifteen of us went," Ivan Koreniuk, a Belorussian resident of the hamlet, later said. "People here are interested when something happens. We buried them. All of them were without clothes. The police—probably not the Germans—took all of the clothing. Then they were put in a pit without a marker."

The three brothers were devastated; they traveled to Konstantin Koslovsky's home, where they mourned for the dead—particularly, of course, their young wives. The next morning, however, they saw a horse and sleigh approaching. Miraculously, Sonia Boldo, Haya, and Salanter were alive. Asael and Zus were stunned. "It's like they'd arrived from another world," said Zus.

But Tuvia's wife, Sonia, was not among them. Tuvia couldn't be comforted. The next morning he and Zus mounted their horses and took off into the snowy countryside.

They rode for days, wandering without any destination. Finally they returned to the bases at Perelaz and Zabelovo, where they resolved to improve intelligence-gathering techniques and increase perimeter security measures. The Chrapinyevo attack had been a stunning blow to everyone's sense of safety. Any sense that they were invulnerable was now gone forever.

As always, the community continued to grow. Jews arrived at all hours of the day and night, sometimes in groups, sometimes alone. Camp residents invariably quizzed them about conditions in the ghettos and the health of surviving inmates. Since weapons were so hard to find, the appearance of a Jewish fugitive with a gun was a particularly happy occasion. The brothers were always eager to add fighters who could defend the camp.

One man who arrived in January, Isak Nowog, a thirty-year-old escapee from the Nazi labor camp in Dvorets, a small town a few kilometers southwest of Novogrudek, told Tuvia about a group of twenty Dvorets escapees, some of whom were armed, hiding on an isolated farm near the hamlet of Abelkevitch, not far from Dvorets.

Tuvia, who had already heard about the group from Viktor

Panchenkov, asked Nowog if he knew how to find the group. He said that he did.

"Then we will visit them," Tuvia said. "It's a great opportunity to increase the number of armed men in our unit."

Late in the evening, the three Bielski brothers and nearly a dozen other men set out on horses and sleighs. As they passed the German outpost at the Yatsuki railroad station, the fighters jumped off their horses and walked through the danger zone. "The Germans were nestled down in their bunkers, warming themselves by their hot stoves," Tuvia later wrote. After traveling all night through the countryside, with Nowog serving as guide, the men arrived just before dawn at a farmhouse with a barn. Both were nearly buried in snow.

Guards were placed around the property, with the promise, because of the frigid temperatures, that they would be replaced soon. The rest headed to the farmhouse, where the farmer greeted them and offered breakfast. After the meal, the partisans mentioned that they had heard that Jews were hiding in his home. "What? I know nothing about Jews," he said, making the sign of the cross. He was pressed further. He denied all until Tuvia pulled a pistol on him.

"Look in the barn," the man said.

The group marched into the barn and called out to their fellow Jews. There was no response. They looked around for evidence of inhabitation and found, under a bale of straw, what looked like the entrance to an underground cellar. One of the Bielski men, Ben-Zion Gulkowitz, opened the door and shouted in Yiddish: "Jews! Do not fear! Come out!" No answer.

Gulkowitz, taking his pistol in hand, climbed down into the

enclosure and discovered several partisans standing with guns at the ready. "Comrades, Bielski, the Jewish partisan commander, would like to speak to you. Why not come up?"

A sleepy Israel Kessler, the leader of the group, showed himself and agreed to the request.

After the two men exchanged pleasantries—Kessler had heard of Bielski and his unit—Tuvia was invited into the cellar to meet the rest of the group. Several two-tier bunks lined the edge of the room. In the center was a table surrounded by chairs. The commotion had shaken everyone from his slumbers, and now they were agitated and confused.

Kessler lighted a kerosene lamp, and Tuvia made out some of the faces peering at him.

"I am Tuvia Bielski," he said, "organizer of a Jewish partisan group."

"Tell me, comrade, are you David's son from Stankevich?" a man asked.

"Yes, and who are you?"

"I am Avremel, the brother of Mishke from Butskevich."

"Ah, yes!" Tuvia said.

They enjoyed a pleasant morning, chatting warmly. A few of the Bielskis' men settled down to get a little sleep. Later in the day, after everyone was rested, Tuvia spoke of more serious matters.

"This place isn't safe," he said.

He told them that local farmers could inform the Germans about this hiding place at any time. A few well-thrown hand grenades would kill everyone.

"I have a large group and I want you to join us," he said. "Bring your women and children, all your supplies, and we'll be free as birds. There is no ghetto and there is no fear."

Then Tuvia added one further incentive: Our Russian friend Viktor Panchenkov has decided to kill you all.

Kessler scoffed. "We have rifles too!"

"Enough of living like this," Tuvia said. "Bring everything and let's go!"

Kessler asked if he could have time to discuss the matter with his men. He returned with a counteroffer. Four of Kessler's men would travel to the Bielski base and decide whether it was worth moving everyone to the new spot.

"Have you studied the Bible?" Tuvia said. "Joshua sent spies to Jericho and they fell into a trap. They had to use the help of a whore to get away. With me, you won't conquer Jericho. You are coming to join us. We have rules and order and you'll live like us. There is no need to negotiate."

They talked among themselves again, and finally agreed to the transfer. "It will be safer there," Kessler told his people. "Bielski is right."

Kessler asked Tuvia if his group could remain together in a separate dugout at the Bielski base. Tuvia shrugged. "Why not? The forest is big enough for another dugout."

With the tension diminished, handshakes were exchanged and a few jokes were cracked. Then Kessler asked for silence. He spoke of a local man who was responsible for delivering many Jewish men, women, and children to the Germans. His house was nearby, Kessler said, and it was likely full of weapons. Everyone understood what he was suggesting. Tuvia liked the idea of joining with the new comrades in a strike against the enemy.

Leaving under the cover of darkness, the group set out toward the village of Abelkevitch. When they arrived, the partisans stopped at the first home they came upon. They asked the gentile there a few logistical questions—about the location of the Germans and partisan forces, about the roads and where they led—revealing nothing of the nature of their operation. Then they moved through the dark village, which looked the picture of slumbering idyllic country life. *It's as though there isn't war going on,* Tuvia thought. *It looks like nothing has ever disturbed this place.*

The group then proceeded to the informer's house, which was on the outskirts of town. Once they found it, they posted guards and selected a few men to speak to the master of the property. The fighters put on red armbands, on which they had drawn black swastikas, and walked to the entrance.

Ben-Zion Gulkowitz knocked several times before a balding, middle-aged Belorussian shouted through the door, "Why all the noise? I'm coming."

"Are there any strangers in the house?" the men asked.

"No."

They entered. Pesach Friedberg sat down on the bed next to the man.

"How are things going?" Pesach asked.

The man responded with an anti-Semitic rhyme, which spoke of how "we are alive and we are killing Jews."

"We are also catching Jews," Pesach said. "But I want to know why you are dragging your feet? So many Jews are on the roads. Why haven't you captured more than you have?"

"I've nabbed plenty," the man insisted. "A few days ago I turned in two women, two children, and two men. I tied them up like sheep and kept them overnight in my barn. They nearly froze to death. Then I took them to the police station. A few weeks ago, I found, I think, eleven people. Then I caught another two—one had a revolver—and turned them over to the police."

While the man spoke, his wife stood at his side, showing pride in his accomplishments.

Pesach looked at Tuvia and detected nervousness in his demeanor. The commander paced the room.

"He is our man," Pesach said to Tuvia, calling him by a Russian first name. "See what immense work he has accomplished."

Pesach asked if the informer had enough weaponry to carry out his duties. "Oh, yes." The man asked his son to retrieve his machine gun and revolver. As the guns were produced, Pesach looked up at Ben-Zion Gulkowitz, who was standing near the door. He saw the impatience in his eyes.

"But how are you able to do it?" Tuvia asked. "How can a man with a conscience turn over people that will be killed? Why are you doing this?"

"What do you mean, sir?" the man replied. "It is the law. We have to obey the law."

"Do you know who I am?" Pesach demanded, unable to hold back any longer.

"Who?"

"I am a Jew." He slapped the man across the face. The rest of the group angrily revealed their Jewish identities and, as Tuvia called it, a "bloody concert" commenced in the peasant's home.

The entire family, forced to lie on the floor, was strafed with bullets. "The family was killed," Tuvia later said. "No living soul was left, not even a cat or a dog."

The men searched the house and found clothing adorned with yellow stars. After seizing the man's horse and taking his weapons, the partisans set the house on fire. In front of the burning structure, Tuvia placed a large sign, on which he wrote a message explaining that the family had been executed for helping the

Germans catch Jews and that a similar fate would befall anyone who did the same.

The burning house illuminated the entire area. As they prepared to depart, Tuvia suggested that they avoid traveling through the heart of the village. A back route through the woods would be safer, he said. Asael dismissed the idea. "We will go right through the village!" he announced.

The horses and sleighs were loaded up and the procession moved through town. Just as Asael's lead sleigh cleared the village limits, a group of villagers opened fire on the group. The informer's horse was hit, and the animal and its sleigh were abandoned. The rest of the sleighs sped forward, in a desperate attempt to avoid the gunfire.

Pesach and Zus, who were sharing the last wagon, unloaded several rounds of machine gun fire and hurled a few hand grenades toward the attackers, using nearly all their ammunition. The speeding sleighs made it out of town, with just two men suffering minor injuries.

"Blood was everywhere," remembered Michael Lebowitz, who was shot in the hand and chest. "I told them, 'Leave me behind. I'm finished. My heart is finished. They got me in the heart!'"

Asael didn't need to glance at his wounds to know that Lebowitz would be fine. "If they hit you in the heart," he said, laughing, "you would be dead." Eventually they arrived back at the camp, having instilled fear in any Nazi collaborators in the Abelkevitch area and boosted the size of the Jewish unit by twenty members. It was a successful excursion, the brothers agreed.

In the early weeks of February, a horseman from Viktor Panchenkov's unit arrived at the Bielski camp bearing a letter addressed to the leaders of the unit. The note, sent by Fyodor Sinitchkin, who was identified as the commander of the Lenin Partisan Brigade, invited the brothers and their top commanders to a meeting near the village of Butskevich.

Eight Bielski men, including all three brothers, rode to a small clearing near the edge of the forest, where they found a large gathering of fighters from various units, including Viktor Panchenkov and Fyodor Sinitchkin himself.

"I bring greetings from the motherland!" Sinitchkin said. It was obvious to the brothers what he meant: A partisan leader with a direct link to Moscow had arrived.

The forty-two-year-old Sinitchkin was a Red Army captain of Russian peasant stock who had joined the military in 1919 and served during the Polish-Soviet War of 1920–21. Since his appointment by Soviet officials as the head of the Lenin Brigade in December 1942, he had been organizing partisan units into cohesive networks that could respond to orders from a central command. Now he was expanding his brigade's influence—his headquarters were in the Lipichanska Puscha—into the region west of Novogrudek.

He flattered the brothers by mentioning that he was aware of their activities.

"Our plans are to disrupt the enemy at every turn," he said, turning to the entire gathering. "We will disrupt the railway system, cut telegraph and telephone lines, and burn bridges. We will disrupt the German food supplies. We will try to save as many lives as we possibly can."

Sinitchkin explained that each unit would now be designated as a detachment (*otriad* in Russian) within his brigade and thus be responsible to the dictates of his command. In turn, his Lenin

Brigade was subordinate to the leaders of the Baranovich Branch of the Central Staff of the Partisan Movement, headed by Major General Vasily Chernyshev, known by his nom de guerre "General Platon."

He then asked each commander to provide a detailed description of his unit's manpower, weaponry, and food supply.

Tuvia, speaking in fluent Russian and using the jargon of the party, reported that his Marshal Zhukov group had 250 members, less than half of whom were capable fighting men, and detailed its stock of goods. He emphasized that if he had more weapons, he could send more fighters into battle.

After the other commanders finished, Sinitchkin announced the details of his reorganization plan. It seemed to amount to little more than changing the unit names. A group led by a Russian named Mikorin would be known as the First of May Detachment, Viktor Panchenkov's fighters, previously known as Unit No. 96, would now be referred to as the October Detachment. The Bielski group would be known as the Second Company of the October Detachment. The detachments, Sinitchkin said, were required to stay in close contact with the brigade staff, keeping it informed of fighting activities, new members, and munitions supplies.

It was a slow start in this corner of occupied territory to what Moscow hoped would be the rigid political and military control of all partisan groups. Instead, the day-to-day operations of the units in the Lenin Brigade remained up to the discretion of the detachment leaders, and explicit commands were issued only when a large-scale mission was in the works. During these days, according to Layzer Malbin, Tuvia's chief of staff, "we hardly ever received orders from above about operations."

But the brothers' unit was now officially part of the partisan movement, and its goal of saving Jewish life—saving Soviet life, as Tuvia described it to Sinitchkin and other partisan leaders—was sanctioned by the military authorities. Stalin himself had decreed that the struggle "should include all honorable male and female citizens desiring liberation from the German yoke." In practice, Jews had a much harder time of it. When the brothers visited Sinitchkin soon after joining the brigade to complain about Russian partisans confiscating weapons and clothing from Jews, the commander promised to look into the allegations. Nothing ever came of it.

SIX

FEBRUARY 1943– APRIL 1943

THERE WAS NO MORE magical word to those imprisoned in the Novogrudek and Lida ghettos than "Bielski." It suggested a fairy-tale world where Jews were free from the pain of Nazi oppression, and collaborators cowered before Jewish strength. Just its utterance gave the weary prisoners a sense of hope.

About a thousand people remained in the two ghettos of Novogrudek, half in the courthouse ghetto, home to the skilled craftsmen, and the rest in Pereshika ghetto, which contained the manual laborers. Over three thousand more Jews were living in Lida's single ghetto, where a German leaflet was discovered promising 10,000 reichsmarks to anyone who would aid in the capture of Tuvia Bielski.

Following the slaughter of the previous spring, Lida's Jewish police force had been staffed with new members, and the reconstituted Judenrat reorganized the work details and distributed some of the victims' belongings to the poorest of the ghetto Jews.

The workshops were expanded under the supervision of two Judenrat leaders, the engineer Altman and the merchant Alperstein. The two men believed that the Germans had no intention of killing the skilled laborers, who worked tirelessly to avoid the execution ditch. In the carpentry shop, men built toys for the children of the Nazis, including a train set for the youngsters of Regional Commissar Hermann Hanweg. Leather workers made belts, purses, and wallets, items that received rave reviews from the female staff of the RC. Hanweg often told Altman and Alperstein how pleased he was with the Jews' industry. "Nothing bad will happen to you even if all the Jews in the other ghettos are annihilated," he said. "You will remain alive here."

Not everyone was convinced. Many young men struggled to acquire weapons, often through clandestine barter with gentile peasants. Damaged guns were repaired in the metal workshop, right under the noses of the RC staff members. And occasional escapes to join the partisans were attempted. But most were still hesitant, especially with stories circulating about Jews being ambushed by Russian partisans or turned in by farmers seeking rewards from the Germans.

Whatever else life was like in the Lida ghetto, its inhabitants no longer had to contend with the two most violent Nazis to serve in the city: Rudolf Werner, who loved to sic his German shepherd on Jews, and the fanatical Deputy Regional Commissar Leopold Windisch, who orchestrated the massacres of May 1942. Werner was transferred to a post in Estonia, and Windisch was sent to Riga, Latvia.

The Jews of Novogrudek ghettos experienced no similar relief, however minor. People were killed for the sport of it—a courthouse ghetto guard shot a man who lit a cigarette late one evening, aiming his fire toward the orange glow of the burning tobacco. (The victim lived.) The RC staff, especially the vicious Judenreferent Reuter, bullied the ever-weakening workers into increasing production. Despite threats of retaliation, escapes were attempted frequently, often when the Germans allowed inmates of the courthouse to visit a water pump outside the ghetto walls.

By winter, the Jews of the city learned that they had lost some valuable allies. The Germans killed a Polish couple who aided ghetto escapees—the Bobrovskys, dogcatchers before the war—after it was discovered that they had been assisting Jews. The husband and wife were shot, their home was set afire, and their six children were deported to a concentration camp in Germany.

Konstantin Koslovsky's younger brother, Ivan, was also lost during these weeks. He had been using his position as a Novogrudek policeman to assist in escape attempts and to deliver weapons and intelligence to the Bielski brothers. In his last days, he felt his end inching closer. He would sit silently in his brother's home for hours, staring into the emptiness. Certain that his superiors had discovered his role, he tried to make a run for the forests and the partisans. He was captured, shot, and burned in a shed on the road to Lida.

Then on February 4, 1943—a few days after the German Sixth Army formally surrendered to the Red Army, ending the bloody, seven-month battle for Stalingrad—Regional Commissar Wilhelm Traub decided that he no longer needed the services of the Jewish laborers of the Pereshika ghetto. The entire population of about four hundred Jews was transported to Litovka, near the site of the August 7, 1942, killing, and executed.

That evening, the Judenreferent Reuter visited the courthouse ghetto, which held about six hundred Jews, and announced that the laborers were killed because they failed to meet their work quotas. "They were good for nothing," he said.

．　．　．

For the Soviet Union, the victory at Stalingrad marked a turning point in the war. The Germans, who had lost more than a hundred thousand men during the campaign, suddenly seemed less than indestructible. The extraordinary bravery of the defenders of Stalingrad gave the nation a renewed pride, and a reconstituted Red Army was eager to push the enemy back toward the west. But the Germans weren't yet defeated; they still held huge chunks of Soviet territory.

The British and American campaign against German and Italian forces in North Africa was now leaning in favor of the Allies. The British Eighth Army took Tripoli in January and then pushed west into Tunisia. It looked as though the fascists wouldn't last more than a few months. But the German U-boats prowling the Atlantic were still wreaking havoc on Allied sea transports. In four days in March, the Nazis sunk twenty-seven merchant ships.

Difficult battles were still being fought in the Pacific. American troops on the tiny island of Guadalcanal finally defeated the Japanese in February 1943, after six months of grueling fighting. It was one of the most trying battles of the war. The Americans learned that their enemy in the Pacific would not be easy to defeat. They braced for many more months of difficult clashes.

While the war was starting to turn against the Germans and the other Axis powers by the early months of 1943, the job of eliminating the Jews was becoming an even more urgent priority of the Nazis. They were even willing to divert trains needed for the war against Allies to transport more Jews to the gas chambers. On January 20, 1943, Heinrich Himmler sent a famous letter to the Reich minister of transport: "I know very well how taxing the situation is for the railways and what demands are constantly made of you," he wrote. "Just the same, I must make this request of you: help me get more trains." In this regard, the Germans were experiencing frightful successes: By mid-March 1943, about 80 percent of all the victims of the Holocaust had already been killed.

The Bielski group was now a large gathering of roughly three hundred Jews living in two adjacent forests—Zabelovo and Perelaz—a few long stone's-throws from the brothers' boyhood home. It was evolving into a society of exceptional creativity and resilience, one of the few places in all of occupied Europe where Jews lived with some measure of freedom.

A number of additional wood-and-earth dugouts—the most vital structures of the community—had been built to accommodate the steadily increasing population. Among the nicest was the one constructed by Israel Kessler's group from Abelkevitch. It was full of comfortable blankets and feather pillows, much prized items that rarely made appearances in the deep woods. The living quarters were spread out over a large area of the snowy landscape, so well hidden that newcomers had to be escorted to them.

Close to each structure was a campfire that warmed frozen bodies and cooked the food. Potatoes, a staple of the forest diet, were baked directly on the coals and eaten, if it was a good day, with salt. Large tubs retrieved from the villages were used for every sort of necessity—to take baths, to clean laundry, to prepare soup. A few doctors rescued from Novogrudek helped tend to the sick and wounded, but often the best, and only, medicine for the chills of a winter night was a stiff glass of *samogonka*.

The brothers themselves were now further removed from the mass of the population, distant leaders who carried an air of absolute authority. They could be seen galloping on their horses through the woods or on their way to the villages. Few of the refugees from the pitiful life of the ghettos would ever forget the first sight of these men with submachine guns strapped over their shoulders, Soviet military caps resting confidently on their heads. "If you saw how the brothers went out on their horses, you would think it was Stalin and his assistants," said Ike Bernstein, one of the fighters. "The ground was shaking."

But as imposing as he was, Tuvia didn't neglect his duties to the weakest of the community. He made it a habit to visit each of the dugouts, where he would inquire about everyone's health and welfare or chat about current goings-on. He showed particular concern for the growing number of children. His legendary tears were often shed when he embraced one of them, so moved was he by the suffering they had experienced. He was like a father to everyone.

A major priority of the camp remained the dangerous task of retrieving food. The young fighters, who were only able to work under cover of darkness, sometimes spent several nights on the roads attempting to complete their tasks. It was a messy job that required a willingness to be brutal, a willingness to threaten the life of a peasant who resisted giving up food.

The brothers knew that their success required a willingness to back up threats with the possibility of real violence. They wouldn't survive for long if they hesitated to deal harshly with anyone who threatened their existence. The peasants had to understand that their lives were in jeopardy if they informed on the Jews in the forest.

The group's ability to instill fear in the villagers closest to their bases was enhanced by the capture of two German informers, local men who had actively sought to capture the Bielski brothers.

The first was Vatya Kushel, the Pole from Stankevich whose family had once been close to the Bielskis. During the tsarist times, Vatya's father had helped David Bielski keep possession of the mill when Jews were forbidden to hold rural property. When the Nazis arrived, Vatya joined with the pro-Nazi police force and, in one of his many anti-Bielski acts, pointed out young Aron Bielski to the Germans on the street in Novogrudek, which nearly led to his death.

One night a few Bielski fighters entered a home owned by two Polish sisters and asked, as was the custom, whether any strangers were staying on the property.

"Vatya Kushel from Stankevich is here, and he's asleep," one of the sisters said.

The fighters dragged the man from bed, bound him head and feet, and marched him off to Asael, who was preparing to burn down a small wooden bridge—an attempt, however minor, to disrupt German transportation routes.

"We have a present for you," the men said.

Asael questioned his longtime neighbor and ordered his execution without hesitation.

"One of the fellows then chopped his head off with an axe," said Aron. "I remember it like yesterday. I was fifteen feet away. He chopped his head off with a single chop."

The men then threw the lifeless body onto the bridge, which they set afire.

The second was Aloysha Stishok, the son of the Bielski family's longtime mill worker, Adolph Stishok, who had sneered at Beyle and David Bielski when the Germans carted them away to Novogrudek. Both men had begun working with the occupiers soon after they arrived. But the elder Stishok was nowhere to be found. He seemed to have fled the area for good. Aloysha, though, was found by another group of Bielski fighters.

The young man was accosted and escorted to the Bielski camp. During questioning, he admitted that he once led a group of twenty-five Lithuanian auxiliaries into the woods in search of the brothers' location. "I deliberately took them to the wrong place," he pleaded. "I've been forced to cooperate with the Germans. I didn't want to do it." He was fed a hearty meal, during which he tried to talk his way out of his predicament. As his fate became obvious, he wept and sputtered and begged for his life.

When Aron walked in on the scene, Aloysha recognized the boy he had known since childhood and his mood brightened. But Aron was neither willing nor able to save a man he regarded with contempt. Tuvia ordered some fighters to take Aloysha deeper into the woods, where he was hanged from a tree.

Despite the brothers' best efforts, they knew it was nearly impossible to keep enemies at bay, especially with so many people now living in the forest. And in February of 1943, trouble arrived in the forests of Zabelovo and Perelaz. A simple act of human error led the enemy directly into the Bielski refuge.

Early on February 15, after a night of searching the countryside for food and supplies, a group of Bielski fighters returned to the Zabelovo base. It was a successful mission, with the booty piled high on the wooden carts. But in the darkness, the men hadn't realized that an animal they had appropriated from a farmer and killed before starting the journey back was dripping blood onto the snow. The job of the pro-Nazi police on that cold morning couldn't have been easier. All they had to do was follow the trail of blood and they would find a partisan base.

That's what they did. Later in the morning, a contingent of the enemy, riding in horse-drawn sleighs, entered the Zabelovo Forest and came within sight of one of the Bielski perimeter guards, Shmuel Oppenheim, an escapee from Novogrudek who was situated about a kilometer from the base. He took one look at the parade nearing him and assumed that Tuvia Bielski and other detachment leaders were returning to camp. In a flash, a policeman hopped from a cart and opened fire on the outmatched guard.

Hit in the face, Oppenheim fell forward into the snow, creating a puddle of blood around his head. One of the men from the attacking force stood over the body and kicked at it with his boot. "He's done," he said. Another man rifled through Oppenheim's pockets, looking for valuables.

The rest of the force rushed toward the partisan hideout. But before they were able to reach it, a second Bielski guard appeared and immediately began discharging his weapon. The exchange between the lone guard and the police force, which may have numbered as many as a hundred men, signaled to everyone in the distant encampment that an attack was in progress. Layzer Malbin, the highest-ranking officer at Zabelovo, urged everyone to run deeper into the woods.

Guards protecting the second Bielski base farther away in Perelaz, where Tuvia and his brothers were conducting an inspection, heard the volleys of gunfire and understood what was happening. An immediate evacuation was ordered, and people grabbed whatever they could—a piece of dried meat, a pair of underwear—and fled in every direction.

The police force easily killed the brave second guard. Facing no further resistance, they entered the Zabelovo base, which was now completely deserted. With nothing better to do, they set about ransacking the place, lobbing grenades into dugouts, and kicking over kettles of soup. On the way out, they grabbed anything of worth, including several farm animals and horses.

After the police retreated, Tuvia and his brothers arrived to survey the now destroyed camp. They then rushed to the third forest location, the first-aid center, which, miraculously, had not been noticed by the policemen. The brothers came upon another fortuitous discovery. Resting among the wounded was Shmuel Oppenheim. He described to them how the gunfire had merely nicked the bridge of his nose and how he was able to crawl to the isolated dugout, where a recent addition to the unit, Dr. Henrik Isler, treated his wound.

The lack of casualties represented a stroke of good fortune greater than anything the brothers had yet experienced. But they had little time to think about it. They spent the day searching for the scattered members of the group. Fearing that another attack was imminent, they decided to relocate everyone to the old summer base in the Butskevich Forest—the location of their first organizational meeting in August 1942. They set out with everything they could carry, walking the route in shocked silence. By daybreak, with the weary marchers arriving in growing numbers, breakfast was cooked over hastily built fires. It was so cold that day, one man remembered, that hot soup froze in the bowls.

The sick and injured were taken to peasant homes for greater comfort. Tuvia also went to one of the homes to spend the first night with his new wife, the woman he would stay with until the day he died, Lilka Tiktin.

He had been drawn to the seventeen-year-old, regarded by many as the prettiest in the forest, in the weeks after his wife's death. Tuvia had known her since before the war, when she would serve as a messenger for his then-girlfriend, later wife, Sonia, delivering romantic notes to his apartment in Lida. But he grew to regard her in a different light.

Lilka's feelings for Tuvia had also evolved. She had fallen in love with him at first sight, but over the course of the war she had also come to respect him. Her stepmother, Regina, who was killed at Chrapinyevo with Tuvia's wife, Sonia, had treated her cruelly and Tuvia understood the trauma that she was undergoing. He knew without being told that she was still grieving for her mother, who had died in 1938.

When Tuvia revealed his feelings for her, Lilka didn't resist his advances. Her father, Alter Tiktin, who was just a few years older than Tuvia, put up plenty of resistance. "He thought Tuvia was taking me for a playmate, a game," she later said. "My father was afraid that I would be mistreated, or maybe after the war he would leave me." The two would always celebrate their wedding anniversary on February 15, the day of the first enemy attack on a Bielski base.

In the coming days, the brothers and their top command discussed the group's next move. They decided to pursue a course of action similar to the one that had saved so many people during the Zabelovo attack. The unit would be split into small groups— several discrete divisions had formed naturally over the past few months anyway—and dispersed across wider areas of the forests. As before, meetings would be held regularly to coordinate food missions and discuss enemy activities. The Bielski brothers would continue to carry the responsibility for the safety of everyone.

Although it probably wasn't necessary in such a charged atmosphere, the brothers renewed their call for increased vigilance. The drops of animal blood on the Zabelovo snow had taught them that it didn't take much to be discovered.

But the brothers were now forced to contend with trouble from another source. As if peasant informers, local police, and the Germans weren't bad enough, the Bielskis had to deal with meddling Soviets.

Since the group was now an official participant in the Soviet war effort—the Second Company of the October Detachment within the Lenin Brigade of the Lida District of the Baranovich branch of the Central Staff of the Partisan Movement—it would have to put on a greater show of its loyalty to the Communist cause. Although partisans were heralded in Soviet propaganda as brave warriors defending the motherland, Stalin regarded them with great suspicion. He didn't trust what he couldn't control. And it was hard for him to control a large mass of guerrilla fighters, men and (some) women gifted in subverting established authority, who were spread across a huge territory. They frankly made him nervous.

Stalin did everything in his power to establish a system of regulation. He decreed that every partisan detachment be staffed with a commissar, who was an enforcer of party doctrine, and a "special section" (*osobyi otdel* in Russian) of the NKVD, which was to oversee internal security. He wanted these party stalwarts to ensure that everyone was acting in a manner befitting a loyal Communist or, more precisely, a loyal Stalinist. Since the arrival of Captain Fyodor Sinitchkin, Stalin's representative in the woods west of Novogrudek, the Bielski brothers knew that they would have to transform their group into something that conformed more closely to the Communist model.

Worried that a commissar would be chosen for him, Tuvia named Layzer Malbin, his chief of staff, to the post. Everyone knew that Malbin had no interest in furthering the Soviet cause.

Tuvia also established a Komsomol (Communist Youth League) chapter for prospective members of the Communist Party. He appointed to head the chapter the first gentile member of the Bielski unit, Grigori "Grisha" Latij, a man who was allowed to join the detachment because he was married to a Jewish woman.

The Komsomol cell quickly grew into a hive of opposition to the leadership of the Bielski brothers. Instead of dedicating themselves to Tuvia's larger, graver purpose of saving Jews, they concentrated on undermining the brothers' leadership by attempting to expose the commanders' lack of ideological purity. Whether they were acting out of genuine feeling for the party or out of resentment of Bielski rule is not fully known. Tuvia himself felt they were motivated by simple jealousy.

The most prominent opponents were the gentile Grisha Latij and the Lubchansky brothers (who had already expressed their unhappiness with the style of rule). Though not a member, Israel Kessler, the leader of the group from Abelkevitch, was sympathetic to the group's ideas.

Their first shot across the bow was a protest against the appointment of Layzer Malbin as commissar. They felt he couldn't properly serve in the ideologically important position because he had once been a member of Betar, the revisionist

Zionist youth group. They also charged that the brothers allowed capitalist speculators to operate in the group, including a man who they alleged trafficked in vodka.

The rebels brought up the charges to Fyodor Sinitchkin when he arrived with some of his aides. It was a serious act of opposition that could have led to the dispersal of the Jewish group among more politically reliable Soviet bands. The Jews would've then been forced to cope with the anti-Semitism that was endemic to many Russian detachments.

Sinitchkin, though, wasn't interested in the complaints, and he dismissed the charges out of hand. Frustrated, the Komsomol members took their grievances to one of Sinitchkin's superiors, an officer who served on the staff of General Platon, the ranking partisan in the entire Baranovich region. A meeting was convened with the Komsomol members and Tuvia to discuss the charges.

As he had done in previous discussions with partisan leaders, Tuvia spoke in the doctrinaire jargon of the party, pledging his undying loyalty to the Soviet cause and to the great Stalin himself. He defended his decision to appoint Malbin to the post of commissar. He discussed each of the men in Grisha's group, pointing out their weaknesses as partisans, and suggested that perhaps they should form their own unit.

"We understand you have forty thousand rubles," the Russian officer said. "Don't you know that the money belongs to the Soviet Union?"

Tuvia was stunned by the question.

He explained that cash had been obtained through dealings with peasants and was used to purchase weapons and other supplies. He then outlined all of the group's expenses, down to the

The Bielski property in Stankevich in the early part of the twentieth century. Asael is at the far right; Zus is third from the right. (*Photo courtesy of Aron Bell*)

The handsome and charismatic Tuvia Bielski (*far left*) in Subotniki during the mid- to late 1930s, when he operated a business with his first wife, Rivke. The two men in uniform are Polish policemen. (*Photo courtesy of Michael Bielski*)

Asael Bielski, the responsible brother who wanted nothing better than to take over his father's mill, pictured before the war. *(Photo courtesy of Haya Bielski)*

The brash Zus Bielski, pictured in 1947 with his wife, Sonia, would throw punches first and ask questions later. *(Photo courtesy of Sonia Bielski)*

Young Aron Bielski, the plucky forest scout, pictured after his arrival in Israel in 1945. *(Photo courtesy of Aron Bell)*

Tuvia Bielski as he looked during the war years. *(Photo courtesy of Michael Bielski)*

Asael Bielski before being conscripted into the Red Army. *(Photo courtesy of Haya Bielski)*

Zus Bielski wearing the Nazi jacket he took from a German lieutenant, Kurt Fidler, whom he killed during an ambush on January 28, 1944. *(Photo courtesy of Sonia Bielski)*

The site outside of Novogrudek where 4,500 Jews, including David and Beyle Bielski and Zus's first wife, Cila, and baby daughter, were massacred on December 8, 1941. *(Photo courtesy of Peter Duffy)*

Konstantin Koslovsky, the selfless Belorussian peasant whose home on the edge of the woods served as a way station for Jews fleeing the Novogrudek ghetto. *(Photo courtesy of Museum of Regional Studies, Novogrudek, Belarus)*

Ivan Koslovsky, Konstantin's younger brother. He worked for the Nazi-allied police but grew disillusioned and began aiding Jews. *(Photo courtesy of Museum of Regional Studies, Novogrudek, Belarus)*

Viktor Panchenkov, the young Russian soldier who became an early partisan ally of the brothers. *(Photo courtesy of Museum of Regional Studies, Novogrudek, Belarus)*

Pesach Friedberg was part of the first group to escape the Novogrudek ghetto and join the Bielski brothers' group. He was eventually appointed quartermaster. *(Photo courtesy of Lea Friedberg)*

Layzer Malbin, a former officer in the Polish Army who rose to be Tuvia's chief of staff and one of his most trusted lieutenants. *(Photo courtesy of Raya Kalmanovitz)*

Raya Kaplinski, a young woman who was assigned the role of secretary of the brothers' outfit. *(Photo courtesy of Raya Kalmanovitz)*

Shmuel Amarant, an intellectual who taught at a teachers' college before the war, was named camp historian. *(Photo courtesy of Tamar Amarant)*

Shmuel Oppenheim, a Novogrudek handyman who became one of the most vital members of the Bielski unit: the gunsmith. *(Photo courtesy of Miriam Stepel)*

Solomon Wolkowyski, a lawyer whom Tuvia chose to be the director of the "special section" responsible for internal security of the group. (*Photo courtesy of Genia Pinski*)

Fyodor Sinitchkin was the first Soviet partisan with a direct link to Moscow to come in contact with the brothers. (*Photo courtesy of Photo Archive of the Republic of Belarus*)

A Belorussian native of Dobreya Pole named Yvgeny Shulak points out the spot where ten Jews from the group, including Tuvia's father-in-law Alter Tiktin, were killed in March 1943. (*Photo courtesy of Peter Duffy*)

Krasnaya Gorka, the site of the brothers' greatest escape, as it looks today, no longer an island after governmental drainage projects of the 1960s dried up much of the swampland in the Naliboki Puscha. *(Photo courtesy of Peter Duffy)*

Vasily Chernyshev was known by his nom de guerre "General Platon." To the brothers, he was the "boss over all the woods." *(Photo courtesy of Photo Archive of the Republic of Belarus)*

Sergei Vasilyev, who succeeded Sinitchkin as the brothers' brigade commander, ordered the execution of Asael Bielski. *(Photo courtesy of Museum of Regional Studies, Novogrudek, Belarus)*

The Lida-Baranovich railroad, near the Yatsuki station, was a favorite target of Bielski sabotage activities. *(Photo courtesy of Peter Duffy)*

A photograph of Bielski partisans who were manning the airport in the center of the Naliboki Puscha. *(Photo courtesy of Sonia Bielski)*

Yefim Gapayev, whose nom de guerre was "Sokolov," was the dashing aide of General Platon who supported the work of the Bielski camp. *(Photo courtesy of Photo Archive of the Republic of Belarus)*

A group of Bielski partisans pays its respects at one of the massacre sites near Novogrudek in the summer of 1944. *(Photo courtesy of Larry Rosenbach)*

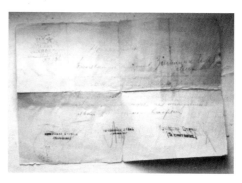

The document issued to Ela Zamoschik on the day the Bielski detachment was disbanded in July 1944. Tuvia's signature is on the left, near the official stamp of the group. *(Photo courtesy of Peter Duffy)*

Sulia Rubin shows off boots that were constructed in a forest workshop. *(Photo courtesy of Peter Duffy)*

Lilka and Tuvia Bielski. *(Photo courtesy of Michael Bielski)*

Sonia and Zus Bielski. *(Photo courtesy of Sonia Bielski)*

Asael and Haya Bielski. *(Photo courtesy of Haya Bielski)*

A group of Bielski partisans, including Michael Lebowitz (*fourth from left*) and Ben-Zion Gulkowitz (*far right, holding the picture*), pose in a displaced persons' camp in Italy with a portrait of Asael Bielski after learning of his death. (*Photo courtesy of Michael Lebowitz*)

A 1960s photograph of the forest leaders, after they helped raise funds to send an ambulance to Israel. *From right to left:* Tuvia, Lilka, Zus, Sonia, Lea Friedberg, and Pesach Friedberg. At the far left is Layzer Malbin. *(Photo courtesy of Lea Friedberg)*

The Nazis of Lida, Rudolf Werner *(left)* and Leopold Windisch, sit in the dock in 1967. Werner was declared unfit for trial. He died in 1971. Windisch was sentenced to life in prison. He died in 1985. *(Photo courtesy of AP/Wide World Photos)*

Sonia Bielski in Brooklyn, New York. (*Photo courtesy of Peter Duffy*)

Lilka Bielski in Brooklyn, New York. (*Photo courtesy of James Estrin/The* New York Times)

Haya Bielski in Haifa, Israel. *(Photo courtesy of Peter Duffy)*

Aron Bell with his wife, Henryka, in Florida. *(Photo courtesy of Aron Bell)*

money they had used to purchase a submachine gun. He emphasized that the unit always offered receipts to peasants after any transactions, as was required by partisan protocol.

Unable to contain his anger, Tuvia charged the informers, as he called them, with callously slandering his group. We have been fighting against the fascists long before we ever received any orders from Moscow, he said. We have caused casualties and we've taken booty. We've attacked German outposts and punished collaborators. And we will continue until the final victory.

The Russian was satisfied with his words. But he suggested that Tuvia work with the rebel group to ensure that allegations of this sort wouldn't be raised again. As Tuvia left the meeting, he felt that a major disaster had been averted and he wondered how he could contain the threat. If the Komsomol members hadn't involved the Soviets in the internal workings of the group, he likely would've just expelled them from the group.

In the coming weeks, Tuvia found a strong ally in this internal struggle. A group of Jews sought entry in the Bielski unit after being discharged from a Soviet detachment, and their leader was Solomon Wolkowyski.

Wolkowyski, a thirty-one-year-old graduate of a Vilna law school who was a practicing attorney in Lodz and Baranovich before the war, had been accepted into the Grozny partisan detachment after escaping with his sister and several others from a German truck bound for the execution ditches. The Russian commander, impressed with his intelligence and erudition, assigned him to an important position in the group, responsible for drafting reconnaissance reports. He and his group of unarmed Jews remained for a few months, until the commander announced that they would have to leave the detachment.

The quiet, self-assured attorney was intimately familiar with the administrative ways of Soviet partisan life. But he was also dedicated to Tuvia's principle of preserving Jewish life. The commander thought he was the perfect person to head the "special section" responsible for internal security, the other important ideological position yet unfilled. The lawyer eagerly accepted the appointment.

Tuvia now had two friends in the sensitive "Communist" posts of the group—Layzer Malbin was commissar and Solomon Wolkowyski was head of the special section. For the time being anyway, he felt protected from the leadership challenges of the rebel Komsomol cell.

He had an immediate assignment for his newest staff member: Keep an eye on the rebel group.

The Bielski brothers now were in the midst of fighting at least four different wars—they had to defend against the possibility of attack from Germans and local police, they had to obtain food from peasants who could easily inform on them, they had to mollify a Soviet command structure that was often suspicious of Jews, and they had to keep tabs on internal dissension that could jeopardize the continued existence of a large, wholly Jewish unit. It was a Herculean effort that required the brothers and their top aides to work to their strengths—Asael, Zus, and Layzer Malbin guided the armed fighters in defense strategies and food-retrieval work, while Tuvia, now aided by the presence of Solomon Wolkowyski, coped with the Soviets and maintained internal order.

But just when one of these four fronts seemed to stabilize, another would flare up and bring the potential for disaster.

In the middle of March, a group of ten Jews, including Alter Tiktin, the father of Tuvia's new wife, Lilka, set out to search for food a few kilometers north of Novogrudek.

Before he left, Alter approached Lilka, who was sitting near a fire with a few of her friends.

Because of his age (late forties) and his close relationship with the commander, Alter wasn't required to participate in the danger-fraught expeditions, usually completed by much younger men. He was also still mourning the wife and stepson he had lost two months ago at Chrapinyevo. But as he told his daughter that evening, he was determined to be useful to the group. He was tired of having others risk their safety for his benefit. He wanted to be a working member of the detachment.

Lilka begged him to reconsider. "Dad, please," she said. "Tuvia doesn't know about it and he wouldn't want you to go. All we have is each other. Do you want to leave me alone in the world?"

The proud man couldn't be swayed. "I must do this." He bid her farewell and disappeared in the night.

A few minutes later, he returned. At the sight of him, Lilka began sobbing. "My words left an impression," she said. "You're staying."

"No, I must go," he said. "But I forgot to kiss you."

He leaned over and kissed her on the forehead. "Good-bye," he said. And then he was gone.

After a night or two of securing necessities, two members of Alter Tiktin's group—brothers Abraham and Ruben Polonski—suggested that the group seek shelter during the daylight hours with a pair of Belorussian brothers whom they knew from before the war. They would surely offer refuge until nightfall allowed them to return to one of the Bielski bases.

The partisans drove their horses and sleighs through the snow to the hamlet of Dobreya Pole, a tiny assemblage of twenty or so homes that was close enough to Novogrudek that its big poplar tree could be seen from the city's Castle Hill.

Vladimir and Galiyash Belous and their families—a total of eighteen people—shared the largest house in the little village, each family with its own entrance. They were simple farmers who, because of their sizable broods, worked from early morning until late evening just to feed every mouth.

At the sight of the Polonskis and the other Jewish partisans, the Belous brothers offered a warm welcome and promised them a place to rest up for the day. But behind the friendly gestures lurked a more sinister impulse: What the Polonskis didn't know was that the brothers had been anything but friends to Jews since the Germans had occupied the area. Vladimir Belous's son Nikolai was a proud member of the police force in Novogrudek that had been so complicit in the Jewish slaughters.

The partisans, exhausted from the trekking, settled in the warm home and were soon sound asleep. That's when Vladimir's fifteen-year-old son Pavel slipped outside, commandeered a horse from one of his neighbors, and galloped the five-kilometer distance to Novogrudek. He found Nikolai and told him about the Jews who were resting in Dobreya Pole.

Later in the afternoon, a motorized contingent of fifty policemen and several German gendarmes arrived outside the hamlet. They turned off the vehicles' engines and approached the Belous house on foot.

The partisans became aware of the impending assault— perhaps they heard the sound of the vehicles, or maybe a member of the Belous family inadvertently tipped them off to the coming danger. They dashed from the house before the soldiers arrived at the doorstep, running in the direction of the nearest patch of forest. It was about three hundred meters away. In order to reach the woods, they had to travel down a small hill and then up its far side before making it to safety.

By the time the partisans reached the upward slope on the distant side of the small valley, the soldiers were in position to fire. In the overwhelming barrage of gunfire that followed, nine of the ten Jews were killed—including Lilka's father. Only Abraham Polonski survived the onslaught.

But rather than return to the forest, Polonski did something completely unexpected. He waited until the Germans and the police left the village, then returned to the Belous house and called out to Vladimir and Galiyash, asking how they could've done something so horrible to their friends. Before he received an answer, he was struck from behind with an axe, killed instantly by one of the brothers.

All ten Jews from the original group were now dead. The bodies were placed on a horse cart by hamlet residents and driven into the forest they had so longed to reach. A common grave was dug in the soft ground, and its outlines were visible for decades to come.

When the team didn't return promptly, Tuvia ordered a contingent to scout the area to learn what they could about the missing men.

In the meantime, with the temperatures beginning to rise, the brothers decided to bring everyone together again in a single forest. Since they couldn't return to the discovered dugouts at Zabelovo and Perelaz, they found a new location in another small forest, Stara-Huta, which, like all the other bases, was not far from Stankevich. By April 15, some four hundred Jews, including about one hundred armed fighters, traveled through the melting snow to the new spot.

The group was becoming better and better known across the countryside. The legend was spreading. Jews who had escaped from ghettos other than Novogrudek and Lida were now walking many kilometers to find this place of Jewish liberation. Soviet partisans and peasant villagers were talking among themselves about the three brothers who were watching over all of the Jews—and who so brutally punished those who crossed them. The local police and Germans were growing more aware of a gathering of people whose very existence represented an affront to their war strategy.

The new base soon began to resemble nothing so much as a small Jewish village. Ghetto escapees who were skilled tradesmen resumed practicing their trade. Shoemakers, using tools obtained from peasants by the fighters, repaired boots, saddles, and harnesses, often in exchange for a little vodka. Tailors mended soldiers' torn shirts and frayed jackets. A team of metalworkers, led by Shmuel Oppenheim, the former Novogrudek bicycle-repairshop owner who'd been injured during the February 15 raid at Zabelovo, worked on broken pistols and rifles. Even a barbershop was opened. It proved quite popular, with people waiting in line for their turn in the chair.

The armed men, whose importance to the survival of the group increased with every new member that arrived, were reorganized into fighting squads of eight to ten men each. Although he was the second in command, Asael Bielski personally took charge of one of the squads, preferring to be out in the thick of the action rather than back in the (relative) safety of the camp. He had no interest in sorting through the problems of Soviet bureaucracy. Neither did Zus Bielski, who directed the activity of cavalry reconnaissance teams that were formed to gallop through the villages in search of enemies.

Several partisan actions were launched in the first weeks of spring. Fighters burned a series of wooden bridges situated on roads leading north out of Novogrudek. Telephone and telegraph lines were disabled when the men chopped down the poles that held them aloft.

Tuvia also called for a renewed effort to free those still imprisoned in the ghettos. Since the Lida ghetto had a few thousand inmates—far more than Novogrudek's six hundred—fighters were instructed to see if it was possible to bring Jews from Lida to the woods.

Bielski fighters with relatives still imprisoned in the city often led the missions. One route involved sneaking to the city's still functioning Pupko Brewery—it churned out a steady supply of beer for the Nazis—which was located just down the street from a wooded area. Staffed by several Jews who received a special dispensation to live within its confines, the brewery provided the partisans a place to rest while they disguised themselves in yellow star–adorned clothing. They would then walk into the ghetto, acting as if they were returning from a forced-labor assignment.

A partisan named Moshe Manski led one of the rescue operations. After he slipped past the ghetto guards on a warm April day, he had little trouble finding people willing to make the return trip to the woods. One of them was a young man named Eliahu Damesek, who decided with great regret to leave his elderly mother behind. He packed a bag, containing clothing and several hand grenades that he had been hoarding over the months. Late in the evening, he slipped from his house and snuck to a spot near the fence where the escape group was to meet. It included several people, including five women, who hadn't been invited on the trip by Manski.

But there was no turning back. The men dug a small hole under the barbed wire, and as soon as everyone had crawled through, they packed the dirt back into the hole, hoping the ghetto guards wouldn't notice it. After clearing the city, they marched through the fields, passing at times through swampland that nearly submerged them in muck. But Damesek didn't feel a bit tired, so energized was he to be out from under German domination.

Then a voice penetrated the darkness. "Halt! Who goes there?" someone shouted in Russian.

"We are part of the partisan group commanded by Bielski," one of the Jews responded.

In seconds, several Soviet partisans surrounded the escapees and greeted them with enthusiasm. They were members of a detachment that was part of Fyodor Sinitchkin's Lenin Brigade and they knew all about the Bielski brothers. "Come, we'll help you cross the river," one the partisans said, referring to the Neman River.

The wanderers traveled through the countryside for another two nights—hiding in the forest during the daytime hours—before coming upon a peasant house that was known as a partisan outpost.

Asael Bielski, who was visiting the house with several comrades, heralded the arrival of the Lida refugees. The peasant couple prepared a meal of sour milk and potatoes for the weary travelers. The escapees were then escorted through the forest to the Bielski base, a walk of about an hour, where they found several hundred people casually going about their day. The fighters were resting in tents and dugouts after a long night of searching for food. Women were preparing meals in a primitive cookhouse featuring a few large pots being warmed over campfires.

Damesek looked in the distance and saw what he described as "the commanding figure of Tuvia Bielski himself, broad of shoulder, a giant of a man." Tuvia approached the new arrivals, shook each of their hands and offered a brief word of introduction.

"Where were you all this time?" he said, in his pull-no-punches manner. "Why did you delay your coming? Why did you wait until members of your family were slaughtered?"

After lunch, the newcomers watched as everyone was given assignments for the coming evening. Perimeter guards were directed to their posts, fighting groups were told of that night's destination, and noncombatants were sent to care for the sick and wounded. As night arrived, family and friends of the young soldiers grew steadily more concerned about their safety. The agitation mounted until the moment when everyone strolled into camp the following morning (or two or three mornings hence), with, if they were lucky, a cart full of goods or a tale about a successful act of sabotage.

By the middle of April, fighters had returned from Dobreya Pole with news about the ten missing Jews. The brutal tale, which the men had heard from peasant contacts, was told to the brothers, who decided upon a swift and merciless response. Their decision had little to do with the carefully mapped-out war strategy. The brothers were angry, and they wanted revenge. They felt that these people must be taught that Jewish blood doesn't come cheap.

"We will avenge the deaths of our people," said Tuvia, who had lost his father-in-law, Alter Tiktin. "But that is our only purpose. Do not take anything from these brothers. I don't want anyone accusing us of banditry. Don't give them an excuse to call us Jewish thieves." This, he said, is a "sacred mission of blood for blood."

Asael assembled a group of thirty men. Dr. Henrik Isler, one of a few detachment doctors, asked to join so he could be on hand to officially pronounce the murderers dead. The unit arrived in the hamlet on the evening of Friday, April 23, by coincidence the day when Orthodox Christians commemorated the death of Christ (and the time of the year when Christians throughout the ages, angered after once again hearing the story of their savior's death, incited pogroms against the "Christ killers," the Jews). The holiday guaranteed that a large number of Belous family members would be at home.

They arrived in Dobreya Pole at around midnight; Asael instructed his men to surround the house and prepare to enter at his signal.

Asael then dismounted and approached on foot. He pounded on the door and stormed into one entrance of the house with Pesach Friedberg, Michael Lebowitz, and a few others.

While the stunned family leaped from their beds to discern the nature of the commotion, one of the Belous brothers—it's not known which one—attempted to flee through a cellar door. Lebowitz, who stood little more than five feet tall, lunged at the man, grabbing him before he was able to escape. The two then wrestled on the floor, each struggling desperately for advantage, while the Bielski men took aim.

"Don't shoot," Lebowitz shouted. "You're going to hit me."

Asael ignored the warning and blasted away, striking Mr. Belous in the neck. His shot was followed by many more. A massacre was under way.

Acting quickly, the men searched the house for any hidden family members. They failed to find anyone. Lebowitz, who had barely escaped Asael's bullet, found a black wool jacket. In defiance of Tuvia's order, he decided to wear it back to camp.

The partisans set fire to the Belous house and placed a sign in front of it that promised similar treatment to anyone who betrayed them.

The fire destroyed several structures on the Belous property, the gentile neighbors remembered, and even spread to a few of the neighbors' homes. A total of ten Belous family members were killed on that day while as many as five people escaped through a passageway in the roof, they said. The conflagration also killed horses, cows, and other farm animals.

With the brutal mission now completed, the Bielski group made its way back to the Bielski base at Stara-Huta. Along the way, Michael Lebowitz reached into the jacket he had confiscated and found a letter written in German. He shoved it back into his pocket and didn't think about it until they reached the base.

Upon arrival, Lebowitz offered it to Tuvia, who also recognized it as written in German. He handed it to the lawyer Solomon Wolkowyski, who translated its message. Written by Wilhelm Traub, Novogrudek's Nazi regional commissar, the letter thanked the Belous brothers for turning over the forest bandits and offered the two men fifty reichsmarks for their cooperation. "When you help us again," it said, "you will get more."

The note served the detachment well a few days later, when Viktor Panchenkov confronted Tuvia about the revenge mission in Dobreya Pole. The Russian angrily pointed out that partisan procedure requires that accused collaborators be put on trial to authoritatively determine guilt. You can't kill someone without just cause, he said.

"They killed ten of our men!" Tuvia said.

"You must follow procedures!" Viktor said.

Tuvia produced the letter, which served to quiet Viktor's complaints. Tuvia then broke out a bottle of vodka, and the men enjoyed a few peaceful drinks together.

SEVEN

MAY 1943 – JULY 1943

EVEN AS A FEW HUNDRED new Jews arrived in the Bielski camp in Stara-Huta in the spring months, many of them from Lida, there remained a sizable contingent in the Lida ghetto who believed that the escapees (and the partisans assisting them) were endangering the lives of the entire population. It had been a year since the mass killings of the previous May, when some thirteen thousand Jews were murdered during five days of slaughter. Perhaps this meant that there would be no more such massacres—so long as the Jews didn't rock the boat.

"Jews, you are bringing catastrophe upon yourselves," said Lida's regional commissar Hermann Hanweg in a talk he gave to the laborers of the workshops after learning of the surge in escapes. "You want to suffer hunger, cold, when they are unnecessary? After all, you are a wise people. Do you think that with your rusty rifles you will be able to sabotage the German army that has conquered all of Europe?

"I can promise you that in the city of Lida not a hair will fall from a Jew's head. Those who had to be liquidated have already been liquidated. I did it in a humanitarian fashion. Why anger the Jews a number of times by executing them one group after another? I carried out the program all at once and you who have remained can now live quietly. I will build a large kitchen. I will prepare a bath in the ghetto and set up a ritual bath for the religious Jews, so that you will be able to live hygienically.

"Only one thing I demand of you—work well and diligently. In order to prove how much I am your friend I am ready to pardon Jews who return from the forest."

Speeches of this sort would have been less persuasive to the six hundred Jews living in the courthouse ghetto of Novogrudek. A major massacre had been committed about every six months in the city since the first one on December 8, 1941, killing between eight and ten thousand Jews.

Then, early in the morning of May 7, 1943, the Jews of Novogrudek were assembled in the courthouse's courtyard for a roll call, as was the routine each day. An unusually large crew of German gendarmes, Nazi commandos, and local police was present in the yard. They moved among the gathering, striking the Jews with their weapons and shouting curses at the tops of their voices.

The Nazi Judenreferent, Reuter, assisted by a Belorussian adjutant, selected about half of the group, the most essential of the skilled workers, and ordered them to return to the courthouse workshops. Once they were gone, the remaining Jews were told to lie face down on the ground, understanding what was to befall them. "Run!" one man yelled. A few of them did, only to be met by a storm of machine-gun fire.

Once order was restored, the Germans approached the remaining Jews and, with swift kicks, got them to stand. Then, in groups of twenty-five, the Jews were marched outside of the courthouse complex. They walked a short distance down the road and then up a slight incline off to the side. There they took off their clothes, tied them up into bundles, and were shoved toward a large ditch. They lined up in front of the holes, and an execution squad machine-gunned them to death. The process lasted for four or five hours. The gunshots were easily heard by those still in the ghetto.

Later, several SS men entered the courthouse and one of them grabbed a woman from Lodz, Poland. When she tried to fight the soldier off, he grabbed her by the hair and dragged her to the ditch, where she was killed. When the woman's five-year-old girl cried for her mother, the other SS soldiers called out to her. "Come, come, your mother is here." The girl was lured outside and taken to the ditch, where she, too, was killed.

Reuter appeared in the workshops to speak to the survivors. "You will remain alive," he told them. "You are vital workers."

The massacre left the ghetto with just about 250 inhabitants. The survivors had their daily food allowance reduced to what amounted to starvation rations: a piece of bread (mixed with straw) and a bowl of watery soup. Few believed Reuter's promise that they would be permitted to live, and a committee was organized to plan a mass escape to the forest.

Six weeks since setting up the Stara-Huta camp, the Bielskis' mini village now included a staggering seven hundred Jews, and, just as Tuvia Bielski had decreed nine months earlier, they were a varied lot: young and old, sick and healthy, armed and unarmed. And in keeping with Tuvia's philosophy, the number of old women sheltered exceeded the number of German soldiers killed.

Tuvia now faced a new diplomatic challenge: how to govern such a diverse assemblage, full of people who brought a variety of prewar religious, political, and social beliefs with them to the forest. "You don't think politics existed in the woods?" said one forest survivor years after the war. "They certainly did." Some complained among themselves about the brothers' manner of rule—they were power-hungry, they drank too much vodka, they favored their family and friends, they didn't distribute the food fairly enough—without fully recognizing the extraordinary survival apparatus that the three men had willed into being.

But Tuvia, especially since the explosive challenge from the Komsomol members, was keen to maintain a strict military-style organization of the group. It was a structure that naturally elevated the importance of those involved in food and sabotage missions. They enjoyed a better quality of food and accommodation than the more vulnerable members, just as those with higher ranks in an army might be afforded greater privileges than enlisted personnel. The society created by the Bielskis was by no means a utopian community of enlightened democratic and egalitarian governance.

In fact, the brothers sought to run the group much like a typical detachment within the Soviet partisan movement. Tuvia saw at close proximity how his ally Viktor Panchenkov, the young Communist idealist, directed his unit, how he wouldn't hesitate to mete out severe punishment to any of his men who violated the rules of partisan life. When two of Viktor's fighters were found to have stolen goods from a peasant, the Russian called his unit together, read an order about the nature of the offense, and then had the two partisans shot to death. It was a rough system that showed little patience for those who didn't toe the line.

Even though the brothers' group was markedly different from

the average partisan unit, Tuvia understood the necessity to run the base with a firm, sure hand. "There must be discipline," he said. "You must obey even if you know you will get killed. You're told to go there, you go there. It is prohibited to say no." When one young Jewish fighter, Peretz Shorshaty, left without permission to join a Soviet unit because he wanted to concentrate more on fighting than on finding food, he was captured by Bielski soldiers, questioned by the commanders, and chained to a piece of farm machinery that had been dragged into the forest. He was certain they planned to execute him. After two days without food, he was finally released—and cured of any desire to join another unit.

To Tuvia, this sort of total control kept the group united in its purpose and gave its members a better chance of surviving the war. And if he and his brothers conveyed an air of menace, well, that made the job all that much easier. The Bielski brand of authority was bound to create friction. But complaints and leadership challenges were always muted when danger lurked.

As the month of May 1943 progressed, the brothers grew concerned once again about the safety of the camp—especially since the rapid growth of the population had made their location widely known. First, a German plane swooped in low and shot off a torrent of bullets. Then, one of the mounted guards came thundering into camp and announced that German trucks were entering the forest. Tuvia immediately dispatched the noncombatants to retreat further into the woods, while the fighting men took up positions to defend against the enemy force.

Without warning—and without a shot being fired—the trucks stopped far short of the base and reversed direction, leaving the forest via the same route they had arrived.

It was a clear sign to Tuvia and his brothers that it was time to move again. How long before the Germans realized their mistake and made a return trip into the Stara-Huta woods?

Everyone gathered around the commanders, and Tuvia stepped forward to say a few words. "I can't promise anything," he said. "We could live a day. We could live longer. But we have to go to a different forest because they have found out we are here. We don't have to be heroes. We just have to live through this war. Whoever will make it, he is the biggest hero."

Years later, one of the young women in the group, Leah Kotler, remembered the leader becoming emotional as he spoke. "This giant of a man had tears coming down his face," she said.

Everything that could be packed up was placed on horse-drawn carts, and a slow procession began toward a small forest called Yasinovo, a few kilometers away. They headed out in a single file as evening descended, with each person told to follow the person directly in front of him. The line stretched out for more than a kilometer. A collection of horses and cows strolled alongside the parade.

After they arrived in a dense forest full of young poplar trees, several communal kitchens, consisting mostly of fires warming a profusion of metal pots, were set up to feed the collection of humanity. Small groups worked to create temporary shelters using tarpaulin and wood, but many simply found a leafy bush and tried to fall asleep underneath its cover. The prospect of creating another base out of the raw woods was wearying for many. The Stara-Huta camp had started to feel something like home. Now we must do it all over again, they realized with exhaustion. But how long before the Germans find us here?

Not long, as it turned out.

Within days of arriving at the new location, Tuvia and his

brothers were hearing rumors from peasant contacts about the possibility of more German excursions in the woods. *How long can we keep this up?* Tuvia wondered. *How long will we be able to protect such a huge collection of people?* They had only one option when they learned about the possibility of another attack—it was time to move again, deeper into the forest.

Just as they made the decision, Tuvia received a message instructing him to travel to a meeting coordinated by Fyodor Sinitchkin, the commander of the Lenin Brigade that the brothers' detachment belonged to.

Tuvia mounted his horse early in the morning and prepared to ride to the rendezvous point several kilometers away.

"The two of you should move everyone out tomorrow morning," Tuvia said to Asael and Zus. "I don't think we can wait around any longer." They agreed it was a good idea.

After Tuvia left the camp, Zus, Asael, and several men set out on horseback to scout the nearby countryside for any dangers. They returned late in the evening and decided to get a few hours of sleep before dealing with any evacuation plans on the morning of June 9, 1943.

A half an hour after he fell asleep, Zus felt Asael shaking his foot.

"What?" Zus barked.

"The Germans are coming," Asael said abruptly.

Without wasting a second, Asael left his brother and ran throughout the camp, shouting about the imminent arrival of the enemy. Several mounted guards then galloped into base, just as the violent sounds of roaring German vehicles could be heard in the distance.

It was only then that Zus was wrested from his slumber. He

jumped up and shouted at Asael: "Is this the way to set off the alarm?!"

But the camp of hundreds was already devolving into utter confusion and hysteria. Asael tried to organize some sort of coherent evacuation, urging his brother-in-law Abraham Dziencielski to direct a large group deeper into the forest. Shrieks filled the air as people struggled to follow orders. An organized evacuation was impossible.

Zus and the fighters grabbed their weapons and lined up to mount a defense, even though the enemy was not yet visible through the thickness of the forest. Then the roar of the German trucks gave way to the clatter of gunfire. In an instant, one of the mounted guards had his horse shot out from underneath him, and he and the beast fell to the ground in a violent tumble.

Zus ran toward the man. Just as he arrived, a thunderous barrage of German machine-gun fire and mortar shell bursts crashed upon the base. Now able to see the Germans through the trees, Zus estimated that the attacking force included more than a hundred men. They were fast approaching the brothers' position.

"Everyone must retreat!" shouted Asael. "Get out of here now!"

Hundreds of camp residents ran deeper into the forest, directly away from the sounds of the German attack, abandoning horses, cows, cookware, and everything else that they had collected over the last few months. Within minutes, the sound of gunfire stopped, but the flight for safety continued. Over the next hour or two, the terrified throng somehow organized itself into several large groups, scattered across a wide area of the woods.

Zus and Asael searched through the woods for each group

and eventually they could account for nearly everyone. After canvassing the group leaders, they discovered that five or six men had been killed during the initial onslaught and that three women and one child were shot while they were trying to retreat. The Jewish force, they knew, had not likely killed any Germans.

Ten casualties—a tragedy, but it could've been much worse. The Bielski brothers knew they had averted another disaster.

Zus, however, was angry. The disorganization of the noncombatants had prevented an organized military defense of the base, even if the enemy force was overwhelming. He felt that it was now time for the brothers to split the group into two parts— one for the noncombatants, the other for the fighters. The soldiers had to be given some opportunity to fight without having to worry constantly about the safety of the civilians. *We are all going to be killed if we continued this way,* he thought.

Since he was several kilometers away during the time of the attack, Tuvia had no knowledge of what was happening. A messenger interrupted his meeting with Fyodor Sinitchkin with the news, and the Soviet commander urged Tuvia to return to his people at once.

He galloped back to the base, which he found deserted. Only a single group member had remained, the man who was assigned to tend to the horses. His name was Lippa Kaplan, although everyone knew him as "Lippa the Black," so named because he rarely took baths. He had climbed a tall fir tree and watched from above as the Germans entered the area and searched for any remaining Jews. After coming across a few more stragglers, Tuvia and the small group spent the night in the forest before returning to the spot near the Neman River where Zus and Asael had gathered much of the group.

After conferring with his brothers, Tuvia spoke about the newest plan of action. He was opposed to Zus's idea of splitting up the group. Instead, he felt it was time to move to a distant location, a Promised Land for partisans, where the large group could live as it had lived during the past year—together.

He spoke in front of the entire assemblage. "Such a large group cannot hide like this," he said. "The last attack wasn't so bad, but we have heard that the German army is bringing reinforcements to fight the partisans. Soon they will be searching for us. So we have decided to move to the Naliboki Puscha."

The *puscha* was located about thirty kilometers to the east of Novogrudek, a primeval forest filled with canals and swampland that was a hive of partisan activity since the earliest days of the war. For hundreds of years, rebels and outlaws had used the *puscha* as a base for actions of one sort or another against whoever happened to be ruling the city. And with good reason: It's difficult to get into and, once you penetrate it, difficult to find your way around.

Reaching the great woods would require a perilous journey across occupied territory, but the brothers felt it would be far safer than the small forests where they had been living for the last year. The transfer also meant leaving an area that was as familiar to them as anything in their lives, a region where they had established gentile allies and cowed potential informers. But the Germans would surely think twice about entering such a heavily guarded forest. Perhaps they could finally find a modicum of safety.

Tuvia rode his horse in front of the group and waded into the river to measure its depth. He found a section that looked shallow enough to cross and slowly walked his animal into the lazily flowing river. The rest of the group formed a human chain and followed behind him. Children were carried on their parents' shoulders while the fighters helped the elderly negotiate the current. Tuvia joked that he was leading his people across the River Neman.

But no one was in a joking mood, as Tuvia recalled it. Food and weapons were scarce, and many were growing sick from constant exposure to the elements. So much of what they had accumulated had been lost at Yasinovo. Now they had to cross through unfamiliar territory at a time when rumors swirled about more German manhunts.

While the journey continued, small groups of fighters were sent to find stragglers who might have been lost in the aftermath of the attack. After four or five days of marching through the evenings and resting during the days, nearly everyone from the group reached a village on the northern edge of the *puscha*. Several Russian units were based there, and they looked sympathetically on the bedraggled lot that limped into the village. "Don't worry," one partisan leader told them. "The leaders are thinking about you. We will all survive this."

In a few days, the unit moved out again, bound for a location in the southern part of the *puscha*, Lake Kroman, a trip that took them through the heart of the great forest. It was an entirely different experience from the previous journeys of the Bielski unit. The brothers had always located their camps close enough to a village that it could easily be reached by the fighters. But this wilderness was far larger, with very few roads and little sign of peasant life. The marchers felt as if they were entering another world, a place that hadn't been touched by the evil of the German occupation. As they continued forward, they heard wolves howling in the distance and were warned about black bears. A young man from Lodz attempted to lift everyone's spirits by singing songs and telling jokes.

Finally, they reached the shores of Lake Kroman, where the group collapsed in fatigue. As always, food was the greatest concern. In the meantime, a nearby Russian unit gave the Jewish group several bags of rye. They mixed it with flour and water to produce a watery porridge, which was cooked twice a day to feed the Jewish population. Unappetizing though it was, it kept eight hundred people from starving to death.

The fighters now had to travel all the way back to the unit's old area. Fyodor Sinitchkin, the brothers' brigade commander, had earlier ordered that the Bielski group only take food from specified villages. The brothers knew that if they retrieved food from the villages ringing the *puscha*, the partisan leadership would accuse them of robbery and, possibly, strip them of their command. So the fighters—Asael led a group of fifty men—were sent back without delay.

Soon after arriving in the *puscha*, Tuvia received word that he was to report to the headquarters of the highest-ranking partisan for hundreds of kilometers, General Platon.

The brothers called the burly, dome-headed Russian the "supreme partisan commander," but his official title was secretary of the Baranovich Underground District Committee of the Communist Party of Bolsheviks in Belarus. He had been parachuted into the region several months earlier to take command of all partisan operations in an area from Lida in the north to Baranovich in the south, from Ivenets in the east to Shchuchin in the west, a vast terrain of forests, countryside, and small cities that stretched for 135 kilometers from east to west and 100 kilometers from north to south. By the end of the year, Platon's region was divided into four districts that had a total of 23 brigades, which were made up of 116 detachments (the brothers' unit being one detachment).

Two years older than Tuvia, Platon had been a Communist Party member since he finished military school in the late 1920s and had held a number of party positions prior to the outbreak of the war. In matters martial, he was known to be strictly no-nonsense. In all other areas, he was jovial and lighthearted.

"He had a big stomach," said Grigori Shevela, a Russian partisan comrade of Platon's. "He was always trying to push it in, to pretend it wasn't there. He had a great way with jokes. I remember once two men on guard duty shot at a low-flying German plane. Somehow they hit the gas tank and the plane fell. It was a miracle. When he gave them a medal, Platon said, 'How dare you shoot down a German plane when you are supposed to be on guard duty!' The men laughed and promised, 'Never again.' He was a merry man. He was open to everybody."

But Platon also had a black mark on his military career. In 1937, an anonymous accuser had denounced him for some perceived slight against the state and he had been exiled to a far eastern portion of the Soviet Union as punishment. Over the previous six years, he had slowly regained the confidence of his superiors. His high position in western Belarus represented a considerable rehabilitation of his reputation.

With a small force accompanying him, Tuvia galloped off to a spot in the northern part of the *puscha* where Platon's command center was located. He was hoping to make a good impression on General Platon. He wanted to communicate to him the importance of the Jewish group's contribution to the partisan struggle and to convince him that their purely Jewish struggle was also a Soviet one. But he also wanted to register a complaint about the increasing number of stories he was hearing about Soviet bands attacking small Jewish groups. They were often forced to give up their weapons, which effectively left them powerless against the Germans and other enemies.

The Jewish partisans thundered into the base. After passing through a checkpoint, Tuvia was shown into General Platon's headquarters, which looked nothing like anything Tuvia had yet seen in the forest. It was the office of a real army officer, full of maps and newspapers, walls lined with parachute silk—an expensive and hard-to-come-by commodity. Binoculars, compasses, pistols, and other pieces of war paraphernalia were lying about, and radios were crackling with communications from distant fighting units.

Platon welcomed Tuvia into the room and introduced him to a number of his subordinate commanders.

"Please," Platon said, after the small talk was out of the way. "Tell us about your detachment."

Tuvia outlined how the group was started, how it worked to rescue "Soviet" citizens from the ghettos, how it punished collaborators and attacked German infrastructure and outposts. He said that the unit now included 800 members—far larger than the average partisan detachment of about 150 members—but he noted that many of them were unarmed.

Platon was impressed with the presentation. "You are a determined fighter and a good Bolshevik," he said, offering the sort of praise that made Tuvia feel as though he had gained a valuable ally. "The rest of the commanders should follow your lead. We have to keep fighting forces alive to carry out comrade Stalin's orders."

The Jewish commander then mentioned the reports about anti-Semitic attacks on Jewish bands. Platon agreed that the matter was serious and he pledged to investigate it in the near future.

The general then told Tuvia that the brothers' detachment was receiving a few cosmetic changes. From now on, it would be called Ordzhonikidze (ord-jon-eh-keed-ze), in honor of Grigori Ordzhonikidze, an early Soviet leader and Red Army commander who died under mysterious circumstances in 1937. The name of Fyodor Sinitchkin's brigade was being changed from Lenin to Kirov. Its membership continued to include the brothers' unit, Victor Panchenkov's October Detachment, and three other groups.

The general, though, had far more pressing matters to discuss with Tuvia and the other commanders. The Germans were coming. They were coming into the Naliboki Puscha and they were arriving in numbers not yet seen in this region.

"It is time to prepare for a huge attack," he said.

Platon turned the meeting over to one of his senior aides, a tall, bearded Russian with fiery eyes, named Yefim Gapayev and known by his nom de guerre "Sokolov."

He outlined a plan to fortify the forest. Brigades were given sections to defend and detachments within those brigades were to defend parts of each section. After Sokolov had finished speaking, Tuvia noted that since his group had a large population of elderly and children, it would need help to hold its section. Sokolov then assigned fighters from another Russian unit to assist the Jewish group.

Tuvia left the meeting stunned by the idea of having to cope with another attack, one that would make all the other incursions against his unit look like child's play. Instead of finding a safe haven in the *puscha*, he had led his group into its gravest danger yet.

He and his men sped back to the base. After arriving, Tuvia ordered a team to assist a Russian unit in cutting down trees to block the Germans' entry into the woods. Foxholes were built at the edge of the forest and mines (built by a member of the Bielski group who learned the art from a Soviet fighter) were placed along the roads.

The morale in the Jewish group had sunk to its lowest ebb. "What will we be able to do with so few arms against such a strong and fearsome enemy?" someone asked Tuvia. The truth was, he didn't know.

EIGHT

JULY 1943–
SEPTEMBER 1943

THE GERMAN ATTACK was sizing up to be everything that Tuvia feared.

Nazi general Curt von Gottberg was sending a large battle group of seasoned partisan hunters to snuff out every "bandit" in a wide swath of territory from the Lipichanska Puscha to the Naliboki Puscha. "Partisan groups are to be annihilated, their camps and bunkers to be destroyed, and their provisions to be seized," read a July 7 order issued to Nazi commanders partici-pating in Operation Hermann, the code name for the coming action. The attack would also include raids on villages deemed friendly to the partisans, during which livestock and produce were to be confiscated and peasants were to be killed or sent to Germany to supplement the slave labor force. It would be, as the Nazi orders stated, a "ruthless deployment of forces."

The Nazi fighting units had spent much of the previous year combing through the occupied territories and conducting scorched-earth campaigns against anyone they decided to call partisans. Many of the troops had taken part in the earlier Jewish slaughters in Belarus, Lithuania, and the Ukraine as members of

SS-Einsatzgruppen formations. After the task of eliminating the Jews of the Soviet Union had largely been completed, the murderers were transferred to the battle against partisans.

The most notorious among these units was an SS-Sonderkommando (special commando) unit led by SS-Obersturmbannführer (lieutenant colonel) Oskar Dirlewanger. Consisting of nearly nine hundred men divided into six companies, it had been formed in 1941 at the behest of Heinrich Himmler, the Reichsführer-SS, who stocked it with men he had released from German prisons. Dirlewanger was as bad as any of them. Even Himmler regarded him as "a bit of an oddity."

With sunken, malevolent eyes, Dirlewanger was a decorated veteran of World War I who joined the Nazi Party, eventually becoming a member of the SA storm troopers in 1934. Later that year he was arrested for engaging in sexual relations with a minor, an infraction that led to his being thrown out of the Nazi Party for the "lowly nature of the crimes" and the "inferior character which shows from his actions." After serving twenty months in prison, he spent two years fighting with a German unit in the Spanish Civil War.

By 1940, following a successful campaign to have his criminal conviction overturned, Dirlewanger was welcomed into the SS and put in charge of Himmler's criminal regiment. In early 1942, after serving for a time in Poland, the unit was transferred to the occupied Soviet Union, where it began the fight against partisans and had no compunction against targeting civilians. Dirlewanger arrested women and children and forced them to march through minefields. He set fire to entire villages and massacred their civilian populations, often after the slightest hint that the residents were sympathetic to the enemy. For all this he was commended by Berlin. During the course of the year, Dirlewanger was presented with four medals saluting his valor, and several of his men were rewarded with promotions.

Throughout the first half of 1943, Dirlewanger and his men pillaged and burned and murdered their way across Belarus, as part of a campaign that led to the deaths of tens of thousands of Belorussian and Polish peasants and the destruction of hundreds of villages, many of which were never rebuilt. During a two-day period in February, the unit destroyed four villages, and on a single day in March it "cleansed," in the euphemistic words of a battlefield report, another three villages. During early May, Dirlewanger reported that his men had killed 386 partisans and 294 civilians while only three of his men suffered injuries, the kind of numbers that led military historians like French MacLean to conclude that the unit was simply conducting mass slaughters.

Operation Hermann would be Dirlewanger's sixteenth large-scale antipartisan campaign. His unit was joined by several other fighting units with similarly cruel reputations. One of them, the SS-Police Regiment 2, had teamed with Dirlewanger for two massive operations in April, including one to root out hostile fighters hiding in the ruins of the city of Minsk. Operation Hermann would also include an SS infantry brigade, riflemen regiments, gendarme platoons, a Polish sharpshooter unit, SD commando units, Lithuanian police regiments, and Luftwaffe air fleets.

The troops were expected to follow the guerrilla fighters wherever they fled, which meant tromping through forests and swamps and risking exposure to mines and booby traps.

"It should be noted, particularly from previous encounters with partisans, . . . that as soon as the partisans realize they're being attacked by Germans [they will] try to hide in impassable swamps or disguise themselves as peaceful inhabitants," the Nazi orders for Operation Hermann state. "In this territory, dissected by swamps and flowing water of all sizes, the troops must be prepared to use waterways and auxiliary bridge construction."

The German forces marched into battle on July 15. It would take another several days before the enemy would close in on the Bielski group huddled near Lake Kroman in the Naliboki Puscha.

The brothers and their fighting men heard the thunderous sounds of battle long before they witnessed any action. The approaching Germans used heavy machinery to push aside the downed trees that blocked the dirt roads leading into the *puscha*'s heart. The path was cleared in the waning days of July and armored vehicles rumbled into the woods. The Bielski noncombatants were sent deeper into the forest, while about one hundred Jewish partisans, joined by two hundred Russian allies, waited to spring a surprise attack on the enemy approaching from the east.

But before the Germans arrived within the range of fire, a Russian partisan—a traitor, it was later learned—let loose a single rifle shot, alerting the Germans to the impending ambush. The Nazis jumped from their trucks and fired in every direction, while the partisans abandoned their positions and dashed into the forest.

The Bielski fighters returned to the location where the noncombatants were huddled. The mood was understandably tense. Soon word arrived from Soviet scouts that the *puscha*—which was, of course, unfamiliar territory to the brothers—was being completely surrounded. The Germans were occupying all the small villages that ringed the edges of the great forest. First, the town of Naliboki, a few kilometers to the east, fell to the invaders.

Then the hamlet of Kletischa, a few kilometers to the north of the brothers' positions, was taken. The noose was tightening.

The German forces then turned to penetrate into the forest, and General Platon's partisan fighters put up a spirited defense. But within hours it became apparent that the Nazi troops would have little trouble moving deeper in the woods. The partisan forces were retreating farther by the hour.

With the battles still roaring in the distance, a Polish partisan commander rode to the brothers' encampment bearing news about the Germans: They are now just two kilometers away from us.

"Be brave, sir," the Pole said, extending his hand to Tuvia. "We are surrounded on all sides." He then rushed back to his men, while the brothers mulled their next action.

But they were uncertain of how to respond. After a few hours had passed, Tuvia and Asael galloped to a nearby Russian unit, in hopes of learning more about German movements. They were informed that the Polish commander's group had already been overrun, and that the Germans were now expected in the area of the Bielski base by the following morning.

"What are you going to do?" Tuvia asked the Russian commander.

"We need to get out of here!" the man said.

"But to where?" Tuvia asked.

The man offered little advice, finally telling Tuvia to act "as you see fit."

Tuvia and Asael returned to the camp, where a nervous gathering of eight hundred people—combatants and noncombatants —was waiting for direction. Russian partisans on horseback were galloping past the encampment at top speed, making it feel as though a battle was imminent. Tuvia knew everyone was looking for him to offer some sort of plan. But he didn't have one. Instead, he tried to communicate a sense of control. He knew he could not allow the group to descend into hysteria.

He announced that it was possible to elude the Germans. It was possible to survive this trial. "What we need is quiet courage," he said.

Not everyone was reassured. Grisha Latij, the gentile who was a leading member of the Komsomol rebel group, took a few allies and walked out of the base, intent to fight on their own. The action caused an immediate panic. A huge crowd attempted to follow Grisha and his men, since they actually seemed to know what they were doing.

Taken aback by the commotion, Tuvia knew that he had to stop this act of insurrection. He rushed in front of Grisha's group and ordered everyone to return to the encampment. "Night is coming," he shouted. "The Germans won't attack at night. That's when we will escape! Everyone must return!"

Miraculously, they all did.

Over the next few hours, partisan groups continued to pass nearby, bound for positions deeper in the woods. As darkness fell, the sounds of gunfire tapered off. As Tuvia had predicted, the Germans were settling in for an evening of rest.

Since Tuvia had promised an escape plan, he knew he would now have to come up with one. He was increasingly embarrassed by his lack of imagination. Then two men came to him with an idea. Unlike so many in the Bielski group, Michel Mechlis and Akiva Shemonovich had an intimate knowledge of the *puscha's* terrain. Mechlis had been a forest surveyor before the war, and Akiva had been a merchant who conducted business near the *puscha*.

"We know where to go," Mechlis told Tuvia. "It's a difficult route through the marshlands. But if we make it to an island, Krasnaya Gorka, we might be able to survive."

"How can you be sure the Germans won't also get to the area?" Tuvia asked.

"There is no guarantee," Mechlis said.

There was no other option. The decision was made to travel that night through the swamps to Krasnaya Gorka. Tuvia addressed the group.

"The enemy is very close but we have decided to move deeper into the forest," he said. "We will be crossing difficult and muddy terrain. We must maintain absolute silence and everyone must obey orders. Leave all extraneous things behind—we don't want to discard items along the way and leave a trail for the enemy. Take as much food as you can carry and that's it."

Everyone stuffed his pockets with grains of wheat and rye and handfuls of dried peas and moldy turnips, while the cows and horses that had been obtained over the past few weeks were abandoned to the wilds of the *puscha*. Then this extraordinary mass of humanity followed Mechlis into the swamplands. Many took off their shoes, thinking that it would be easier to push through the mud barefoot. Children were carried on the backs of their parents.

Slowly and silently, on a night that was eerily without wind, the group of eight hundred strong moved through the marshes, one person after another. The only sounds came from the squishing of bare feet sinking into the swampy muck and the lowing of the cows wandering somewhere in the distance. The water was at times as high as chest-level, while at other times it barely cleared the walkers' ankles.

At around midnight, the sound of a loudspeaker echoed in the distance. The words came first in Russian and then in Polish. "Partisans! You know you cannot fight a war against our tanks and cannons. When daylight comes, throw down your guns and surrender."

Just before dawn, the group reached a dry spot among some bushes and many dropped onto the ground in exhaustion. But they hadn't yet reached the island of Krasnaya Gorka. The ordeal was far from over. Still, some fell asleep. Anyone who snored was awakened, to prevent the broadcast of unnecessary sounds. Sitting in silence among his people, Tuvia was reminded of the days when the group first went to the forest, back when they had to fret about every sound they made.

When the sun had risen, Tuvia, Asael, and the guide Mechlis found a dry path that would lead them back to the camp they had abandoned the previous evening. They decided to see where the Germans were located.

They crept toward the old camp and for a fleeting moment Tuvia thought that perhaps the danger had passed, that perhaps the Germans had retreated. Then, in an instant, the sounds of heavy gunfire pulsed through the air. The three dove into the bushes and waited for the shooting to stop.

It was obvious to Tuvia that the shots came from Germans who were at or near that very base. As soon as there was a halt in the shooting, the three rushed back toward the group.

By the time they had made it a few hundred meters, the gunfire began again. "I thought it was over for us," said Tuvia. He estimated that the Germans were about half a kilometer away, and he was sure that the three had been spotted.

They again dove to the ground, where they heard the shouts

of the Belorussian volunteers serving as the Germans' advance guard. "Catch the animals!" they yelled. "Catch the animals!"

Somehow avoiding detection, they scurried back to the assembled group, which was once again in a fit of panic. A mother begged her young child to stop crying; an old man mumbled prayers under his breath. German mortar shells hit nearby tree-tops, causing sparks to fly everywhere.

Tuvia urged everyone into the swamp. The tense journey to Krasnaya Gorka resumed.

Luck was with them. The portion of the swamp that the group waded into was overgrown with tall grasses, and the hundreds of people now fleeing the enemy were able to hide their escape in the vegetation. Luftwaffe planes circled above but none of them spotted the long line of marchers. German voices could be heard in the distance—"Heinz, catch the horse!" a man shouted—but none of the soldiers spied the hundreds of fugitives sweeping through the grass.

As the hours passed, exhaustion hobbled several of the marchers, who had to be urged to continue. The meager supplies of food neared depletion and everyone suffered from pangs of hunger. Women leaned on the men in front of them and fighters tried to keep the elderly from falling into the water.

When evening arrived, the unit reached a forested area, which, although it was submerged in water, provided decent cover. "I tied my belt and weapon's holster together and strapped myself to a tree trunk and dozed fitfully," said Tuvia. "Soon most followed my lead, while others climbed the trees to find solace."

Of those who didn't sleep, several scrounged for food, and they succeeded in finding some raspberry bushes. "We had absolutely no food, nothing," said Leah Johnson, née Bedzovsky.

"When we found berries from the trees, we didn't know if the berries could be eaten. It was terrible." The night passed slowly and, extraordinarily, in silence. The children remained quiet throughout the ordeal.

The mist rose off the swamp the following morning and the group roused itself to resume the march north, toward Krasnaya Gorka. Good fortune was again with them. The island was just a few hundred meters away, and before long, eight hundred people were lying on a tiny landmass surrounded on all sides by swamp.

But the sounds of artillery fire continued to fill the air. Even though the group had reached what seemed to be a safe haven, the danger hadn't yet passed.

Now what? Tuvia's plan was to stay on this island in the middle of the swamps, in the middle of the huge *puscha*, until the Germans ended the siege. But how long would that be? And, most pressing, how would they find food? They had little when they began the journey to Krasnaya Gorka. Now they had next to nothing.

After everyone settled in, the brothers conducted a roll call and discovered that six people were missing, including a father and his two children and an old man named Shmuel Pupko. Three men agreed to conduct the search for them. By evening, they returned with all the stragglers.

As one day and then another passed, the food dilemma grew worse. Even a stale piece of bread had become a prized delicacy, to be eaten by its owner behind a tree or a bush, far from prying eyes and hands. Some started to lose their strength, and they would lie on the ground in exhaustion. Signs of starvation began to appear, including puffiness around the eyes and flaking of the skin. "It just came off our bodies," said Murray Kasten. "Peeling off like paper."

The German attack continued all around them, its sounds echoing over the swamplands. The fighters couldn't yet risk traveling to the villages ringing the *puscha*.

After another day passed, Tuvia decided to send the scout Akiva Shemonovich and a few others to see whether it was possible to approach the nearest village, Kletischa. Several hours later, they returned with the news that the Germans were everywhere.

By the time a week had passed, people started to lose hope, and several worried that Krasnaya Gorka would be their final resting place.

Some of the fighters began talking about breaking through the blockade, no matter where the Germans happened to be stationed. A blustery Zus was vocal in his insistence that it was time to risk a journey through Nazi positions. "Staying there and dying of hunger was not what I wanted," he would later say.

"He said to me," said his wife, Sonia, "'I cannot take the hunger. I cannot take it. Who is going with me?'"

Eighty fighters left with Zus, who threatened to shoot anyone who tried to follow them. His plan was to slip through the German attack lines and travel all the way back to the brothers' former theater of operations in the region around Stankevich, where he knew food could be found. If Zus and his men saw that it was impossible to pass through the Nazi positions, he would send a scout to Krasnaya Gorka to instruct everyone to remain there. But if within two days a message hadn't been received, the group at the island was to assume that the unit had found safe passage. Everyone would then follow a similar route back to the Stankevich area.

It was a highly risky plan. If the Germans wiped out Zus's group, preventing him from sending a scout, then the Krasnaya Gorka unit would walk into a deadly trap. But the brothers felt there was no other choice. Either we leave soon or we die anyway.

After two days passed with no word from Zus's men, an exodus of small groups of twenty to thirty people began, each headed by experienced partisans like Yehuda Bielski, Pesach Friedberg, and Yehuda Levin. The last group to leave was led by Tuvia, Asael, and Layzer Malbin, and it included the weakest and the sickest of the noncombatants.

The groups traversed across the territory with great care, passing through the swamps toward the *puscha*'s edge. They stumbled upon discarded packs of German cigarettes, piles of used Nazi cartridges, and even crumpled-up German newspapers. It seemed as though the Germans had at least partially abandoned their positions.

Finally, the small Bielski units reached the river that marked the *puscha*'s western boundary. One man drowned; everyone else made it out of the Naliboki Puscha safely. Few were in the mood for celebration, but they knew something extraordinary had been achieved. For nearly two weeks, a tired and starving group of eight hundred people eluded the most lawless troops Hitler ever threw into battle. It was one of the great escapes of World War II, a flight of such daring and luck that it made all the other miraculous Bielski escapes seem like dress rehearsals.

But no one was much thinking about it as they traveled back to the region around Stankevich. After all, they were returning to an area they had fled two months ago because *it* had become too dangerous. Many thought they were walking back into the arms of death.

* * *

One of the small Bielski units—it included about thirty people—
decided not to return to the Stankevich area. They stayed in the
puscha with the idea that they would prepare a base for the larger
group in the event that it was still unsafe in the former territory.
The unit was led by Israel Kessler, the man who had been discovered by the brothers hiding with several of his followers near
Abelkevitch and who had found common cause with the members of the Komsomol rebel group. He was a native of the village
of Naliboki and he felt comfortable with the puscha surroundings.

The brothers were growing worried about Kessler, who,
according to rumors, had been a thief before the war, even serving time in prison. But so far he had proven himself an important
addition to the unit, and he had the brothers' blessing to remain
behind in the puscha. Tuvia asked that he send a messenger with a
progress report to the brothers' yet-to-be-established headquarters by September 1.

Kessler's unit wandered within the confines of the puscha,
dodging stray German forces, in search of any kind of nourish-
ment. They came across a horse that had been shot. "Starving and
afraid to make a fire, we cut the meat up and ate it raw," wrote
Isak Nowog. Then, a group of eight of their number approached
a peasant home and, although they were shot at and chased by
dogs, successfully made off with a healthy supply of food.

A few days later, while the group was resting, Kessler leaped
to his feet and declared that he smelled smoke. He quickly
climbed a tree to get a better view of the surroundings.

"Everything is on fire!" he yelled from the heights.

It was obvious that Kletischa, Naliboki, and several others
communities surrounding the puscha were being ransacked and

burned by the retreating Nazi forces. The peasant inhabitants were being killed or carted off in trucks bound for Germany.

The Kessler group set out to explore the villages. In each one, the partisans discovered the same scene. Not a single structure was left standing and not a single living inhabitant could be found. It seemed as though the Germans, unable to kill as many partisans as they hoped, had taken their anger out on the peasants.

To Kessler's men, the destruction of the villages, although a catastrophe for the peasant population, was a wonderful stroke of luck. Not only did it mean the end of any potential or real informers; it also meant they could seize the food and supplies that the Germans were unable to cart away. And it was quite a bounty.

In the ruined towns the partisans found chickens, pigs, and cows ambling everywhere. They raided beehives for honeycombs and rooted through cellars for potatoes. They discovered vegetables in the gardens ripe for picking and wheat in the fields ready for harvesting. Wagons, sewing machines, cobbler's tools, and threshing machines were theirs for the taking. Most of what they had lost during the harried retreats from the Germans during the last two months could now be replaced.

Over the course of several days, everything was taken to a small base they established not far from the island of Krasnaya Gorka. The fighters ate like forest kings and danced around the fire, lifting Kessler up onto their shoulders. On a journey to partisan headquarters, they offered one of Platon's deputies a supply of cherries preserved in honey.

But at least one member of Kessler's group, Abraham Weiner, was becoming uncomfortable with the leader's behavior. He noticed how he would ransack peasant homes for jewelry, watches, and other valuables, instead of taking only items needed for the group's survival. It was the kind of behavior that could cause problems with the Russian partisans.

"Kessler returned to his old profession," Weiner said. "The thief who sat in jail and only learned to write his name in block letters in the forest was now out of control."

Unaware of the fortunes of Israel Kessler and his men, the small Bielski units made the roughly forty-kilometer journey back to the old area. Once Tuvia, Asael, and Layzer Malbin's group arrived near Stankevich—they had been the last to leave the *puscha*—the commanders attempted to make contact with all the other units. In the warmth of August, the scattered groups had created their own small camps, which consisted of a few tentlike shelters and a campfire, in the small forests where the brothers had been based before the journey to the *puscha*.

The fighters promptly sought to obtain food from their old peasant allies, and they discovered that Operation Hermann had also caused much destruction in this area. The population was reeling from the violence, and many Soviet partisan detachments were in disarray after the battles. It created a highly charged situation in the countryside, and the fighters had to work especially hard to secure sustenance. Instead of comparatively luxurious items like cows and chickens, they were coming back with lots of potatoes. After so long with so little in their stomachs, many had trouble digesting even such simple fare.

In the chaos of these post-Hermann days, stories were surfacing about lawless Soviet partisans, many of whom had become separated from their units during the attacks. Jews often bore the brunt of their brutality. In one instance, a partisan killed a Bielski group member who refused to hand over his weapons. Then a group of Soviet fighters robbed young Aron Bielski and a few other Bielski men, taking their weapons, watches, and several pieces of gold.

The three brothers were outraged and immediately organized a force of seventy armed fighters. "We will fight if the weapons are not returned," Tuvia told the troops. "This is happening too often for us to ignore it."

The partisans stormed into the Russian camp, and Tuvia, Zus, and Asael proceeded to the commander's hut. Since he was sleeping off a hangover, his deputy asked what the commotion was about. "Are you planning to attack us?" he wondered.

"Yes, you son of a bitch," Tuvia responded. "If necessary, we'll fight you."

"Who gave you orders to disarm my people, my brother?" the Jewish commander continued. "Do you know who Aron Bielski is? Do you know what this boy has done for the motherland?"

The Russian tried to calm Tuvia, but the latter was so incensed that he couldn't be soothed.

"I want our weapons now!" Tuvia said. "Where are they?"

"Hold on. I don't know anything about it," the Russian said. "Wait, wait, I'll get our leader." He then awoke the commander from his slumber.

After rising from his bed, the groggy Russian listened as Tuvia told the story of the confiscation and demanded that everything be returned. "If one bullet is missing, we'll kill you all," Asael piped in.

The commander pledged to do what he could. He left his hut and ordered his troops to line up. The men sauntered into position and Aron identified the thieves, eleven men in all. Then the

Russian commander spoke: "I give you five minutes to produce the weapons." In quick order, everything was returned and the belligerence of the Bielski brothers melted away.

As Tuvia was leaving the base, the Russian commander chided him for getting so upset. "We could've solved this quietly and amicably," he said.

"Yes, I was a little overwrought," Tuvia admitted, shaking his hand. "But I must fight for what I believe is right."

The Bielski anger, so potent when aroused, could also be directed at those within their own group, and during these stressful days Zus turned his vicious temper on another Jew.

He became enraged when he heard stories about a man named Kaplan, a leader of one of the small Bielski units. It was said he had allowed his fighters to steal from the peasants, with one man taking a fur coat. Zus also heard that Kaplan struck one of the female members of his group, and forced the woman and her child to remain behind when he and his people moved to a new location. Zus rushed to confront the man he saw as besmirching the brothers' reputations.

An argument between the two ensued, during which Zus castigated Kaplan for his poor treatment of the woman. Kaplan accused the brothers of being more interested in gold than in helping people. Zus moved to strike him. When Kaplan turned to flee, Zus aimed his gun and ordered him to halt.

Kaplan ignored him.

"Don't do it!" Asael yelled to his brother.

But Zus opened fire and killed Kaplan. The dead body was buried where it fell.

It was an upsetting incident for many. The idea of a Jew killing another Jew, especially during a time when Jewish life was so endangered, was hard to accept. Those who were naturally suspicious of Bielski leadership regarded this as an outrageous act of criminality.

But the brothers felt the killing was justified by the man's participation in activities that endangered the unit. It was the sort of brutal act that had so far worked in the group's favor— it was one of the tools that allowed such a large gathering to continue to exist in such a lawless world. In practice, however, the brothers' increasingly strict manner of rule could be a messy thing to behold. Most of the group, so thankful to have the brothers' protection, didn't want to think about it too much.

At the end of August, Tuvia gathered together the entire eight-hundred-member group—excepting Kessler's unit, which remained back in the *puscha*—and told them the news that would forever alter the history of the detachment, an upsetting change in the manner of its operation.

Fyodor Sinitchkin, the commander of the Kirov Brigade and the brothers' immediate Soviet commander, had been replaced by one of his lieutenants, Sergei Vasilyev, a pug-faced former Red Army tank commander who had escaped from German captivity in August 1942. The thirty-nine-year-old Russian was putting into place a plan that would divide the huge unit into two sections—one for the fighting men and the other for unarmed men, women, and children.

The idea was to keep the combatant group in the brothers' original area of activity around Stankevich. It would retain the name Ordzhonikidze and be commanded by a Soviet partisan. Zus would be its deputy commander and chief of reconnaissance.

The noncombatant unit, which would be based in the distant Naliboki Puscha, would maintain Tuvia as its commander, Layzer Malbin as its chief of staff, Pesach Friedberg as quartermaster, and Solomon Wolkowyski as head of the special section. It would be known officially as the Kalinin Detachment, named for one of Stalin's top deputies, M. I. Kalinin, the chairman of the Presidium of the Supreme Soviet of the USSR.

Asael was being assigned to neither of the two units. He was being sent to Sergei Vasilyev's Kirov Brigade staff, where he would serve as a reconnaissance officer.

Not only was the group being torn apart, but the three brothers were forced to separate.

Tuvia strenuously opposed the breakup plan when Vasilyev told him about it. From the earliest days of the war, he had argued that the Jewish group was strongest when it was largest. Now, thanks to the interference of the Soviets, everything would be jeopardized. Without its armed protectors, the noncombatant group would be vulnerable to attack. With a Soviet commander, the fighting group would no longer be committed to the preservation of Jewish life. And Asael, the trusted leader of the young soldiers, would be lost to partisan bureaucracy.

To Tuvia's mind, the unit would now be forced to act in greater consonance with Soviet war aims. And Jews weren't exactly at the top of the partisan movement's list of priorities, despite Stalin's public statements about the role of every Soviet citizen in the battle for the motherland.

Tuvia struggled to come up with an alternative plan that would be satisfactory to the Soviets. He even considered removing the entire unit from Vasilyev's purview and relocating it to a new zone of operation, far from the Novogrudek-Lida area. But after consulting with his brothers and top aides, he conceded that he had to follow the command. He told Vasilyev he was "a true and loyal Soviet citizen," ready to follow orders.

The new brigade commander gave Tuvia five days to effect the transfer.

"What?" he said. "It is not possible to move hundreds of people without adequate preparations, without food and a command structure."

When Tuvia suggested it would take two weeks, a brusque Vasilyev told him he had a week to complete the task.

Immediately, unit members were assigned to collect food and supplies for the long return trip to the *puscha*. Many of the fighters packed up their belongings in anticipation of joining up with their new commander, a Ukrainian captain by the name of Mikhail Lushenko. Tuvia couldn't abide the idea of losing all the fighters, so he quietly approached several of them and urged them to defy orders and stay with the noncombatant unit. Most of them agreed to his request.

About half the total number of Bielski armed men, around a hundred soldiers, reported to the first meeting of the fighting Ordzhonikidze Detachment. Joining Captain Lushenko at the gathering was a Russian named Vasily Kian, who had been appointed commissar for political affairs, and another Russian, Petr Podkovzin, who was the chief of staff. The Soviet commanders divided the Jewish fighters into two sections, one of unmarried men and the other of married, and appointed section commanders and deputies. Among the new unit's soldiers were a few of the agitators of the Komsomol rebel contingent, including the gentile Grisha Latij, who was appointed deputy commissar.

The fighters were told that the detachment would operate

much like a typical Soviet group. During the evenings, the men would engage in partisan activity and during the days they would rest up in friendly peasant homes. The unit would also resume its occasional alliance with the brothers' earliest partisan ally Viktor Panchenkov's October Detachment, which had remained in the area during the turmoil of July and August.

Unlike his older brother, Zus approved of the plan to separate the main group into two parts. He had first thought of the idea after the disorganized retreat during the German attack on the Yasinovo Forest on June 9. He felt the noncombatants had prevented an organized counterattack, jeopardizing everyone's safety. But since he deferred to Tuvia on organizational matters, his view didn't result in a rift with his brother. He would never support splitting up the group over the objections of either Tuvia or Asael. But when the Soviets ordered the change, he didn't lodge any objections.

The new unit also provided him with a strong leadership role, greater than the one he was afforded in the larger group. Captain Lushenko and the Russians couldn't match his leadership abilities or his knowledge of the area. "On paper, only Lushenko was the leader," Zus said many years later. "Truthfully, I was the leader."

The brothers' world had changed markedly in just a few weeks. Zus's new group was preparing for its first Soviet-supervised actions, while Asael reported for his duties at Sergei Vasilyev's command post, and Tuvia's noncombatant group began its slow journey back to the Naliboki Puscha. About seven hundred Jews were returning to the place where they had hoped to find safe haven two months earlier. After a weary summer of running from the Germans and coping with the orders of the Soviets, they were praying they would find it.

NINE

SEPTEMBER 1943

BY THE SUMMER of 1943, the war was turning in the favor of the Allied forces. The Germans had regrouped after Stalingrad to score a victory at Kharkov but then lost a mammoth battle in early July at Kursk, where more than 1.3 million Red Army soldiers faced nearly a million German fighters, in what historian Richard Overy described as the "largest set-piece battle in history."

Soon after the Soviets won at Kursk, British and American forces invaded Italy, after finally vanquishing the Axis forces in North Africa. The Anglo-American campaign resulted in the fall of Mussolini, but it was by no means an easy victory for the Allies. As they pushed toward Rome, they were met by strong German counterattacks and the progress was slowed. In the meantime, the Nazis were suffering other difficulties, including a successful effort by the Western powers to greatly diminish the effectiveness of Nazi U-boats in the North Atlantic.

In the Pacific, the Japanese were on the defensive, having withdrawn from the Aleutian Islands and suffered setbacks at New Guinea and New Georgia.

The destruction of European Jewry continued without any

letup, even as many brave attempts at resistance were undertaken. The most famous, the Warsaw ghetto uprising, began in
April 1943, when more than seven hundred Jews with makeshift
weaponry heroically fought off more than two thousand German
and German-allied soldiers for twenty-eight days. Finally, on May
16, after brutal house-to-house fighting, the Germans announced
that they had quelled the rebellion. Several thousand Jews were
killed during the fighting, while more than fifty thousand surrendered and were shot or sent to death camps. The Germans
claimed that they only lost sixteen men, although many believe
the number to be as high as several hundred.

But nothing could stop the murderers. In June 1943, after a
fourth gas chamber was opened in Auschwitz, Himmler ordered
that all the ghettos of Poland and the Soviet Union were to be
cleared of Jews as soon as possible. Hitler, it was now certain, was
bound to lose the war against the Soviet Union, Great Britain,
and the United States. But he was determined he was not going
to lose the war against the Jews.

Any attempts to flee the Lida and Novogrudek ghettos were put
on hold during the great battles of Operation Hermann in July
and August of 1943. But by early September, small groups, particularly in the Lida ghetto, were again risking trips to the partisans.
Many of the young people, inspired by the successful escapes of
the past year, struggled to locate arms and convince aged relatives
to make the journey.

Layzer Stolicki, commander of Lida's Jewish police force,
aided the escapees by plying the gentile guards with vodka and
showing would-be partisans the way to the woods. Others continued to resist the urge to leave, believing the Nazis' lies about

no harm coming to those who worked faithfully for the Reich. "For the older people it was easier to think that surely a miracle would happen than to get up and leave in great poverty for the unknown forest," wrote Liza Ettinger. Still others, believing the end was near, were preparing for the inevitable day when the Nazis would arrive for the next mass killing.

That day would soon come. On September 17, the Germans and their collaborators surrounded the Lida ghetto—which had a population of "more than two thousand," according to a German document of two months earlier—and broadcast a message over loudspeakers. "You will not be harmed. We need workers for the war effort. You have two hours to pack your belongings." The troops then charged into the ghetto and lined everyone up in groups of fifty. Some attempted to hide, certain that another killing was imminent.

Liza Ettinger, carrying a loaf of bread, matches, and some gold coins, descended with a friend into a bunker underneath a house. From her spot, she could hear the screams of the ghetto inmates as the Germans began shooting into the air and shouting orders at the top of their lungs.

The Germans marched the inmates through the ghetto gates. "It was the same route as May 8," said Willy Moll, then thirteen, referring to the massacre of Jews in 1942. "As we walked, a lot of the people in town, the gentile people, the Polish people, were standing and watching. Some had smiles on their faces and some you could see were quite sad."

As the march continued, Moll slipped out of the line. "I walked about half a block and this woman recognizes me and she starts screaming, 'A Jew! A Jew!'" Alerted by her cries, a German soldier ran after the young boy, who darted into a back lane and jumped into an outhouse. "Through a crack in the outhouse I could see the Nazi running this way and that way," he said. A young Polish man who had been watching the scene unfold told the German where the young Jew had found refuge.

"He rips the door open and he pulls me out and puts me against the wall of the shed," said Moll. "I'll never forget the sky, because I was too chicken to look at him standing with the gun. I looked up. It was such a beautiful day, so sunny, and the sky looked so beautiful. I was positive he was going to shoot me, but instead he pushes me and tells me to walk. So I walk."

The two returned to the line. "We need to keep an eye on this little Jew," the German said. When the group rested farther down the road, young Willy slipped away a second time and this time he wasn't captured. He hid in a field until nightfall, when he started journeying toward the Jewish partisan camp he had heard about, the one organized by the Bielski brothers.

The rest of the marchers were soon aware that they weren't being escorted to the execution pits of May 8. Instead, they were bound for the train station, part of an evacuation process that continued over the next two days, September 18 and 19.

When seventeen-year-old Mike Stoll arrived with several family members, he saw that the Jews were being packed into fifteen to twenty train cars. "They threw us into a car and we were standing there frozen, wondering what to do next," he said. "We knew they would kill us. We knew we'd go straight from the transport train to the ovens. There were all kinds of rumors. Some people didn't believe what was going to happen. Some people said there were camps where you worked and would survive. I knew we had to find a way out of there."

Stoll and the others in his car scrambled to devise some sort of escape plan. His sister, Bella, spied a Yugoslav auxiliary, a man she had befriended during the occupation, and asked him if he would give her an axe, which the group hoped to use to chop through the car's wooden floor. "A crazy idea, but maybe something," said Bella. "He said, 'Are you going to kill me?' I said, 'Why should I want to kill you? We want to save ourselves. You know we are not going any place where they will let us live.' He mumbled a little bit and then said he would look around in the shed." He eventually produced an axe with the handle removed. Others from the train spoke to a local policeman who, after being given jewelry and watches by everyone in the car, agreed to leave the train door unlocked.

Once the train left the station in the late afternoon, the group discovered that the door was firmly locked. They abandoned the plan to cut through the floor as too dangerous. Instead, they focused their attention on a small, barred window near the roof of the car. Using Bella's axe, the men were able to remove the bars and, after a discussion, Stoll crawled out the window.

"I couldn't fall down because my father and sister were in the car," he said. "I stepped down and turned myself around. I walked over to the latch by the door. There was a wire there and to this day I don't know where I got the strength, but I worked on the wire and I finally pulled it open."

He reentered the car, and all prepared to make the jump. After three people exited, the sounds of gunfire punctured the night air. Stoll returned the door to position and everyone in the car began praying. Then they began arguing over what to do next. Before they could come to a resolution, the train's speed lessened as it entered a station.

Once it ground to a halt, policemen conducted an inspection, and came upon the unlocked door. "Who's missing!" one of them demanded.

"We're all here," someone said. "Who would jump out of a train?"

The policemen cursed and screamed and promised to put them all to death. But in the end they simply closed the door, making certain that it was firmly locked.

"It didn't faze me," said Stoll. "I was like a wild animal. I had to get out."

In the darkness, the soldiers hadn't seen that the bars had been removed from the window. So after the train started up again, Stoll worked his way outside and balanced himself in front of the door.

"By now I was already an acrobat," he said. "I knew what to do. So I got to the door. I pulled the wire, slid open the door, and jumped inside. I said, 'Let's go.'"

Several people leaped from the train, including Stoll, his father, and his sister, Bella. "We jumped and rolled over, sideways and downhill," Stoll said. They made it out safely and without hearing gunfire. "All I remember is a mouthful of gravel," said Bella. "I was scared stiff. I lay there until the train passed. It was making a lot of noise. I thought I would never hear the end of it." Then they began walking back toward Lida and to the Bielski base.

Stoll and his fellow escapees were the lucky ones, some of the few Jews in the history of the war to escape from a train bound for a concentration camp. The trains were headed for the gas chambers at the Maidanek concentration camp, located outside the Polish city of Lublin. Over the course of nearly three years, more than 300,000 people were killed in the camp. Included among them were the last residents of the centuries-old Jewish community of the city of Lida.

In Novogrudek, which once had two ghettos populated by thousands of Jews, the single courthouse ghetto now contained some 250 inhabitants. Several began plotting a desperate and ingenious breakout plan following the May 7 killing, the city's fourth major slaughter.

A plan to storm the ghetto gates, using guns purchased from the local police, was abandoned as too risky. Then a man named Berl Yoselovitch, a photographer before the war now working as a locksmith, came up with the idea to dig a tunnel to freedom. The news was kept from an Austrian Jew, who, it was feared, was an informer.

The hole was begun in the Jewish living quarters closest to the northern wall of the ghetto. The plotters, knowing that the guards rarely visited the vermin-infested barrack, dug directly down for a meter and a half and then began hollowing out a long passageway toward the ghetto fence. The dirt was concealed in the barrack's rafters.

"I was one of the strongest diggers," said Eliahu Berkowitz, who used special tunneling tools smuggled out of the ghetto workshops. "Why? Already when we had reached two meters deep, there was a shortage of air, and the heavier-built men had problems working because they needed more air and we dug lying down. I was one of the smaller men among the diggers and the lack of air did not bother me. We actually had to work naked or in a robe especially made for digging."

Every day the hole was extended by about two meters and soon the tunnel's dirt ceiling was nearing collapse. Wooden

planks were taken from the workshops and used as reinforce-
ment columns to hold it in place. The planks were also used to
build additional spaces within the living quarters to conceal the
ever-increasing amount of dirt.

As the tunnel lengthened, the workers found it difficult to
transport the dirt back to the barrack. So carpenters built a rail
track, upon which a cart could travel, pulled by a rope made of
tied-together rags. Kerosene lanterns were used to help diggers
see their work, but a lack of oxygen caused them to keep going
out. The problem was solved by cutting small vents directly
through to the surface every few meters, allowing air to circulate
in the damp space.

An electrician named Rakovski then devised a plan to eliminate the need for the kerosene lamps. He tapped into a live current he found in the ghetto and ran an electrical wire into the
tunnel. Lights were strung up every few meters of its length.

By July, after two months of work, the tunnel had extended
some hundred meters. But heavy summer rains caused it to partially flood. The carpenters added more wooden beams to prevent
collapse, and additional tunnels were dug off the main passageway
to catch the water. "We prayed to God that the Germans wouldn't
decide to kill us before we were finished," said Sonya Oshman.

It was a reasonable worry. On July 9, an SS-Hauptsturmführer (captain) attached to the SD outpost in Baranovich arrived
in Novogrudek with a platoon of thirty-six men, mostly Latvian
auxiliaries. Due to a mixup in communication, Wilhelm Traub,
Novogrudek's regional commissar, wasn't expecting the commando squad in the city.

Traub, who the SS man said was "astonished" by the unit's
arrival, nonetheless mentioned a few "security police matters"

that required immediate attention. One had to do with Polish partisans. The other concerned the ghetto. He wanted the Jews removed.

Traub said that he feared the Jews were planning an escape, although he knew nothing of the tunnel. "He believed he could assume with certainty that the partisans intended a large liberation attempt at the camp," the SS-Hauptsturmführer, Artur Wilke, wrote in his report of July 11. Traub suggested that the Jews be transferred to the Baranovich ghetto, a request Wilke declined because he feared that the Jews of Lida, who had not yet been transported to Maidanek, would learn about the move from peasants and interpret it as "an execution." "About a thousand Jews in Lida would head for the partisans in the forests for sure," he told Traub.

In the coming weeks, the Nazis of Novogrudek put aside the question of the Jews and focused attention on Poles they deemed troublesome. On the evening of July 17, scores of Polish men were arrested, apparently against the wishes of Traub. A week later, he ordered many of them released, while the rest were sent to Germany to work as forced laborers. On July 31, eleven Catholic nuns were taken into custody. It was rumored that the sisters had aided the partisans, a story denied by Rev. Aleksander Zienkiewicz, the nuns' chaplain. On the following morning at four A.M., they were shot near Skridlevo, the location of the December 8, 1941, massacre of Jews.

By September, rumors were reaching the Novogrudek ghetto that the Germans were planning another Jewish killing. One story had it that the Nazis wanted to eliminate all but twenty of the most highly skilled craftsmen. Then news circulated that the Jews of Lida had been taken from the city. Surely the Jews of Novogrudek were next?

A meeting was held on September 19 to gauge how the ghetto inmates felt about escaping through the nearly completed tunnel. About twenty percent of the 250 people expressed opposition to leaving, according to Jack Kagan, a boy of fourteen at the time. The reasons varied. One man felt that the tunnel, which now extended some 250 meters, would collapse. Others were sure the Germans would discover the plot. "The atmosphere was electric," said Kagan. "When the escape committee said the tunnel was ready, it was a ray of hope."

The plotters decided to leave on a rainy night. When a storm struck on Sunday, September 26, the decision was made. By the early evening, the electrician Rakovski cut power to the searchlight, darkening the guard towers, while the lights in the tunnel remained on. The nails in the barrack's tin roof were loosened, allowing the pounding torrents to create a loud racket.

"We assembled in a long line, according to the instructions given," wrote Kagan in his memoir of the war. "We waited for about an hour. It was very quiet, and you could just make out the faces in the semidarkness. I sat quietly . . . and thought about my family and what had happened to us in such a short time. My only wish was not to be taken alive by the enemy."

Several of those who had opposed the plan changed their minds in the last minutes, putting the total number of conspirators at around 240. Only 10 remained in the ghetto. "Children, you go," one elderly man said. "I have nothing to go for."

Then the long crawl through the tunnel began, with one person following after another. A man of about fifty tied a rope between himself and his two daughters, so he wouldn't lose them on the other side.

By the time Kagan, one of the last to leave, was set to descend into the tunnel, he heard the sound of gunshots. "There was no question of stopping," he wrote. "We had to go. When I came out of the tunnel I could see the whole field ablaze with flying bullets."

"It was pouring and thundering," said Rae Kushner, also toward the end of the line. "Everyone got out of the tunnel. They became confused and started to run in different directions. Maybe it was the excitement of freedom or the instinct of survival that made them run off instead of staying together. They lost one another."

The brightness of the electric lights in the tunnel made it difficult for the escapees' eyes to quickly adjust to the darkness. More than a few ran back toward the ghetto fence in confusion. About ninety were killed by the guards, who likely thought that the partisan liberation attempt that Traub feared was in progress. Among the dead was the plan's mastermind, Berl Yoselovitch.

Later in the evening, policemen searched the buildings but were unable to find a single person. The ten Jews who remained behind were hidden within crevices in the structures. On the day after the escape, German trucks arrived in the ghetto and carted away all the workshops' tools and machinery. Then swarms of peasants visited the courthouse complex to inspect the site of the Jews' extraordinary escape.

The 150 who survived wandered the countryside looking for food and shelter. Sonya Oshman and a few others were chased away by a number of farmers before an old Belorussian man, slightly demented, agreed to let them stay in his home. "I know that you escaped from the ghetto," he said. "I just heard it on the radio. Don't be afraid. I will help you." Kagan and another boy walked for several nights before hearing Yiddish spoken by passing partisans, who turned out to be members of Zus Bielski's Ordzhonikidze Detachment. Soon Oshman, Kagan, and Kushner—indeed, many of the tunnel escapees—were on their way to the safety of the Bielski family group.

Hiding in an attic in the nearly deserted ghetto, Eliahu Berkowitz, one of the original tunnel diggers, and a few of his relatives remained undetected for several days. Eventually they decided to flee for the woods, leaving on another rainy night. After several days of wandering, they discovered the home of Konstantin Koslovsky, the brothers' steadfast ally. He offered them bread and a place to sleep and then directed them to the Bielski unit, which was then making its journey back to the Naliboki Puscha.

TEN

OCTOBER 1943 – JANUARY 1944

As EACH OF THE three brothers embarked on their separate missions as ordered by the Soviets, the thoughts of many in both the fighting and the non-fighting groups shifted to the soon-to-arrive high holy days. The first night of Rosh Hashanah was to fall on September 30, and the holiest day of the Jewish year, Yom Kippur, the Day of Atonement, was to be marked on October 9, 1943. More than a few in the Bielski contingent, however, had no use for the expression of religious observance. They were more concerned with simply surviving. They were also angry. Where was the benevolent Creator when the Nazis were conducting the slaughters?

Others couldn't forget. In the face of annihilation, they had to reaffirm who they were.

On the eve of Yom Kippur, a group of young men and women from Tuvia's noncombatant unit approached a peasant home with the intention of preparing the traditional holiday meal, a festive occasion that precedes the solemnity of the arrival of Yom Kippur (and its daylong fast) at sundown.

One of the men found a chicken, handed it over to Raya Kaplinski, who had been with the brothers since August 1942, and told her to make the feast. Although she wasn't much of a cook, she started preparing the food with help from her friends.

Then Kaplinski and the others heard Germans nearing. They all ran outside and hid in the bushes. After a short while, when it became apparent that the Germans had moved on, the group returned to the home. The cooking was completed and they enjoyed a bounteous meal of chicken and potato soup.

Afterward they left the peasant's home and began to walk through the forest. "I remember that it was very cold," said Kaplinski. "The sky was clear and there were big, big stars." Since nightfall indicates the arrival of Yom Kippur, it was suggested that they all recite the Kol Nidre, the prayer that begins the service, ushering in the holiday. A congregation's cantor chants the prayer's haunting melody, repeating its Aramaic words three times, each time with greater intensity.

"We didn't remember the words," she said. "But everyone knew the tune of the prayer, and we sung it from memory while we thought of our families. I remember looking up at the trees and it was as if they were singing with us."

At the base Israel Kessler had established in the Naliboki Puscha, a group member with a melodic singing voice substituted for the cantor during the recitation of the Kol Nidre prayer. The man led the partisan assembly while wearing a prayer shawl that had been found at Krasnaya Gorka at the height of the German manhunt. It was a discovery that confounded everyone. By what happenstance had a traditional item of Jewish worship made it to the most isolated corner of an impenetrable swamp during the dire days of a world war?

Forty fighters from Zus Bielski's Ordzhonikidze Detachment were unable to mark the holiday—which requires Jews to abstain from eating, drinking, washing, wearing leather, and engaging in sexual relations—in any traditional fashion. Instead, they prepared an ambush on Germans traveling on the Novogrudek-Lida highway. Alas, the road was empty and they returned without striking at the enemy.

Tuvia's noncombatant group, which had been traveling back to the Naliboki Puscha from the region around Stankevich following the Soviet-initiated split, started arriving in numbers by the second week of October. Sheep, cattle, and horses walked alongside the creaky wooden carts, which hauled bags of grain, flour, and other goods. They found a site a few kilometers from Kessler's base, and the commander instructed everyone to begin construction on a new base. Since it would be used for the upcoming winter, the base would need wooden dugouts like the ones in which they had survived the previous winter. Many more of them would need to be built to comfortably house a much larger group of Jews.

Fighters were assigned to obtain tools and equipment from peasants, and carpenters were directed to build temporary shelters until more permanent dugouts could be constructed. Tuvia also ordered the establishment of a small second camp to store food and supplies. But the work proceeded slowly, with everyone worn out from months of living like nomads.

Tuvia visited Israel Kessler's camp, which had about fifty or sixty members. He agreed to allow it to be a satellite of the much larger base, even though he was hearing worrisome reports, from members of Kessler's unit and from Soviet partisans, that Kessler robbed peasants.

Then the Jewish commander spent weeks traveling through the region to locate stray Jewish groups and bring them back to the new camp. He even journeyed to the area around Stankevich to pick up noncombatants who had failed to make the earlier trip. Since the base was now officially designated as a place for unarmed Jews, members of General Platon's staff also directed any small Jewish groups to its location.

The newcomers arrived to discover feverish activity. Workmen were trying to complete the dugout accommodations, designed to house fifty people each, before the arrival of the cold weather. The quartermaster Pesach Friedberg supervised the building, promising extra rations and clothes for the laborers. Horses dragged blacksmiths' anvils and makeshift sewing machines, items retrieved from the burned-out peasant villages, to the locations where workshops were being readied. And despite the demands of the Kirov Brigade commander Sergei Vasilyev that the *puscha* base be reserved for nonsoldiers, fighting men that Tuvia had asked to defy Soviet orders were assigned to new squads.

Although still angered by the involuntary breakup of the group, Tuvia was starting to feel more positive about the new base. With the Germans unlikely to launch another huge operation like Operation Hermann, the Naliboki Puscha could finally offer the protection he and the group were hoping for when they first ventured there.

By November 7, the base was presentable enough to host a celebration of the anniversary of the October Revolution, which was attended by partisans from throughout the *puscha*. Commanders gave speeches about the bravery of their comrades as their fellow partisans drank from a barrel of *samogonka*. After a toast to the Red Army, everyone joined in the singing of rousing partisan songs and in spirited dances around the fire.

Back in the area near the brothers' boyhood home in Stankevich, the fighting Bielski unit—rarely called by its official title of "Ordzhonikidze"—immediately began participating in partisan actions. No longer required to procure huge amounts of food, they were able to concentrate all their energies on attacking the enemy. Zus Bielski, in particular, enjoyed the opportunity to be a full-time soldier. It was what he had always wanted. Now he could devote himself exclusively to exacting revenge.

The men acted under direct orders from Sergei Vasilyev, who was also supervising the actions of four other detachments in his Kirov Brigade. Vasilyev's staff provided the Jewish group with explosives and weapons to complete the missions and offered intelligence reports that aided in decisions about when and where to strike.

But overall the Jewish soldiers acted according to their own understanding of partisan warfare. Zus developed an equitable working relationship with his nominal leaders. "What I said to him, he never contradicted," he said, referring to the detachment commander, Mikhail Lushenko. "He always agreed with me. Even when there was a difference of opinion during a meeting with Russian partisans, he always was with me and not against me."

As the original Bielski group had done in the first days of its fighting work, the Ordzhonikidze unit focused on the areas to the west and northwest of Novogrudek. The detachment particularly concentrated attention on the railway that ran north from Baranovich to Lida and on the highway that traveled from Novogrudek northwest to Lida.

With the unit's more formal ties to the Soviet structure, each of its deeds was now dutifully recorded in reports sent to the partisan command. In one of the first reports, Zus reported that three small groups of Jewish fighters were sent to lay mines on sections of the railway near the Yatsuki station. Each group performed its task as ordered and a total of 260 meters of rail line were destroyed. A few days later, two groups led by the gentile Grisha Latij laid seven mines along a stretch of the line, which resulted in the destruction of 80 meters of track. Three days after that action, another operation dislodged 130 meters of rail line.

Mines were created in a variety of ways. "We made the mines out of cigar boxes," said Murray Kasten, an Ordzhonikidze fighter, describing one method. "We took a fuse from a grenade and four sticks of dynamite, and the fuse was pushed down in the dynamite sticks. When it was detonated, all four sticks exploded. We planted them on railroad tracks and we planted them on roads. I remember we dug a hole in a road, a gravel road, and we put the mines in the hole and used branches from the pine trees to cover the mines, to masquerade them."

The unit was also collecting food from peasants—"economic missions" in the words of the reports—and meeting with the local population to discuss political matters—"propaganda work" that emphasized the importance of supporting the Soviets over the fascists. "We talked to the peasants of the village of Stankevich, Big Izvah, and Small Izvah on the topic of how to save such property as grain, clothes, cattle, and so on from the German occupants and how to prevent being taken as slave laborers to Germany," according to one report. Every so often, a group of fighters would deliver a supply of food to the Bielski base in the *puscha*.

During September and October, the detachment participated in several economic missions, propaganda visits, and stealth bombing expeditions. Fewer in number were face-to-face confrontations with the Germans or local police. With an increasing number of partisans now operating in the area, the Germans rarely traveled between cities without a sizable contingent of armed escorts. In many instances, Ordzhonikidze fighters abandoned a planned ambush on the Novogrudek-Lida road because, as one report put it, "the enemy's force exceeded our own." Germans also increased their surveillance of the rail lines.

Then, on November 2, a group of anti-Soviet Polish partisans attacked a small unit of Ordzhonikidze fighters led by Grisha Latij while they were crossing the Neman River on the way to conduct a sabotage mission on a railroad. The surprised Jewish group tried to return fire, but they were overwhelmed and had to retreat. One of the Jewish fighters was injured, and Latij, the gentile who had been instigator of the Komsomol rebellions of a few months earlier, was killed instantly. His body was put on the back of a wagon and driven to a nearby village, where he was buried with full military honors. Yet many of the brothers' allies were relieved that he was gone: Now he could no longer cause us trouble, they thought.

Asael was experiencing a different sort of life at the command center supervised by Sergei Vasilyev, the Kirov Brigade commander. Like Zus, he was being utilized by the Soviets for his extensive understanding of the regional terrain and his obvious abilities as a partisan commander. But instead of participating in the war against the Germans and their collaborators like his younger brother, he was serving as a protector of high-ranking Soviet partisans. He loathed it.

Soon after he reported for duty, he was sent into action.

When a contingent of local police was spotted heading for Vasilyev's headquarters, Asael quickly organized a retreat of all the top staff, escorting them through the woods to a place of safety. It was a close call, but all the officials made it out unharmed. An overjoyed Vasilyev credited him with saving his entire command.

But Asael hated the idea of being a glorified bodyguard for the Soviet partisans. And he hated being away from his fighters and his wife. He knew that Tuvia, who wasn't nearly as close to the armed men as he was, needed his military leadership in the *puscha*. He was like a family man who had been torn away from his family.

When Sergei Vasilyev ordered him to supervise construction of a new base, he finally had enough. He wasn't about to create shelters for a group of people he didn't care about, especially when people he did care for needed his help much more. Without telling anyone, he walked out of the partisan command center and journeyed all the way to Tuvia's new base in the Naliboki Puscha.

The fighters and his wife, Haya, were overjoyed to see him. So was Tuvia, who understood his brother's importance to the fighting and food operations. He immediately was restored to the post of second in command and put in charge of military expeditions.

But his sudden appearance came with grave concerns. Asael had acted recklessly, with Bielski-like disdain for anyone who dared to tell him what to do.

Tuvia knew the risks of defying the command of a leader of Vasilyev's stature. Partisans were put to death for far lesser infractions, things like sleeping on guard duty or contracting a venereal disease. Desertion was considered such a serious offense that some detachments maintained a list of a partisan's family members, who themselves would be threatened with execution if a soldier went missing.

He had to do what he could to keep his brother out of danger. It would require a new, intensive diplomatic initiative with Russians. But it was something he was willing to do to have his brother back at the camp.

At first, he proceeded lightly. On November 23, Tuvia wrote a letter to Vasilyev updating him on the progress of the camp, which, he wrote, had 804 residents. "At present the work has just started and the personnel is very small and that's why I ask you . . . to leave my brother Asael, a scout whom I need very much, here at the . . . headquarters," he wrote.

The base was slowly taking the shape of a forest shtetl, a Jewish village in the heart of Nazi-occupied Europe. For the first time since the brothers had begun hiding in the woods, the group wasn't constantly worried about being attacked, protected as it was by the growing strength of Platon's partisan movement. The measure of stability gave the eight hundred inhabitants the freedom to build a mini-civilization, a small-scale replica of what the Nazis had succeeded in destroying throughout the towns and cities of western Belarus, indeed much of Europe.

While the dugouts were being completed, the workmen concentrated on building structures of necessity. The kitchen was a priority. Its centerpiece was a huge pot that continually cooked potato soup, a staple of camp fare. The fire beneath it was kept burning by several young men assigned to the task. At each mealtime, people fought to get to the head of the line, where they stood a better chance of receiving a helping that contained an actual bit of potato rather than just watery broth.

After some fighters found a meat-grinding machine in one of the villages, work began on a sausage-making facility and smokehouse, headed by two ritual butchers who strived to maintain the kosher laws. Soviet partisans would bring animals to the facility to be processed into ready meat products.

A small mill was constructed to grind wheat and other grains. Instead of being powered by flowing water, like the old Bielski mill in Stankevich, the churning wheel was set in motion by a horse walking in a circle. The flour created by the mill was passed to the bakery, which was equipped with an oven constructed from bricks retrieved from the villages. Run by a gruff man who was said to be rough on his young helpers, the bakery produced bread of varying quality.

The herd of cows provided the camp's supply of milk. Several teenage boys tended to the animals, taking them out to pasture each morning in a nearby field. Sometimes at night wolves ventured too close to the cattle, and the perimeter guards fired into the air to scare them away. The camp's water was obtained from a well that was dug in the forest floor and encircled by a wooden fence.

The most popular product of consumption among the fighting class was something a bit stronger, *samogonka*. The liquor was obtained during the normal course of food missions, and it was carried in old bottles of many shapes and sizes.

"Listen, we were drinking *samogonka* like water," said Michael Lebowitz. "Before we went on a mission, so we should be fearless. Tuvia used to come to me and say, 'Michael, you have a little *samogonka*?' And we used to sit down and drink."

The fighters devised ways of tricking the farmers into revealing where the higher-quality batches were hidden. A partisan would stagger to a peasant's door, pretend to be gravely wounded, and ask for something to ease the pain. His comrades would then watch as the man went to the spot where he kept his personal supply of liquor, which was invariably better than the weaker stuff he gave to partisans.

A bathhouse was built near the flour mill to ensure the hygiene of camp inhabitants. Its chief purpose was to rid everybody of lice, which carried the dreaded infectious disease typhus. "It was just like a sauna," said Peretz Shorshaty, who made it to the *puscha* after a long journey from Warsaw. "They would heat the stones and pour water over them. We would have twigs and we would use them to zap at the lice." People lined up for their turn as early as six o'clock each morning. They sometimes cleaned themselves with dark brown soap with the consistency of dough, made by one of the camp residents. The attendants often gave special preference to the fighters, who reciprocated by offering them goods obtained during their travels.

Two separate medical facilities were established—a small clinic for the sick and wounded and a quarantine hut for those suffering from typhus. A doctor named Hirsch took over the role of camp physician from Dr. Henrik Isler, who had joined Ordzhonikidze. He was a familiar figure, walking throughout the camp with his medical bag, rumpled clothes, and perpetual grin.

With expertise in obstetrics and gynecology, the bespectacled doctor was called on to perform a number of abortions, since many women were horrified at the prospect of bringing a child into a world of war. (He also delivered a few children.) He accepted all sorts of payment for his work, especially from those who he knew had the ability to pay. Tuvia remembered that he once refused to perform an abortion until he received a new pair of boots.

But without much medicine, the doctor and his patients

often had to improvise. "I remember many people got blisters between the fingers," said Jack Kagan. "It itched like mad and was very easy to pass on to another person. A remedy was found. We removed the wheels from the carts and slathered the grease on our hands. It stunk, but it solved the problem." The doctor also created a salve, a putrid mixture of pig fat and dynamite sulphur, to be rubbed on skin infected by mites and other parasites.

A female dentist from Minsk joined Dr. Hirsch on the forest medical staff. "My teeth were falling out," said Murray Kasten, who would occasionally visit the *puscha* with other Ordzhonikidze fighters. "There wasn't much salt: If you don't have it, your teeth fall out. They rot away. So the dentist told us to cook chestnuts and use the chestnut juice to wash our mouths. When you cook it, it comes out like blue water, dark blue." And it helped.

While the structures providing for the health and welfare of the residents were being completed, construction was continuing on workshops that would make the name of the Bielski base known far and wide among partisan circles.

The largest building was designed to house several light in-dustries. With its high ceilings, large windows, and several stoves, the structure served as the headquarters for more than a hundred workers. Wooden barriers separated the workspaces of each trade.

Eighteen tailors toiled under the direction of Shmuel Kagan of Novogrudek. The men worked to patch up old clothing and to stitch together new garments. Soviet partisans regularly stopped by to request an alteration, often in exchange for guns or food. Twelve women worked as seamstresses, utilizing the two sewing machines that represented the height of forest technology. The women transformed coarse cotton material found in the villages into precious commodities like underwear.

Situated opposite the tailors in the building were the shoemakers, whose importance to the quality of life of the camp cannot be overestimated. Twenty-odd workers labored to maintain
the footwear of the entire camp, many of whose residents had
spent upward of two years walking through the woods on whatever they could strap on their feet. Long lines of people waited to
visit the cobblers, who were continually complaining about the
number of orders they received. For those who could pay, service
was rendered with greater speed.

In another spot, leatherworkers created bridles, ammunition
belts, and saddles for the fighting and riding men. Nearby, three
barbers offered haircuts and shaves to hirsute camp residents.
The barbershop evolved into something of a social gathering
spot, where people traded gossip and told off-color jokes. The
barbers' razors were dull, however, making the forest shave a less
than pleasurable experience. In the carpentry section, window
frames and rifle stocks were produced. An elderly carpenter kept
his rifle near him at all times, waiting for the time when he could
use it to defend himself.

Near the building's entrance sat the watchmakers, who bus-
ied themselves repairing timepieces, and the hatmakers, whose
services were especially vital with the approach of winter. It was a
nook of fervent political discussion, with the foreman of the
watchmakers, Pinchik, and a hatmaker named Lebowitz engaging
in frequent dialogues. A former member of the socialist Bund
Party, Pinchik thought that immigrating to Palestine after the war
wouldn't solve the problems of the Jewish people, while
Lebowitz, an inveterate pessimist, felt that the Russians would
lose the war and that Jews would have no future anywhere.

Other workshops were set up just outside the main camp

area. A tannery was constructed to produce the hide required by the shoemakers and leatherworkers. The animal skins given to the tanners by the butchers were submerged in six wooden tanning tanks. Several of the tanners were devout Hasids, and the workshop became a de-facto synagogue where the men would quietly conduct services among the drying skins.

Shmuel Oppenheim, the Novogrudek man who had been shot in the bridge of his nose at the attack on Zabelovo/Perelaz on February 15, established a metal shop near the bathhouse. He supervised the repair of damaged weapons and construction of new ones from discarded parts. "He had hands of gold," said Jack Kagan. "His creations were sometimes better than the originals." The shop was a particular favorite of the Soviets, who were happy to trade spare weapons for a proficient repair job on a prized firearm. Oppenheim seemed always in the middle of intense negotiations.

Nearby was a forge, where blacksmiths did all sorts of forging work, including shoeing horses for mounted partisans. The sounds of their hammer blows could be heard in every corner of the camp.

In addition to the workshops, other institutions of civil society were created. Two teachers, one of them a woman named Tsaysha Genish, instructed the camp's many children in a dugout school, which avoided non-Communist subjects like Zionism. "She taught us every Russian song that was popular in those days," said Ann Monka, who was then thirteen. She also led the children in games, taking them on short field trips and providing them with glasses of milk. But the school was less about instruction than keeping the children busy and out of trouble.

The camp even had its own jail, built near the blacksmiths' forge. It was a dark, unventilated dugout that was watched over by an armed guard. The lawyer Solomon Wolkowyski was responsible for investigating crimes and setting prison sentences. Something as minor as milking cows without permission could lead to a few days' imprisonment.

Near the center of the forest village was the commanders' office, the *shtab*, as everyone called it—Russian for "headquarters." Tuvia, Asael, Layzer Malbin, Pesach Friedberg, Solomon Wolkowyski, and Tanchum Gordon, a recent escapee from the Shchuchin ghetto who had been named acting deputy commissar by General Platon, conferred within its confines each day. The camp secretary, Raya Kaplinski, aided by two assistants, was present to take the minutes of meetings, draft letters to partisan leaders, and type up reports of fighting actions with a typewriter retrieved from one of the villages.

"It contained two rooms," said Kaplinski of the *shtab*. "The larger room had a big table, and that's where I kept my typewriter. On the wall was a picture of Stalin, drawn by a girl in the camp who was fourteen or fifteen years old. The Russian partisans thought it a wonderful picture of Stalin. One side of the face was swollen, and a Russian asked why. The girl said it was because he's swollen with joy because he was about to banish the Germans."

All of her clerical work was done in triplicate—one copy for the base records, another for Platon's staff, and a third to be buried in the ground. She also aided Malbin in supplying the Soviets with extensive lists of the unit membership. She was jokingly referred to as the rabbi because she would record a couple as married even though they hadn't been officially wedded. All the documents included the signatures of Tuvia and Malbin and the official stamp of the Kalinin Partisan Detachment.

Directly in front of the *shtab* was a town square that served as a gathering spot for the entire unit. This is where fighters met before going out on missions and where the commanders collected the entire community for important announcements. It also hosted delegations of visiting Soviet partisans, on hand to celebrate Communist holidays and other festive occasions.

"Tuvia said that it would be good if when the Russians come we could provide some entertainment," said Sulia Rubin, who had seven years of ballet training before the Soviet invasion in 1939. Under her lead, a performance troupe was formed to provide entertainment for the events. She devised a variety show that included folk dances, popular songs, and theatrical skits. There was no theater building; the spectators sat on the ground.

"The skits were usually about liberation, about fighting, about love," said Rubin. "I did Shakespeare, who cared? We did anything. We sang partisan songs, Russian songs. We played the accordion, sometimes spoons and whistles. We made flutes out of wood! We told jokes. The show sometimes came from the visitors, because there were many talented people among the Russians. They had beautiful voices and they knew different songs. They needed laughter and we did too."

Rubin translated Hebrew songs into Russian and taught them to the partisan spectators, who never knew they were singing Jewish songs.

"It would get wild, absolutely wild," said Ann Monka, one of the singers. "Of course, before the show, the Russians would really get into the mood. They were full of energy and hope, and I guess the drinking helped."

Rubin met a man with a beautiful singing voice who had spent time in the camp jail, and she recruited him to sing solos during the performances. She urged a young Jewish partisan serving in a Russian unit, Sol Lapidus, a gifted dancer, to perform for the crowds.

Rarely were the performances planned. Rubin and her crew would start a show whenever enough people were around to watch. Someone would begin playing accordion, and Sol Lapidus would start dancing with Rubin. After the dance, a song or two would be sung and then someone might tell a story.

The youngsters from the school formed a choral group, and they were often featured performers during the shows. "I remember we used to sing a Russian song that tells the story of a woman making contact with a partisan and being grateful to be among them," said Monka. "Around the Russians we had to sing about Stalin.

"But among ourselves we had other songs. For instance, there is a song in Yiddish called 'The Jewish Child,' about a mother who wants to save her child from the massacres. She decides to bring him to a Christian family to hide among Christian children. Then she tells the child the reason he is hiding is because his life is threatened as a Jew, and he has to be on his best behavior and not reveal in any shape or form that he is a Jew. Naturally, the child cries, but she has no choice and she leaves. It was a very popular song. A sad song."

The visitors marveled at this bustling village in the heart of Naliboki, and it was the subject of much talk among the peasants. Some gentiles disdainfully called it "Jerusalem," a description used by the "big anti-Semites," according to Tuvia, because it implied that they weren't committed to fighting the war. But many Jews took pride, even comfort, from the appellation.

"It seemed like a fantasy from another world," wrote Liza

Ettinger of her arrival at the base. "The same people—flesh and blood—but stronger and freer. A kind of gay abandon filled the air; biting frank talk spiced with juicy curses; galloping horses and the laughter of children. Everything seemed to float and get mixed up. Suddenly I saw myself as an extra in a Wild West movie with many participants. I didn't know whether to laugh with everyone or cry alone."

The accommodations for the huge group were still being completed as the snows began to fall. The dugouts lined both sides of the main road that ran roughly from one end of the camp to the other, passing through the central area containing the main workshops and the assembly area. The avenue came to resemble any major thoroughfare of a community. Fighters returning from missions would pose with newly obtained Russian (and occasionally German) army gear. Young women lucky enough to get a new pair of boots would parade their wares before jealous neighbors.

The dugouts were numbered and divided along the same social lines as the rest of the camp. People hailing from the same village or sharing the same profession would sometimes live together. Dugout Number 11 was reserved for the "intelligentsia," including Solomon Wolkowyski, Dr. Hirsch, and others. The commanders' accommodations, as might be expected, were without rival. Tuvia and Asael each had a private dugout, which they shared with their wives, Lilka and Haya. Tuvia's dugout was comfortable enough to host meetings with visiting Russians, during which his wife would serve snacks and drinks.

Each day, a man named Max Potashnik walked throughout the dugout areas and demanded in blunt language that fires be extinguished to prevent the base from being spotted by German planes. Enemy aircraft did swoop close to the camp during these months, but with the structures well hidden within the thick forestation, little came of the overflights. The forest was so dense that to glimpse a bit of sunlight, even during the day, required craning one's neck skyward.

In time, each resident discovered a niche within the base structure. Those with few skills served on guard duty or were assigned to collect firewood. Young women were often issued guns, sent to the outer parts of the camp exterior, and told to watch out for enemy activity.

Shmuel Amarant, an expert on Jewish history and Zionism who received a doctorate when he was only twenty-three years old, was appointed camp historian, with the responsibility to collect information about ghetto and forest life. He conducted interviews in his dugout each day with unit members, eventually collecting sixty-five notebooks' worth of material. He also delivered lectures on subjects related to the war.

Among the most restless of the camp inhabitants were its handful of young teenage boys. Although they were assigned a variety of duties, including serving as workshop apprentices, the boys found time to hang around the fighters or trail visitors as they made their rounds. There wasn't a corner of the camp they weren't familiar with or a piece of gossip that they hadn't heard in several different versions. They also picked up the ribald partisan slang that, to the horror of many, became the lingua franca of camp life.

A lonely teenager named Yankel was thought to be the only mentally ill person at the base, his disability caused by a severe beating he received at the hands of the Germans. He wandered around in tattered clothes with a wild look in his eyes. "Yankele, why don't you mend your sleeve?" someone would ask. "I want to shake you out of my sleeve," he'd say. "How can I do it if it is sewn?"

The older people, and there were residents as old as eighty, did their best to contribute in areas in which they had expertise. But mostly they were supported by the work of others. So too were the smaller children, the three- and four-year-olds who were watched over by their mothers.

"I was with my baby a lot," said Fay Druck, an escapee from the Lida ghetto. "We used to go around in the woods. We would search for cranberries, which we would eat. There were mushrooms and we ate the mushrooms."

By December, Tuvia had learned that Sergei Vasilyev hadn't forgotten that Asael had left the Kirov Brigade headquarters without permission. The Russian was incensed by his insubordination. He saw him as nothing better than a deserter and demanded that he receive the executioner's bullet.

Petrified for his brother's safety, Tuvia penned a letter to General Platon, Vasilyev's superior, requesting that the Jewish group be removed from Vasilyev's brigade and thus be insulated from any orders regarding Asael's status. He argued that since the *puscha* group was so many kilometers from the other detachments in Vasilyev's Kirov Brigade (which included Zus's Ordzhonikidze unit), it should be placed under the jurisdiction of a Soviet commander located nearby.

Before he would get a response, Tuvia received a demand from Vasilyev that infuriated him. The Russian wanted fifty of Tuvia's best fighting men to leave the *puscha* base and report for duty at the Kirov headquarters.

Tuvia and several men hopped on their horses and galloped

to General Platon's headquarters many miles across the *puscha*. The Jewish commander was hopeful that Platon would lend an understanding ear to his plight. He couldn't allow Vasilyev to rip his group apart again.

"If I accede to Vasilyev's order," Tuvia told the Russian commander after his arrival, "I will once again be defenseless. I will not be able to maintain the cohesiveness of the group and I will have to resign. Vasilyev's plan is not in accordance with the goals of the motherland, and the hundreds of people with me would eventually perish."

Platon chuckled, conceding Tuvia's point. He agreed to rescind Vasilyev's orders regarding the execution of Asael and deployment of the fifty men.

Relieved, Tuvia returned to the base and sent two horsemen to Vasilyev with Platon's statement. The two returned after several days with word that Vasilyev was outraged by Platon's order and that the Russian had reiterated his assertion, in language filled with venom, that Asael deserved to be killed. Tuvia also learned that Vasilyev had appropriated food from a group of Bielski fighters.

Once again appalled by Vasilyev's behavior, Tuvia stormed off for another meeting with Platon, bringing with him food that had been prepared in the base kitchen. Tuvia spoke of his continuing problems with Vasilyev, noting the brigade commander's unrelenting call for Asael's head and his confiscation of goods meant for unarmed "Soviet citizens."

But Platon was not interested in issuing any orders on that day. He was eager instead to visit the Bielski base personally to see just how life was progressing for the Jewish group. He would arrive, he said, on December 31, 1943.

Noticing that the general was wearing frayed trousers and damaged boots, Tuvia said that a man of his stature deserved much better clothing. "I can help you," Tuvia told him. "And you will be satisfied."

Platon was pleased by the offer.

"We have in our Torah, 'Don't take a bribe,'" Tuvia later said. "But it's not written that you can't *give* a bribe."

After Tuvia arrived back in camp, he ordered a massive beautification campaign in preparation for the general's arrival. It was a great opportunity to prove the camp's utility in support of Soviet war aims.

On the appointed day, the "boss over all the woods," as Tuvia referred to him, rode into camp accompanied by forty partisans equipped with the latest in modern weaponry. Platon was escorted to the *shtab* and served a princely meal of sausages, pickled meats, stuffed cabbage, and plenty of *samogonka*.

Following the meal, Tuvia took the general on a tour of the camp facilities. As they entered the light-industries building, a worker called the laborers to attention. Platon asked everyone to remain at ease and proceeded to move through the space, stopping at each one of the workstations. To one of the leatherworkers, he remarked that every saddle produced in the base was the equivalent of an ambush on the Germans. To one of the barbers, he mentioned that the partisans at his headquarters were due for haircuts and invited him to make a visit in the future.

Before exiting the building, Platon complimented the tailors on their handiwork and expressed surprise at the workmanship of the watchmakers. Tuvia and the general then walked outside to Shmuel Oppenheim's metal workshop before moving in the direction of the tannery. The Russian noticed that several religious Jews were immersed in their afternoon prayers. He stopped. "What is this?"

"Don't you know?" Tuvia responded. "They're learning the history of the party."

The two men laughed heartily, and continued on to the forge. One of the workers was performing the difficult task of fashioning a rifle breech. Platon listened as the worker explained what he was doing.

"Many breeches to attack the German fascists!" the Russian said. He was equally impressed by the sausage-making facility. "Visit us often," Tuvia said, "and we will gladly share our bounty with you."

The tour moved along: the jail, the bakery, the food-storage area, the soap-making shop, and the flour mill. He visited the infirmary with Dr. Hirsch, who complained about the lack of medical supplies.

Once the tour was completed, the two partisans returned to the *shtab*. Platon spoke for thirty minutes about the importance of the camp's work and pledged to aid in the unit's difficulties with other partisan groups. He announced that the base would serve as a "quartermaster corps" for the partisans of the *puscha*, a supply-and-repair depot that tended to the needs of the fighting men. "It is what every army requires!" he said.

To Tuvia, it was a triumphant moment. If Platon supported the work of the Jewish camp and understood its utility to the partisan war, he would surely protect it from Soviet partisans like Vasilyev, who saw Jewish noncombatants as useless in the fight against the Germans. And if the base was now largely safe from Soviet interference *and* German attack, two of the great battles in the Bielski war were nearly won. Could it be that all his diplomatic efforts with the partisan leadership were paying off?

But Platon hadn't yet decided whether Tuvia's group would remain under the jurisdiction of Sergei Vasilyev.

After his talk, the Russian requested that Tuvia and a few of his men travel with him to some nearby partisan camps.

The group left that afternoon and soon arrived at a base that was preparing for a New Year's Eve celebration. Putting aside official duties, the men indulged in the festivities, not to mention many rounds of vodka. They woke up the next morning, imbibed a few more drinks, and rode off to visit one of Platon's trusted lieutenants, Yefim Gapayev, who was known as Sokolov.

The men reached Sokolov's base by the afternoon and launched into another party. Late that night, everyone sat down to discuss business, and the meeting lasted until the morning of January 2.

During the discussion, Tuvia reiterated his desire to have the family unit removed from Vasilyev's jurisdiction. He also suggested that it be renamed "Platon" in honor of the commander. Platon nixed the idea of the name, but he gave his consent to removing the unit from Vasilyev's supervision.

Tuvia spoke about his brother Asael, noting how gifted he was as a military leader and how important he was to the smooth operation of the fighting forces. "Without this force," Tuvia said, "I cannot maintain the integrity of our group and we know how important it is for our group to continue to exist. Our productive and loyal citizens are certainly worth preserving."

Platon agreed to issue another command rescinding any orders regarding Asael's execution.

Next day, January 3, 1944, Platon signed a typed statement formally removing the unit from the Kirov Brigade. Instead of reporting to Vasilyev, Tuvia would now be subordinate to Sokolov. The unit was removed from the brigade structure altogether and made an "independent" detachment.

The final paragraph of the "strictly confidential" dispatch outlined how Platon saw the Jewish group as functioning:

> I assign this task to the commanding staff of the detachment: To provide the family population in the detachment with provisions and armed guards. To find means for arming those capable of battle. To involve those armed in destroying communications, bridges, and roads and to carry out reconnaissance missions. To form at least two to three diversion groups out of the 150 armed detachment members in order to blow up railways, military trains, road trucks and other military technology. To form ambushes to destroy the battle force of the enemy.

Zus's Ordzhonikidze detachment, which had 117 partisans as of the New Year, eight of whom were gentiles, had an easier task in proving its usefulness to the war struggle: Strike at enemies responsible for thousands upon thousands of Jewish deaths. It was a job they pursued with relish.

In November and December, while the base in the Naliboki Puscha was being built, Zus's outfit participated in typical partisan missions. On November 7, four men blew up a railway bridge and burned down a wooden vehicle bridge. On December 12, a group of fighters burned two houses near the Lida-Baranovich railroad, and on December 19, several partisans ambushed an enemy vehicle on the Novogrudek-Lida road, killing the driver.

On December 21, on the morning after a heavy snowfall, Zus's group teamed up with men from the October Detachment led by one of the brothers' early allies in the war, the young Russian Viktor Panchenkov. They attacked a small convoy on the Novogrudek-Novayelna road, killing four Germans, two policemen, and one civilian collaborator. The German force, however, was sizable and it launched an energetic counterattack, sending the partisans fleeing into the forest.

One Jewish fighter was killed and another was injured. Dr. Isler went to work on the wounded man, but his injuries were so severe that he soon died. Still under attack, the partisans had no choice but to flee. On the next day, several men returned to the scene of the confrontation and found the dead man's naked corpse propped against a tree with a bottle of vodka frozen to his hand, placed there by Germans.

But the detachment's luck soon improved. Ordzhonikidze joined forces with Viktor Panchenkov's men for two successful missions in the coming weeks.

On January 5, just days after Tuvia had his adventures with Platon, Viktor led two units from the Ordzhonikidze and October Detachments in an action against the Lida-Baranovich railroad. As evening descended, several fighters dislodged the rail lines from their beds, making it physically impossible for a train to pass.

Then the men waited for several hours, crouched in the snow, until a locomotive pulling seven cars barreled in from the east. After its conductor noticed a problem with the track, the train slowed to a halt.

"I gave the order to fire," Viktor later wrote, "and shooting began. However, from the train we heard the sound of crying women and children, and I ordered the shooting to stop."

A Nazi officer, who was later identified as a deputy to the Novogrudek regional commissar Wilhelm Traub, appeared from one of the cars and shouted something at the partisans. Viktor asked one of his men to translate the German's message, which, he learned, amounted to little more than the Nazi calling the partisans "riffraff." The Russian ordered the shooting to resume.

The partisans beat back the German fighters and occupied the train's cars. Viktor reported that forty civilians were captured and then released, while four soldiers were taken prisoner. The Ordzhonikidze report mentioned that two Germans were killed and thirteen wounded. No one from the partisan force was killed. The booty was significant, with the train carrying forty motorcycles, three cars, and loads of ammunition and rifles. Following the action, the train was set on fire.

A week later, Sergei Vasilyev, who remained Zus's brigade commander despite losing his supervisory role with Tuvia's noncombatant group, issued a report that seemed to greatly inflate the number of enemy casualties. He wrote that twenty-one Germans were killed in the action. (Zus would also later claim a much larger body count, noting that fifty Germans were killed.) Either way, the ambush was a great success. It was the subject of glowing articles in partisan newspapers and the fevered talk of peasants of the region. Commanders from both detachments were presented with awards from the Kirov commander.

A few weeks later, on January 28, another operation was launched, which, the partisans hoped, would top the train derailment. Vasilyev's staff outlined an ambush plan that utilized men from four detachments of the Kirov Brigade. Ten partisans from the Jewish group were to play a key role in the attack.

Upon entering the village of Vasilevitch, the Jewish partisans shouted, cursed, and shot their pistols in the air. The men carried bottles of vodka, from which they drank in large gulps. The peasants grew increasingly agitated by the behavior, thoroughly convinced by the acting of the partisans. For the truth was, the men were perfectly sober. The containers were filled with water.

As the scene played out, more than one hundred and fifty partisans, including an additional ten men from Ordzhonikidze, surrounded the approaches to the village and waited for any sign of the enemy. As the partisans expected, a peasant from Vasilevitch ran off to a nearby German outpost and informed the Nazis of the activities of the drunken Jews. Eventually several vehicles appeared, carrying a total of thirty-four men, including eight Nazi officers.

"We were just lying on the ground," said Sergei Zhigalo, one of Viktor's men. "When I saw them coming up to us, I whistled to the rest of the men."

The convoy stopped at the edge of the village, and the policemen left their vehicles to confer with the Nazi commander. With the enemy so vulnerable, the partisan force pounced, unleashing a thunderous offensive. Though the Germans and their collaborators recovered to fire off some rounds, killing four partisans and wounding three, the enemy fighters were overwhelmed in quick order. Within minutes, dead bodies were everywhere. Each of the Nazi officers and twenty-two policemen were killed. Four policemen, three of whom were wounded, were taken prisoner.

Among the dead was Kurt Fidler, the Nazi lieutenant who commanded the German outpost. "He wasn't a man, but a beast," wrote Viktor. "Not only did local residents fight against him, but even the police fought him."

Zus examined Fidler's broken body and removed his uniform. "It fit me perfectly," he later said. "I finished the war with this uniform." It was one of his proudest moments—a man whose parents, two siblings, wife, and child had been killed by Nazi murderers was now wearing the clothing of the hated enemy. Nothing he did could ever bring his family members back, but at least he could humiliate those who had hurt him.

The cooperation between the Jewish group and its Soviet counterparts wasn't always so productive. Zus's men were well aware of the need to be watchful of everyone, including their allies. Russians regularly threatened Jewish fighters and spread tales about them hoarding gold and other valuables. But the Bielski unit earned a reputation for swiftly responding to any affront. Zus more than once pulled his gun on soldiers who were ostensibly friends.

Of course, Zus's men had plenty of other enemies and their numbers seemed to be increasing every day.

Principal among them were anti-Soviet Polish partisan units, whose strength was growing in the Lida/Novogrudek area during late 1943 and early 1944. Fighters of the Armia Krajowa (AK), or Home Army, were referred to as White Poles, and the Bielski brothers knew them to be vicious enemies of the Jewish people. Indeed, General Bor-Komorowski, the AK's top commander, issued an order on September 15, 1943, calling for the extermination of Jewish partisan groups, which he regarded as bandits.

Some Polish guerillas had attempted to cooperate with the Soviet fighters in the early years of the occupation. But the Soviets responded with "a cocked pistol" when the Poles were resistant to being incorporated into a movement that demanded loyalty to Stalin and Communism, according to one account of a

White Polish fighter from the Novogrudek area. The Poles' willingness to fight the Soviet partisans led to alliances between the AK and the occupying Germans, who offered them weapons, ammunition, and medical care. Cooperation between the two was an open secret in the countryside, and a document written by the Nazi regional commissar in Novogrudek speaks of "our agreements with Polish partisans."

There was another group that directed its fighting power against Jewish and Soviet partisans in the Bielski zone.

Thousands of pro-German Cossacks and their families streamed into the area in the fall of 1943, fleeing their homelands in the Caucasus region after Red Army victories over Wehrmacht troops. Renowned as mounted defenders of the Russian steppes, remorseless protectors of the tsars, and savage tormenters of Jews, the Cossacks are people of mixed Turkish, Tatar, Russian, and Ukrainian ancestry. They were distinctive in their shaggy fur caps, baggy pants tucked into high leather boots, and long sheepskin cloaks. The Nazis rewarded their loyalty to the cause by allowing them to lead their own military regiments and set up "self-governing regions" where they were free to establish their own system of governance.

In the Novogrudek area, a charismatic Cossack named Sergei Pavlov directed an effort to build a school, hospital, and an Orthodox church. Eventually, twenty-five thousand Cossacks moved into the region. Several Cossack regiments of a thousand men each soon joined the struggle against enemies of the German occupation.

If that wasn't enough, a cavalry unit of pro-German Belorussian soldiers, led by Boris Ragula, a Nazi collaborator from Novogrudek, was now active in the area.

Ragula, an ambitious twenty-three-year-old from a family
of Belorussian nationalists, was imprisoned and tortured by the
Soviet authorities prior to the German invasion. A fluent
speaker of German, he joined up with the occupiers soon after
they arrived in hopes of convincing them to give the Belorussian people greater autonomy. He served as a translator for
regional commissar Wilhelm Traub during the first, bloody year
of the occupation.

In the late summer of 1943, he was called into Traub's personal residence to discuss the formation of an anti-partisan
force. The Nazi apologized for the German unwillingness to
accommodate Belorussian nationalistic dreams. "Are you still
willing to form a unit to fight the partisans?" Traub asked,
promising to supply horses and ammunition. Ragula agreed. He
was flown to Minsk, where a Nazi general briefed him on the
mission.

Within weeks, Ragula was leading a 150-man unit dressed
in Nazi uniforms with the national colors of the Belarus on the
collar.

The profusion of German-allied fighters didn't alter the view
of many that the Germans were doomed to lose the war. To add
to the confusion on the battlefield, local policemen allied with
the Germans started defecting to the partisans, figuring the
future was brighter with the guerrillas. Zus himself was sending
messages to Volodiya Picta, the police chief of Novogrudek, a
Belorussian native of Big Izvah who had once been close with the
Bielski family. "Bring twenty or thirty men and join us," Zus
wrote to him. "And all will be forgotten."

Picta, who had previously sent word to the brothers that he
deliberately misfired whenever he came into contact with the

Jewish group, even met with Zus at a neutral site outside the city. Nothing ever came of the talks.

The messages were also coming from the other direction. The top Nazi in Novogrudek sent a note to Viktor Panchenkov promising amnesty to his group if it joined the Nazi struggle. Panchenkov's response, which, according to Zus, was crafted by a Jewish doctor attached to the unit, was rather unambiguous.

Panchenkov addressed him as "Mr. Temporary Regional Commissar" and castigated him for daring to send such a letter. "Think . . . You can't leave the city without an escort of an armored vehicle or tanks. When you were in Novogrudek, you couldn't use a phone and your trains and cars were derailed in the hundreds, as no trains travel at night. You don't control the villages, and every day you have more and more graves."

Just when Tuvia Bielski felt as though he had insulated the group from any trouble with the Soviets, new problems arose to cause him headaches. The timing couldn't have been worse. He had struggled to slip from underneath the thumb of Sergei Vasilyev and to develop a positive working relationship with General Platon. Now he had to deal with internal dissension, which, he felt, threatened to ruin all his work.

The problems came from Israel Kessler, who was still operating the small satellite base a short distance from the main camp. He had long been a critic of the brothers, but his opposition had increased since the new *puscha* base had been constructed. He joined with others who were displeased with Bielski rule and started speaking with Soviet commanders about his grievances.

The rebel group's activity was confirmed for Tuvia when

one of General Platon's deputies summoned him to respond to a report about a group of Bielski fighters acting recklessly after returning from a mission. "There is no discipline and even your people are saying this!" the Russian said. Tuvia regarded the reference to "your people" as a troubling sign that his authority was being undermined.

Then Sokolov, who had direct responsibility for the Bielski camp, spoke with Tuvia about the matter. The Russian had also received reports from Kessler's group about the Bielski leadership.

"Why don't you come to the camp and investigate the matter yourself?" Tuvia suggested to him.

The Russian, an imposing man with a golden beard whom Tuvia praised as "the antithesis of the typical Russian anti-Semite," arrived a few days later and received a welcome similar to the one Platon had enjoyed. Tuvia asked if he would be interested in watching a performance by the base's entertainment troupe. Sokolov said he would. He and his retinue found seats on the ground in the assembly area as a large portion of the camp population joined the visitors.

The show included Soviet songs, folk dances, and a skit that aped a Charlie Chaplin silent film, with one of the older children playing Chaplin himself. Then an eight-year-old girl sang a solo, greatly impressing the Russian commander. He showered her with kisses and promised to fly her to Moscow to study music. It was a promise he fulfilled in the coming weeks; she accompanied a few injured partisans being sent to a hospital in the capital.

Sokolov then met with Kessler and his allies, who muted the criticisms they had delivered in written form to the partisan command. The Russian left impressed with the base facilities and feeling unconcerned about the complaints against Tuvia's leadership.

But the drama didn't seem over. Kessler and his comrades continued to write letters to the Soviets, and several in the camp suspected he was angling for Tuvia's job.

ELEVEN

JANUARY 1944–
JULY 1944

"WHEN I FIRST SAW Tuvia Bielski, he was wearing a leather jacket with a machine gun across his chest. He was surrounded by men on horses," said Charles Bedzow, who arrived in the *puscha* from the Lida ghetto. "He was, to me, the biggest hero in the world. After the ghetto and the killing, after living from hour to hour when we didn't know when the Germans would take us away, it was incredible. It was freedom."

The bustling forest village was indeed a thrilling sight for those Jews who continued to trickle into it, and its imposing partisan fighters provided a profound relief after all they had been through. Some were escapees from ghettos and labor camps who had walked for weeks to find the base. Some were Jewish fighters in Russian bands tired of the bigotry displayed toward them by their comrades. Some were part of small groups attempting to live on their own, ordered by the Soviets to relocate to the acceptable place of Jewish residence.

They all journeyed through a landscape that had been ravaged by the war. They passed villages filled with burned-out homes, decomposed human and animal bodies, and feral cats scavenging for sustenance. Some suffered the gibes of Russian fighters, who wondered why they had worked so long for the Germans in the ghettos, or the taunts of disdainful peasants who refused to give them food.

Then they entered a haven where their people were living in safety and eating hearty meals. Over and over, the new arrivals wept in disbelief; the rumors they had been hearing, the stories that had been told about the Bielski brothers' kingdom of the Jews, were true! No one was cowering before the whips of Nazi thugs. No one was whispering under his breath, praying that he wouldn't be overheard. It wasn't a fairy tale. It was a real place.

Many described what they saw in language tinged with religious imagery. An oasis in the midst of hell, they would say; and Tuvia Bielski, who indeed rode a white horse for a time, was a messiah rescuing his people from evil. "I consider that he was sent by God to save Jews," said Beryl Chafetz, a rabbinical student before the war who became a rabbi after it. "He wasn't a man, he was an angel," said Isaac Mendelson.

But since the end of the Novogrudek and Lida ghettos— aside from the Bielski settlement, these were the last major concentrations of Jewish life in the region—fewer sizable groups were arriving in the Bielski camp. The last great influx included sixty or seventy Jews who had escaped from the Koldechevo labor camp near Baranovich in March. The horrible truth was, there weren't many left.

The community was evolving through the first months of 1944. Despite the harsh, snowy weather, people were improving their dugouts—there were about twenty of the large communal structures, which held some fifty people each—and building their own cooking facilities.

A group of six people, including the camp historian Dr. Shmuel Amarant and his wife, constructed new living quarters on higher, drier ground, after receiving permission from the base command to make the move. The Amarants' small home had tree stumps for chairs, a large window looking out onto the forest, and a small tub used for cooking, bathing, and laundering clothes. It was the envy of the forest. Before long, others were building their dream homes in the exclusive neighborhood.

The wives and girlfriends of the fighters and commanders were preparing food over fires near their dugouts, making them less reliant on the base's communal supply of food. Cooking pots were forged by the blacksmiths from material taken from the roofs of the abandoned houses in the village of Naliboki. The base kitchen continued providing food for those who had no other options, but the overall quality of life had improved remarkably, and the proportion of residents who relied on the base kitchen was lower than ever.

During the day, small groups tromped through the snows looking for birch trees, which they cut down, sawed into small pieces, and transported back to the camp. The wood was burned in the dugout stoves, bringing warmth to the damp interiors. People passed the time by trading gossip or staring silently at the roaring flames.

The camp's residents were usually in bed by nine P.M. A few fires were permitted to keep burning to prevent those on guard duty from freezing. "If anyone wanted to attack, they would have to come through us first," said Meyer Bronicki, an escapee of the Dvorets labor camp who joined the Bielski group in April 1943.

"But we didn't have any problem in those days, because the snow was probably ten feet deep and we were so far in the forest."

The month of February was a particularly frigid one, and blinding snowstorms blanketed the *puscha* in white powder. The temperatures exacerbated health problems, especially with medications still in short supply. With predictable gallows humor, people joked that Dr. Hirsch only had two diagnoses: You're going to live or you're going to die.

Everyone feared catching typhus, which was carried by the lice that were impossible to completely banish from the base. The bugs nested in the seams of shirts and pants; even submerging the fabric in boiling water didn't dislodge the vermin. A typhus outbreak materialized after a Soviet group donated supplies to the Bielski unit, with several people coming down with the ailment soon after the clothing, food, and weaponry arrived. A man was assigned to transport the sick from the base to the quarantine hut in a horse-drawn sleigh.

Those who contracted the disease were forced to be quarantined for twenty-one days. Most survived the ordeal, returning to the camp in a pitiful state of depletion. At least one person died. The death, along with other casualties of illness and injury, led to the creation of another staple of any community's life: a cemetery.

Despite the deep snow and health problems, the unit upheld its responsibilities to the larger partisan effort. Tuvia was instructed by General Platon's staff to send a team of workers to a site in the *puscha* where a landing strip for airplanes was being prepared. It was a sign of how strong Platon's partisans had grown in the last few months—they now felt that the Germans wouldn't attempt another excursion into the *puscha*.

About a day's journey from the camp, the facility required several dugouts to house the airport staff and the wounded fighters waiting for air transport to hospitals in the east. Among the workers were partisans from a detachment of a few hundred Jews commanded by a Minsk carpenter named Shalom Zorin. He had established a *puscha* base a few kilometers from the Bielski location, making it the only other Jewish camp of significant size.

The primitive "airport" was really nothing more than a clearing in the woods. After the dugouts were built and a runway smoothed out, the Red Army supply planes started arriving in the evenings. They were guided into position by huge fires placed around the perimeter of the field. To prevent German trickery, the number of fires was communicated by radio: The flyers didn't land unless they saw the agreed-upon number of fires.

The pilots brought with them badly needed weapons and medicine, as well as less desirable propaganda pamphlets and songbooks. They also brought stories from the distant front, tales of Red Army victories over an increasingly beleaguered Wehrmacht. The talk grew louder: Could this war be coming to an end?

The Jewish group's commanders were also instructed to send as many fighting men into the field as possible.

The force of fighters, including a unit of ten to twenty men led by Asael Bielski, were in continuous action. General Platon's partisan command ordered them to carry out their food and combat missions in the area around Stankevich, which put them in the vicinity of Zus's fighters. The men sometimes spent a week or two on the road completing their work, all of which took Asael further away from the day-to-day operation of the base.

The most successful strike against the enemy happened on February 4, when a group of eight Bielski men struck a blow against the Germans that rivaled the Ordzhonikidze successes of the previous month. The men planted a mine, built by the unit's explosives specialist Lev Ferdman, on the Lida-Baranovich railroad, not far from the Yatsuki station. At about eight-thirty P.M. a train traveling northwest toward Lida was sent reeling by the explosion. Seven train cars were destroyed and four were damaged. Rail traffic was halted for fifteen hours. There were no partisan casualties.

As the weeks wore on, Tuvia was becoming steadily more concerned about the activities of Israel Kessler. Now a leader of over nine hundred people, he was unsettled by the idea of an active opponent among the ranks. Though the threat of a destabilizing insurrection seemed to have dissipated in the last few months, Tuvia worried that Kessler's opposition could result in his being stripped of his command by the Soviets. If Kessler's charges were given credence and Tuvia was found to have been disloyal to the Soviet enterprise, he could face possible execution.

Kessler felt that Tuvia's pledges of loyalty to Communists were all a ruse—which was true. He was also heard saying he believed Tuvia was really a capitalist speculator—an absurd charge. One thing was clear: The rebel was busily searching for others who opposed the Bielski rule.

The situation reached boiling point when Tuvia learned that Kessler had been absent from the base without permission, a violation of protocol—ironically, the same violation of protocol that nearly led to Asael's execution. The lawyer Solomon Wolkowyski, the director of the "special section" responsible for internal investigation, said he thought Kessler was meeting with Sokolov's staff, filling their ears with his grievances about Tuvia.

When Kessler eventually returned to the camp, he and his wife were ordered to report to the *shtab* to speak with the leader. Kessler produced a note written by Sokolov that explained he was at brigade headquarters to discuss "service matters."

After clearing the room of all but a few men, Tuvia demanded of Kessler: "Who gave you permission to leave the camp and visit Sokolov?"

"I see no reason for explanations," Kessler responded. "I brought a note from Sokolov. This is sufficient."

Tuvia didn't say a word. Instead, he struck Kessler in the face with the butt of his revolver, drawing blood. The husband and wife, both of whom were carrying revolvers, were disarmed, and Kessler was escorted to the jail dugout. His wife, Rachel Rieff, refused to leave his side, and she was also incarcerated.

Back in Kessler's satellite camp, one of his deputies, a man who had helped Kessler write letters to the Soviets, grew agitated at the news of his leader's arrest. To the others in Kessler's base, he seemed primarily worried for his own safety, now that his leader was in trouble.

Soon thereafter, Asael and his fighters returned from a mission in high spirits. They enjoyed an evening of singing and dancing around the fire. But when the deputy commander was told the news about Kessler, Asael's mood darkened.

"We must execute him now!" he said.

Tuvia counseled patience. He sent Wolkowyski to the partisan headquarters to discuss the charges leveled by Kessler and his allies. The lawyer was shown a petition signed by rebels and their allies that alleged the leadership wasn't sufficiently Communist and that the commanders were out for personal gain rather than the general good of the population.

Wolkowyski returned in a state of anxiety. He told Tuvia that the base leadership would be threatened if the rebellion were allowed to continue. He recommended that Israel Kessler be executed. The other commanders agreed with his judgment.

The men marched to the jail and ordered the several prisoners to line up in a row. Employing a technique he learned in the Polish Army, Tuvia asked each one of them to explain why he was incarcerated. The last to be questioned was Kessler. "You know why I am in jail," he said. "It is unfair."

Asael pulled out his pistol and shot him where he stood. He had to be restrained from attacking Kessler's wife.

"Leave her be," Tuvia said to his brother.

A short time later, a trial was held to judge one of Kessler's allies, a barber who, it was charged, had aided the Nazis of Lida. He was also found guilty and sentenced to death.

Tuvia felt certain about the need to eliminate men whom he regarded to be as dangerous as any of the group's external enemies. In all his writing and interviews, he never expressed doubt about the propriety of the move. Many agreed that the situation in the forest was too fraught with danger to allow such open dissension. "He was a troublemaker," said Jack Kagan. "If Kessler succeeded and a Russian commander took over, then problems would arise. Tuvia understood that. We had all lived through the Russian occupation, when the biggest fear was informers. You could be sent to prison and never know why it happened."

"You can't let everything go," said Beryl Chafetz. "You have to show your power. It was too risky to let these things happen."

Kessler's supporters were incensed. They felt that the brothers were now so drunk with power that they would eliminate anyone who challenged them. Many stewed in silence at the strong-armed ways of Tuvia and Asael. Kessler's widow, Rachel Rieff, would forever regard the two as monsters. "I have nothing good to say about them," she said decades later.

But however jarring the killing, it ended any further problem with the Soviets. Solomon Wolkowyski traveled to partisan headquarters to explain the incident to Sokolov. No disciplinary action was taken against Tuvia.

For the Ordzhonikidze fighters, the challenges came mostly in the form of external enemies throughout February, March, and April. The group was growing steadily more successful as a fighting band, becoming one of the few wholly Jewish fighting detachments to operate on an equal basis with Soviet units. Zus's men were participating in an increasing number of large-scale ambushes and eliminating more and more enemy fighters.

In one attack, on March 5, the unit participated in a joint attack with Russian bands that eliminated forty-seven White Polish fighters and injured twenty more. Later in the month, on the 22nd, some twenty Jewish fighters laid an ambush for a Nazi convoy and succeeded in killing twelve Germans.

But dangers still lurked. Five partisans were killed during actions in March, and seemingly friendly peasants occasionally caused difficulties. On one evening in April, several members of the unit were staying in a Polish man's home on the outskirts of a small hamlet. As usual, guards were posted around the property to keep a lookout for enemy activity. In the early morning hours, one of them, Avram Movshovich, was discovered dead, apparently from a blow with a steel pipe.

Officials from Sergei Vasilyev's brigade staff conducted an investigation and concluded that the Polish homeowner and his son knew nothing of the crime. Unsatisfied with the verdict, Zus requested permission to interrogate the Poles with Vasilyev's men present as witnesses. Eventually the truth emerged: The old man confessed that his son had murdered the Jewish guard.

Vasilyev ordered the deaths of the man, his son, and a third accomplice. The sentence was carried out on April 27 in front of the entire unit.

Zus and his men were also continuing to rely on the assistance of the oldest and best ally of the brothers Bielski, Konstantin Koslovsky, who had remained a vital supporter since the first meeting in the summer of 1942. He had assisted in the rescue of perhaps one hundred Jews—possibly more—who had fled Novogrudek in search of the brothers' camp, hiding them on his property or behind the house, serving them food and vodka from his kitchen, and offering them clothes from his wardrobe. He was a saintly man who never spoke of his good deeds and never sought reward for the danger in which he had placed himself and his several children. His assistance hadn't wavered even after his policeman brother, Ivan, was murdered for aiding the Jews of the ghetto and the forest.

But by the spring of 1944, word of his activities had reached the enemy.

A contingent of local police appeared outside Konstantin's house near Makrets. Although the forty-seven-year-old Belorussian wasn't at home, several of his children were present. They quickly found a place to hide.

The men stormed into the house and shouted for Konstantin. Unable to locate him, they smashed the family's possessions, and Konstantin's then-six-year-old daughter Taisija recalled how they broke a kitchen table in two.

The policemen left the house and descended on the family's barn, where they shoved sticks into the hay to discover if anyone was hiding in the stacks. Taisija ran to a nearby home shared by Konstantin's two brothers, Mikhail and Alexander, and their families. She hid underneath a bed with one of her cousins.

Konstantin Jr., Konstantin's oldest son, then twenty, and a few adults remained in plain sight.

With no luck in the shed, the police forced their way into Mikhail and Alexander's house, and demanded that young Konstantin tell them the whereabouts of his father. When he refused to answer, the men placed him facedown on a bench and began whipping him with the iron rods that are used to clean rifles. But Konstantin's son refused to say a word. Finally, he lost consciousness.

One of the policemen spied the young girls concealed underneath the bed. Pulling one of them from her hiding place, he said, "So, you are the Jewish kids?"

"They are our children," one of the older Koslovsky relatives said. "Don't touch them."

"They are just kids," a policeman said to his comrade. "You, too, have children. Let them stay."

The man released the little girl and helped his comrades drag Konstantin Jr. from the property. They threw the young man in the back of a cart and drove him to a nearby village, where they dumped him on the side of the road. Found by a friend, he returned to his father's home and spent months recovering from his injuries.

But the incident rendered the Koslovsky family unable to provide safe haven for the Bielski brothers and any other Jews. Konstantin's children and a few of the older relatives moved into the nearby forests for protection. Konstantin also sought shelter in the woods, hiding himself in the same places where he had delivered Jews who had fled from the ghettos.

On April 17, 1944, Tuvia reported to his partisan superiors that the camp now held 941 people, 162 of whom were armed fighters. The workshops were improving and upgrading, and visiting Soviet partisans were now such a familiar sight that they almost went unnoticed. Using parachute silk dropped from Soviet supply planes, the tailors were making shirts and underwear of a quality not previously seen in the woods. The supply planes were also delivering newspapers, which, coupled with an increase in the number of radios and partisan publications, gave the population a good idea of the progress of the war. Battlefield strategy was heatedly discussed in the central square.

The warm weather made it easier for old dugouts to be improved and for new ones to be constructed. The "untouchable reserve," the storage area reserved for food and supplies that could be used only in the event of an attack, seemed to contain enough grain and potatoes to last another war. The herd of cows now included as many as sixty animals, and the number of horses grew to more than thirty. Aron Bielski, now fourteen, would sometimes round up a few of the children his age and sneak off into the field to teach them how to ride.

Most of the population was intent on contributing to the victory over the Germans by remaining immersed in their work duties. Even the youngest of the residents wanted to pitch in. Willy Moll, the thirteen-year-old who had escaped the Lida ghetto during its final days in September 1943, worked as a carpenter's apprentice, although he had little idea what to do. Even younger children wanted to be counted among the troops. Carmela Shamir's four-year-old son would salute Tuvia every time the commander walked by, silently pledging his allegiance to the cause.

General Platon dispatched Ivan Shematovich, a stout Belorussian from Minsk, to fill the vacant commissar post, which hadn't been filled since the group was split back in the late summer of 1943. It was an appointment that the Soviets hoped would keep the base soundly Communist and ensure against any further Kessler-like troubles. But Tuvia was pleased to discover that Shematovich, who was married to a young Jewish woman, was more interested in drinking *samogonka* than in ensuring the doctrinal purity of the detachment. Still, camp residents avoided any too-outward expressions of Jewish political or religious sentiment. The songs around the campfire would switch from Soviet themes to Jewish ones only when everyone was certain that no Russians were nearby. The prayers of the religiously inclined were performed quietly out of the way at the tannery.

Asael was as busy as ever during the spring, leading a number of missions into the distant countryside. In a stretch of three days in April, Asael directed an extraordinary rampage across the Novogrudek countryside. On the 27th, the Jewish partisans blew up two enemy vehicles with self-made mines, killing three Germans and two policemen. On the following day, he and his men derailed a train on the Lida-Baranovich railway, halting traffic for nine hours. On the 29th, they blew up a truck on the Lida-Novogrudek road, killing one German and two policemen. Asael's men, all of them ghetto escapees, were now some of the most feared partisans of the region.

To so many of the *puscha* residents, the sight of Asael riding his horse through the base after one of his excursions was singularly reassuring. He wasn't as complex as Tuvia, a man who seemed to carry great burdens. The second Bielski brother moved with confidence and ease and, despite his reticence, radiated a sense of openness. It didn't take much to get him to smile. And after so many missions under such tense circumstances, Asael's fighting men adored him. Wherever he decided to go, they would follow.

On May 1, everyone gathered in the *puscha* for a large May Day celebration, held on a beautiful spring day that inspired optimism among the war-weary population. After a lunch during which everyone was given a ration of sausage, the entire group congregated in the central square, which was decorated by scores of flapping red flags. The fighters lined up in a military fashion, while the nonfighters, men and women, young and old, also stood at attention.

Facing the gathering were the commanders—Tuvia, Asael, Layzer Malbin, Ivan Shematovich, Solomon Wolkowyski, and Pesach Friedberg. Holding a message from the Soviet government, Tuvia stepped forward to speak. He announced that the Red Army had retaken the Caucasus region and the Germans were retreating, a bit of news that inspired prolonged cheering.

"This war will soon reach the German heartland and there the Nazi monster will finally be crushed," he said. "The front is approaching rapidly and we can expect difficult days ahead. We must be ready for them. Victory is clearly before us!"

Zus's group was also noticing the signs of the impending defeat of the Germans. The Jewish unit was continuing to attack the enemy—Zus led an ambush that killed eight Cossacks and wounded two in May—but by the end of the month, the roads were filled with large convoys of German vehicles, protected by

Cossacks and sometimes White Poles, retreating toward the German Reich. Zus and his men were told to move into the forest to wait for the arrival of the Red Army. The few missions they conducted involved the collection of foodstuffs. The orders were clear: Lie low.

The Germans had been steadily retreating across the vast plains of the Soviet Union since the loss at Kursk in July 1943. Hitler, not willing to surrender, insisted that his troops fight on. But the defeats were many and they arrived with regularity. By November 1943, the Red Army had recaptured the Ukrainian capital of Kiev—indeed a large portion of the territory that the Germans had occupied since June 1941. Through the winter and spring, Stalin's six major tank armies continued to push to the west.

By May 1944, the last great concentration of German forces, Army Group Center, commanded by Field Marshal Ernst von Busch, was centered in Belarus. Stalin was planning a major assault on it for the middle part of June, to be called Operation Bagration (bah-grah-tee-on), in honor of a Georgian hero of the war against Napoleon. Meanwhile, across the world, the British and American forces were readying their long-awaited amphibious invasion of France, dubbed Operation Overlord, which promised to divert large quantities of German troops from the Soviet front.

On June 6, 1944, the Allies landed a massive force at Normandy, France, adding significantly to the war burden of Hitler's troops. Then, on June 22, three years and a day since the start of the German-Russian War, the Red Army launched Operation Bagration. The Red Army was on the advance.

In the *puscha*, the Bielski residents could hear the sounds of the distant battle, rumbling explosions that sounded to the forest Jews like a beautiful symphony.

Tuvia was summoned to report with his armed fighters to a location near the edge of the *puscha*. He and his men arrived to find many hundreds of partisan soldiers, waiting to hear orders from high-ranking officers from Moscow. A Soviet general rode to the head of the group, accompanied by several of his staff officers. He remained seated on his horse while he spoke.

"Comrades! In 1941, the German army destroyed our western front," he said in a loud voice. "They bombarded our factories and burned our cities and villages. The Soviet people have suffered terribly. But soon victory will be ours!"

He paused. "Long live the Red Army!"

The partisans erupted into a chorus of cheers.

The general took off his hat and raised it high above his head.

"The Soviet Army has surrounded a large German force near Minsk," he shouted. "We are certain that they will try to break out of our trap in small groups and work their way westward toward the forests. Our duty, comrades and fellow partisans, is to prevent the Germans from reaching the forests! I have every confidence that you will carry out this mission completely."

The partisans were organized into defensive forces and deployed along the eastern edge of the *puscha*. The men dug trenches, which they disguised with branches and other overgrowth, and waited for signs of the incoming Nazis. They knew it wouldn't be long. The radio was reporting startling Soviet successes. The Germans were being routed as thoroughly as the Soviets had been during Operation Barbarossa three years ago. By July 3, the Red Army had captured Minsk. The defeated Wehrmacht was moving swiftly toward the Novogrudek-Lida region.

After a day or two of waiting, a group of Jewish fighters got their first sight of a small group of German soldiers heading for the safety of the woods. In a flash, the Jews opened fire. The Germans dropped to the ground in confusion, uncertain where the gunfire was coming from.

For one of the German soldiers, this was the final straw. "I don't want war!" he yelled desperately, preparing to surrender. "I want to live!"

But he wouldn't be allowed to surrender. His commanding officer raised his gun and shot the soldier to death. He then turned the gun on himself.

The Jewish partisans jumped out of the trenches and ordered the surviving Germans to put their hands in the air. Immediately, the soldiers begged to be spared. "We never wanted this war!" one of them said.

Hearing their cries, Isak Nowog, who had been with the Bielski group since early 1943, thought back to the way Jews had begged for their lives before being dragged to the execution ditches. But his bitterness didn't permit him to exact revenge in this instance. The men were taken prisoner and marched to a processing area.

But most of the German soldiers weren't so lucky. Partisans were pitiless toward any Nazi who didn't immediately drop his weapon and surrender. They simply shot him. Within a few days, thousands of German bodies lined the edge of the Naliboki Puscha.

Back at the Bielski base in the heart of the woods, the chaos of the battles threw the camp into confusion. Many of the fighters, eager to take on the retreating German forces, left the base to hunt for the enemy. Pandemonium broke out when four German soldiers were captured. After the lawyer Solomon Wolkowyski and the other commanders interrogated the men in the *shtab*, they were released into the central square of the camp.

A furious mob gathered around them. "Look at us, we are Jews!" one man shouted. "Do you know what you did to us?"

Children spat and screamed about their dead parents. Wailing women slapped and cursed at them. Eighty-year-old Shmuel Pupko repeatedly struck each of the Germans with a large stick. After each blow, he announced that the blow was for his brother or for his sister or for his child.

Three of the Germans begged for their lives, trying to convince the Jews that they weren't murderers. The fourth refused. Instead, he stood at attention and said that the Jews got what they deserved.

The beatings went on for nearly two hours; then the Germans were thrown into an open pit. They died amid a hail of bullets.

The executions proved emotionally wrenching, opening up rage that had been perhaps only barely contained. People swilled large quantities of vodka and began scouring the woods for Germans, itching to take further revenge for all that had been visited upon them. Tuvia and his aides grew concerned about the safety of the base in this atmosphere. He urged people to be vigilant. "The war is not over!" he shouted.

On the following morning, on July 9, at around seven A.M., a contingent of some two hundred Germans broke through the *puscha*'s edge and ran headlong toward the Bielski base. They opened fire on the few remaining perimeter guards and charged through the trees toward the dugouts. Hearing the sounds of gunfire, the camp residents were jolted from their sleep and several fighters immediately began a counterattack.

Realizing that his men had no chance against the German force, Tuvia ordered everyone to disperse. Hundreds of people ran, searching for a place to hide in the woods and nearby marshes. It was sheer bedlam.

The ragged Germans entered the camp, spraying gunfire in a haphazard fashion and throwing grenades into the dugouts. The soldiers searched for food, scrounging for anything that might ease their hunger. They weren't able to look for long. Nearby partisan bands, alerted by the sounds of the shooting, descended, forcing the Germans to run for cover. Several Nazis were killed during the ensuing fight.

Bielski members returned from their hiding places to find that nine of their people had been killed, including deputy commissar Tanchum Gordon, who was hit by grenade shrapnel while crouched in the *shtab*. The medical staff attended the few dozen who were injured, while many of the survivors walked around in a gloomy daze.

It was one of the worst days of the detachment's existence. But it was also to be one of the last. Just a few hours after the attack, news filtered through the base that Red Army troops were traveling through the woods. The Germans had been overrun.

Many rushed to a nearby road to have a look at the Soviet fighters, a steady procession of young soldiers, who were covered in dust after miles of marching. It was an overwhelming sight for many of the Jews, and their pent-up emotions came spilling out—tears, or laughter, or both, as the refrain "the war is over" reverberated. The Russian soldiers eagerly accepted the kisses of the young women.

"You can go home!" one of the soldiers yelled.

·   ·   ·

So it ended.

The following morning, after everything had been packed on horses and carts, the entire group gathered together in the central square. Each person carried a small bag of belongings.

Tuvia stood before the unit for the last time. A community that had begun as a small gathering of relatives in the woods near the Bielski family mill was now a mini-city of a thousand Jews from throughout Belarus and Poland, created from survivors of the most ferocious slaughter of a single people in centuries. For more than two years in the forests of western Belarus, the Jews of the Bielski group had withstood adversity from a variety of enemies. They had been forced to abandon a series of camps in mad dashes from Nazi and police attacks. They had faced these challenges and so many more with vigor and vitality. This place, this haven in the woods, was the living emblem of their bravery, a place where they prayed, worked, sang, and loved.

On July 10, 1944, Tuvia Bielski gave his last speech to his people.

"My dear brothers and sisters," he said. "We have suffered through very hard times together. We have been attacked and blockaded. We have been cold and hungry. We have been in constant fear for our lives. Now we are going to tell the world that we, a tiny remnant of a people, have been struggling to save ourselves and our tortured brethren. We are witnesses to what Hitler and his killers have done. We will bear witness to the murder and destruction, to the suffering that the Nazis brought upon the Jewish people."

Then the convoy started the long walk to Novogrudek. Some partisans remained behind to destroy the camp, which the Soviets feared might be used by insurgent groups opposed to their rule. Tuvia, Asael, and the other commanders inspected the column as it marched by. Slowly, the parade of Jews shuffled in the direction of a new life.

Toward the end of the line was a man who had piled his cart high with goods and supplies, in defiance of an order that called for only personal belongings to be taken from the camp. Tuvia confronted the man, who responded by cursing at him and stating in a defiant tone, "We are liberated and you are not my commander anymore."

Tuvia's temper flared. On the final day in the Naliboki Puscha, he pulled his gun and shot the man. It was an act of pure rage that stunned the marchers, who were chilled by sounds of the hysterical sobbing of the man's wife.

In later years, Tuvia never spoke of the deed in the same way as he did of the Kessler shooting. In 1946, he noted that he killed the man "without hesitation." He didn't elaborate. Many suspected that he regarded it as a mistake brought on by the tensions of the final days of forest life, perhaps even by his sudden loss of stature.

Even Shmuel Amarant, the judicious chronicler of forest life and a great admirer of the brothers' achievements, expressed his dismay over the incident. "This was a tragic end to an endeavor which fought to save Jewish lives from the clutches of the Nazis," he wrote. "The camp ended its existence with the taking of a Jewish life and the destruction of a family."

By the end of the day, the group had reached the edge of the *puscha*, where it decided to rest for the evening. Many rushed into the nearby Neman River and, for the first time in three years of war, they bathed themselves without worry of being ambushed. That evening, they cooked fish that they had caught by tossing grenades into the water.

The following morning, they found a shallow portion of the waterway to cross—the most vulnerable members were transported in rafts—and then continued on through the green countryside. The line of marchers stretched out for more than a kilometer into the distance. As the group passed through small villages, the gentile population left their homes and stared dumbfounded at the huge collection of Jews. "How did you survive?" they asked. "Are you ghosts?"

After a few more days of travel, the convoy caught sight of Novogrudek's Castle Hill. Just outside the city, the marchers set up a temporary camp on a farmer's plot of land.

In the meantime, Zus's Ordzhonikidze unit had traveled to Lida, where it helped put out fires and maintain civil order.

Both groups were soon dismissed from service to the partisan movement. Tuvia reported to his partisan superiors that his *puscha* unit included a final tally of 991 members. Zus reported that Ordzhonikidze had 149 members. The Bielski brothers' detachment then included 1,140 Jews on the day of its discharge, making it easily the largest Jewish partisan unit in the Soviet Union—and in all of Nazi-occupied territory. (Two years later, Tuvia would put the number at 1,230, which likely took into account members of the group who may have left before the official count was submitted to the Soviets.) It was the largest rescue of Jews by fellow Jews during World War II.

Everyone was then issued a document certifying his or her membership in the partisans. Except for those fighters (about one-third of Ordzhonikidze) who were conscripted into the Red Army, they were now free to go.

.   .   .

But go where? The Jews of the Bielski detachment knew they didn't have homes to return to. The only home they had was a camp in the middle of the woods. Everything else in their lives had been destroyed.

After paying his respects at the mass grave on the outskirts of his hometown of Dvorets, an angry Isak Nowog, one of the Bielski fighters, marched into the village marketplace, which was full of people who instantly recognized him. He noticed among the gathering a man who had saved him from death early in the occupation. Quieting the crowd, he publicly lauded the man and his wife for the assistance.

Then he castigated the remainder for standing by while the Jews were slaughtered, for behaving callously toward people they had known for generations.

"But I gave bread to the workers in the ghetto," said one villager.

"I offered them potatoes," said another.

"Those you hated are now in their graves," Nowog said, after asking again for silence. "Only God knows what you did during those times. Judgment is now in His hands."

Raya Kaplinski, the base secretary who had escaped from the Novogrudek ghetto in August 1942, marched to her former home in the city, which she found guarded by a Red Army soldier. She demanded to be let inside. He told her to go away, but she wouldn't be denied.

"I just want a memento of my family—a picture or something," she said. "I have nothing."

Hearing the chatter of the argument, a Russian commander stepped out of the house and asked what all the commotion was about. Raya explained her objective. The man said that the house held none of her family's belongings. "There's absolutely nothing in there," he said. "Come in and see for yourself."

Raya walked into the home where she grew up. Just as the man had said, it was empty. Then she noticed a desk in the middle of the room. It had belonged to her grandfather. Raya could see that a portion of one leg was missing, and that it was propped up with a piece of wood. She instantly broke into tears.

"It was an endless cry," she remembered. "An old general asked how I was doing. I couldn't speak."

The Bielski brothers' sister, Taibe, who had survived in the forest with her husband, Abraham Dziencielski, traveled to the small village where her young daughter, Lola, had spent the bulk of the occupation. The brothers had placed the nine-month-old girl with a Polish family during the first winter of captivity. Now nearly four years old, she had no memory of her birth parents or her Jewish upbringing. She spoke Polish fluently, attended Catholic Church as a baptized communicant, and even parroted the anti-Semitic sentiments she heard discussed around her.

On the day her parents arrived, the little girl was playing with her friends in the yard, while her Polish foster parents were occupied away from the home.

Taibe and Abraham drove up in a car and spoke to an adult who was standing nearby. The topic of conversation, Lola learned from one of her friends, was the baby who had been left with the Polish couple during the winter of 1941.

"It's her!" said one of the playmates, when the Jewish couple requested to be shown the girl.

The two asked their daughter if she would get in the car to tell them how to travel to Novogrudek, forced to kidnap a child that had no memory of them. She would only have to ride with them for a short while, Taibe promised, and she would be given a bag of candy for her help.

One of the neighbors urged Lola to do as she was requested.

The young girl climbed into the car, but as the vehicle began to move she felt uncomfortable. She started crying and hitting her parents, demanding that she be let out.

The young girl was driven to Novogrudek, where the couple had found a place to live. For the next several weeks she struggled to adjust to life without her foster parents. She would drop to her knees to pray whenever she heard the church bells ring and she would beg to be allowed to go to Catholic services.

Desperate, the Dziencielskis worked out an agreement with the foster couple that allowed the Polish woman to stay with Lola on some evenings, an arrangement that greatly eased the girl's anxieties. But the deal was troubling to Taibe, who feared the Poles would run off with her daughter. After the Dziencielskis received the documents that enabled them to leave the country, they took the girl and embarked on their journey without saying good-bye.

Over time, the little girl discovered her true identity as a Jew. She learned her parents' language and discovered her religious background. But for years afterward, she would remember the horrifying sounds of the German bombs and the shiny boots of the fearsome Nazi soldiers who visited her safe home. She would wake up in the middle of the night screaming that the Nazis had arrived to take her away. Like everyone who had survived with the Bielski brothers, she was now free; but neither she nor any of the twelve hundred would ever be liberated from the memories of the three dreadful years from June 1941 to July 1944.

TWELVE

TO ISRAEL AND
AMERICA

FOR THE BIELSKI BROTHERS, the great trials of the war seemed to be over. Each obtained jobs in the fledgling local Soviet government, and the three moved into separate rooms in the same building in Lida with the wives they had married in the forest.

Tuvia was assigned to work in an electric utility, responsible for restoring power to a decimated Lida. Zus was charged with procuring meat and grain for the military, while Asael helped organize a cafeteria for partisans and soldiers remaining in the area. Young Aron, just fourteen years old and without his parents, was enrolled in a local school. It was the saddest time in his life: His brothers had their wives and their jobs. He was a lonely boy without his parents.

Most of those who held leadership positions in the brothers' unit were assigned tasks to help stabilize the region. Layzer Malbin worked as a bookkeeper in Lida, and Pesach Friedberg toiled as an economics officer in Novogrudek. Solomon Wolkowyski returned to Baranovich to resume his legal work. The group's most prominent Russian allies also stayed in the rear zone. Viktor Panchenkov, who disbanded his detachment with 298 mem-

bers, took a prominent party position in Novogrudek. He learned
that the Germans had killed his father and two brothers in his
home region near Smolensk. Vasily Chernyshev, who no longer
required his nom de guerre "General Platon," headed to Baranovich for a similarly exalted party post.

The brothers remained answerable to the government for
the activity of their detachments. Tuvia was criticized for dis-
missing his force before receiving proper permission, making it
difficult (as he had intended) for many of the fighters to be conscripted into the Red Army. He had a simple answer when
queried by the Soviets: "I hadn't asked to assemble them, so I
didn't ask to dissolve them."

Both Tuvia and Zus were ordered to appear in Minsk to fully
debrief the Soviets on all that happened during the war. Accompanied by his chief of staff, Layzer Malbin, Tuvia arrived in the
Belorussian capital in September. On the 15th of the month, he
submitted a handwritten report titled "The History of the Origin of the Kalinin Partisan Detachment, Lida Zone, Baranovich
District," the first detailed history of the life of the group. It outlined the unit's sabotage missions, its executions of Nazi-allied

informers, the establishment of the forest workshops, and the
fighters' efforts to save "Soviet citizens" from the ghettos.

He estimated that sixty children survived in the forest years,
two hundred people staffed the workshops, and twenty percent
of the population was female. In the military sphere, he described
how the Bielski troops destroyed thirty-four train cars, eighteen
bridges, and eight German-run farm-supply buildings. A total
of 261 enemy fighters were killed, he wrote. Others would later
estimate that about fifty members of the Jewish unit were killed
during the time in the woods.

Ordzhonikidze's history detailed its military actions from the fall of 1943 to the summer of 1944. It carried out a total of thirty-three combat missions—both acting alone and with other detachments—that resulted in the deaths of 120 enemy fighters. The Jewish partisans destroyed two locomotives, twenty-three train cars, thirty-two telegraph poles, and four bridges. Zus submitted his personnel file, in which he noted that he personally killed fourteen Nazis, seventeen policemen, and thirty-three pro-Nazi spies and provocateurs.

Both men received awards from the partisan superiors. And both returned to Lida with the growing feeling that it was time to leave the country. They knew there was no future for Jews in the Soviet Union.

During the same period, Asael received a different sort of honor from the Soviet government—a draft notice calling him into the service of the Red Army.

Some said that Sergei Vasilyev, still angry over Asael's avoidance of the death penalty, was responsible; nonetheless, Asael wasn't interested in having the order rescinded. Always the loyal soldier, he told his wife, Haya, that he wouldn't flee. "A Bielski doesn't run from a fight," he said.

The notice reached Asael shortly after his wife had discovered that she was pregnant, and the soon-to-be father was thrilled by the news. Haya swore to him that she would have the baby and wait in Belarus until he returned from the war.

Tuvia, Zus, their wives, and Aron were inching closer to abandoning the Soviet Union for British-controlled Palestine. "We kept thinking of the Land of Israel," said Zus, who had an altercation with Soviet officials after he discovered them searching his room. "Why build something here that wasn't mine? Let's join our brothers." Tuvia received requests to meet with Soviet functionaries for more debriefings and awards, all of which he ignored. He conducted his day-to-day affairs "carefully," as he put it, taking pains not to draw too much attention to himself.

In the winter, a few Soviet officials woke him up late in the evening and demanded to see his documents. After scanning the papers, the men, whom Tuvia had known from the woods, brusquely left the residence. Tuvia felt certain that the visit was a prelude to his arrest. By morning, everyone was ready to run for the border. The radio was still playing when Lilka closed the door to her room for the last time.

The five hopped a freight train heading north to Vilna on a frigid day in December, carrying little more than the clothing on their backs. After arriving in the city, Tuvia spotted a man he knew, a fellow Jew who was now working with the Soviet government. The man arranged a place for the family to stay and set about obtaining documents to allow the Bielskis to travel to Poland. Several days later, the papers were in order and the family took the next train southwest toward Poland.

The documents allowed them to pass through Soviet inspection without a problem. After a stop in Bialystok, they arrived in the Polish city of Lublin, where several Bielski group members were also staying. They made a painful visit to the liberated Maidanek concentration camp and heard tales about White Poles continuing to attack Jews. One Jewish fighter said that Polish partisans were looking for Tuvia.

It didn't require much to convince them to abandon Poland. The family obtained forged documents from an underground Jewish agency that was working to facilitate the immigration of

Holocaust survivors to Palestine. Identified as citizens of Greece, they boarded a train that would take them south, toward Hungary.

When confronted by officials seeking to examine the papers, the Bielskis spoke lines from Hebrew scripture, which they hoped would sound like Greek to the untutored ear of the gentiles. Skeptical, the officials found a Greek man and asked him to translate the words. "I don't understand them," he said. "I am from eastern Greece and they are from western Greece." The family was allowed to continue.

In Hungary, the Bielskis disembarked from the train and discovered a wary local Jewish population. Despite their fluency in Yiddish, the Hungarians wanted proof that they were really Jews. After a week, the family resumed the journey, heading west to Bucharest, Romania. Tuvia and Zus and their wives were admitted to a camp for those seeking passage to Palestine, while Aron, even though he was only fifteen, was sent by himself to a facility for young refugees in Trieste, Italy.

Six months later, legal documents arrived allowing the four adults to enter Palestine. They journeyed by boat across the Mediterranean, arriving in Haifa in October 1945. The ship docked on a Sabbath evening, and the passengers weren't allowed to disembark until the holy day had passed. Aron followed soon afterward, entering the country illegally after a three-week voyage on a tugboat.

Haya remained in Lida, pregnant and alone, feeling as if she didn't have a friend in the world. In the first months after Asael left for the front, the two wrote to each other frequently, sometimes discussing plans for the future. She dreamed of moving to the land of Israel; he said he didn't particularly care where they decided to settle.

Then the letters stopped. Frantic, Haya did everything she could to learn of her husband's plight. She sought out any Soviet official who might be able to give her an answer. Wrapping herself in a fur coat, she traveled to several cities seaching for clues to his whereabouts. No one seemed to know anything. In frustration, she returned to her home. It was there that she discovered the truth.

"I went to an officer to ask what happened to my husband," she said. "He took out a paper that said he was killed on February 7 in Marienburg. I don't even know what happened next. I don't know how I got home."

Asael participated in the Red Army's great siege of Königsberg, the ancient East Prussian city, which began in January. His unit was one of the many that followed the retreating Germans to the area around Marienburg to the southwest, where heavy fighting occupied much of late January and February. The body was buried in a military cemetery along with thousands of other soldiers.

Crushed, Haya packed up her belongings and moved from Lida to Novogrudek, where she still had a few relatives left. By the time she settled in, she was ready to have her baby. Cared for by a nurse who had been in the Bielski group, Haya gave birth on April 7, 1945. The delivery was difficult.

In the first seconds of her life, the infant struggled to breathe, turning blue because of a lack of oxygen. Working furiously, the medical staff coaxed the child to take in air and eventually the danger passed. The twenty-six-year-old widow had given birth to a baby girl. She was named Asaela in honor of her father.

Several months later, Haya and her baby started their journey toward Palestine, a harrowing trip that took them through the heart of a devastated Europe. On a train early in the expedition, she and the baby were forced to hide among the pigs in a freight car. Whenever the police checked for stowaways, Haya would kick the pigs, causing them to squeal, to drown the cries of little Assi.

The war was now over. The Germans, crushed by the Russians from the east and the Americans and British from the west, had surrendered on May 8, 1945—Tuvia Bielski's thirty-ninth birthday. The Japanese, after being soundly defeated in the islands of the Pacific, agreed to an unconditional surrender on August 14, 1945, after atomic bombs were dropped on the cities of Hiroshima and Nagasaki. Before Germany's defeat, however, Hitler effectively wiped out centuries of Jewish life in Eastern Europe. Six million Jews were dead.

Tuvia and Zus and their wives were eager to participate in a Jewish revival. They struggled to establish themselves in a new land. After moving from place to place, they settled in Holon, then a nascent community outside of Tel Aviv, where the couples shared a small house.

The brothers worked with a professional writer to set down their war experiences, the result of which was a slim book written in Hebrew. It gained the notice of Moshe Shartok, a leader in the fight for establishment of a Jewish state, who read it while imprisoned in the summer and fall of 1946 by the British authorities. Following his release, he sought out the Bielskis and promised to help them in any way he could. Tuvia, who had shunned offers to join in the political and military struggles then raging in the country, opened a small grocery store with Shartok's assistance. He just wanted a quiet life.

Zus continued to drive a delivery truck, which he owned, between Jerusalem and Tel Aviv. Both Bielski couples, each now with one child, moved to separate residences in another Tel Aviv suburb, Ramat Gan.

As violence increased between Jewish residents and Palestinian Arabs, Tuvia and Zus participated in the struggle in limited ways. But their involvement increased markedly when neighboring Arab countries invaded the state of Israel soon after its creation in May 1948. Tuvia, Zus, and Aron, now eighteen, volunteered for military service. Each man lived through tense situations that rivaled the difficulties of World War II. Tuvia was even declared missing and presumed dead. After becoming separated from his unit, he reappeared several days later unharmed.

Following the war, Shartok (who had since changed his name to Sharett and been appointed first foreign secretary of the Israeli government) again did what he could to help out the brothers. Having little luck with the grocery store or during a stint as a truck driver, Tuvia asked Sharett to provide him with a hard-to-obtain license to operate a taxicab. Zus also requested a cab license, although he was doing well enough as a truck driver to buy his own home. Both men received DeSotos from their oldest brother, Velvel (now known as Walter), who had immigrated to America before the war, and the cars were converted into taxis.

As in previous ventures, Zus proved a better businessman than his older brother. "How many times my husband picked up people and wouldn't take a penny," said Tuvia's wife, Lilka. "Then he didn't have any money to come home and feed his own family."

As the years passed, Tuvia struggled to make ends meet, and by the early 1950s his health had deteriorated. He was diagnosed with a stomach ulcer—"I was sick in the stomach and sick in the nerves," he said. In 1955, he traveled by himself to the United States to receive the kind of medical assistance that wasn't available in the young state of Israel. The following year, his wife and children followed him to New York, as did Zus with his wife and children. Soon both couples found residences in the Midwood neighborhood of Brooklyn, New York, just a few blocks from each other, and each set about raising families in an environment far from the battlefields of Europe or the Middle East.

The postwar path of most Bielski partisans followed a similar pattern. Few were eager to stay behind in the Soviet Union, instead starting new lives in Israel, the United States, or Western Europe. Many spent years in displaced persons camps in countries like Germany and Italy before being allowed to enter the lands that would become their homes.

Pesach Friedberg and his wife reached New York City, where Pesach, now referred to as Paul, opened Paul's Luncheonette at 147 West 35th Street in Manhattan. Layzer Malbin arrived in Israel and settled in the Negev Desert, where he worked for years as a manager of road construction, unmarried and lonely. The lawyer Solomon Wolkowyski made his home in Brooklyn, where he found a wife and became a financial officer for an organization that provided aid for Israel. Shmuel Amarant, the camp historian, reached Israel after being imprisoned by the Soviet authorities for helping Jewish survivors flee the country. His jailers confiscated sixty-five notebooks containing material he collected during his forest interviews. They have never surfaced.

Haya Bielski remarried after she settled in Israel. Young Assi wasn't aware of her father's identity until she was seven years old, when her mother told her the whole story as they sat on a dock in

Haifa. But the girl couldn't shake her belief that he was still alive. In 1957, when a wave of immigrants arrived from Poland, she met the group with flowers in her hands, thinking that the lost father would surely recognize his daughter.

After establishing themselves in the new world, most survivors concentrated on providing for their families, and several built successful businesses from the barest of starts. Most stayed connected through the power of transatlantic phone calls and the occasional bar mitzvah, wedding, or anniversary celebration. The events were particularly moving to Tuvia, who was overcome by the simple sight of the children of partisans growing into adolescence and adulthood. The tears would flow without much prompting.

In the mid-1960s, a few of the Bielski group traveled to Germany to testify against Leopold Windisch and Rudolf Werner, the two Nazis who had played vital roles in the massacres of May 1942 in the Lida area. The legal maneuvering went on for years before Werner was declared unfit for trial for medical reasons and Windisch, a proud Nazi to the end, was sentenced to life in prison. Werner died in 1971, Windisch in 1985. The two men's commanding officer, Hermann Hanweg, was presumed by German prosecutors to have fallen in battle during the final months of the war.

No similar judicial accounting, however inadequate, occurred in the case of the two detested Nazis of Novogrudek, Regional Commissar Wilhelm Traub and the Judenferent Wilhelm Reuter. Traub died in a prisoner-of-war camp in Yugoslavia in 1946. Reuter's fate is unknown.

Like the Bielski survivors, the Russians from the woods would meet periodically over the years, often during Soviet celebrations of the Great Patriotic War. Photographs show them strolling proudly in veterans parades, balder and paunchier than during their partisan days, with medals pinned to their chests. Yefim Gapayev (Sokolov), a postwar resident of Lida, sometimes marched with Viktor Panchenkov and his men. Vasily Chernyshev (Platon) and Fyodor Sinitchkin, who served as the brothers' first brigade commander, were each given the state's highest military honor, the Hero of the Soviet Union medal. Chernyshev died in 1969. A technical school and a street were named after him in Baranovich. Sinitchkin died in 1962. A street in Slonim bears his name.

Sergei Vasilyev spent his postwar life working as a factory manager. Panchenkov, who supervised construction work in Lida for many years, was diagnosed with cancer in 1976, which marked the beginning of years of health difficulties. He died of cancer in 1996.

He remained a staunch Communist even after the fall of the Soviet Union. In an unpublished memoir, Panchenkov wrote that the war was fought for two reasons: to protect the USSR and to prevent "chauvinism and racism against the Jews." He praised the party for possessing "organizational genius and perseverance" and for having a profound "connection to the people." His wife, Nadezhda, a devout Christian, didn't share his enthusiasm. Following his death she arranged for the lifelong atheist to be interred in a manner befitting a believing Orthodox Christian. Instead of putting a red star on his gravestone, as he wished, she decorated it with a cross.

Konstantin Koslovsky returned to his work after the war and never spoke of his charity toward Jews. His youngest daughter, Taisija Dorozhkina, never once heard him utter a word about it. He died in 1982. Several years later, an effort was made by Jewish survivors from the Novogrudek area to honor him. Yad Vashem, the Holocaust memorial in Jerusalem, granted him the title of Righteous Gentile Among the Nations of the World in 1994.

When independence arrived for Belarus in 1991, some Bielski survivors made the emotional journey back to the old country, often simply to pay their respects at the graves of their relatives. Efforts were organized to install stone markers at the sites of the killings in each of the towns, and trips were arranged to bring extended families to the country for memorial services.

The youngest Bielski brother, Aron, who changed his name to Bell after arriving in the United States, ventured back to Stankevich even before the demise of the Soviet Union. He discovered that the tiny village of his childhood had disappeared, with only the small waterway that powered the family mill remaining. "I will tell you that if I could go and live on that ground near that lake in Stankevich, I would go right now, in the middle of the day or night," he said. "But only if I knew that nobody would touch me. The majority of the people would hate me. There are no Jews there. But that is my home for the rest of my life."

In his later years, Tuvia would speak only of returning to Israel, where he hoped to be buried. He worked as a truck driver, just another anonymous immigrant traversing the highways of the New York metropolitan area. The pain of the war weighed heavily on him, and he never spoke of his forest achievements in a triumphal manner. He was nearly penniless when he passed away in 1987. A year later, his body was exhumed from a Long Island cemetery and reburied in the Har Hamenuchot Cemetery overlooking Jerusalem, during a service that included an Israeli military honor guard.

The last of the three brothers, Zus, who called himself

Alexander in the United States, operated a gas station in Brooklyn before selling the business to start a trucking and taxi company. He died in 1995, not long after giving an interview to representatives of the newly established United States Holocaust Memorial Museum. Slowed down by the ravages of the aging process, the eighty-two-year-old had difficulty following the line of questioning. But when asked what he remembered about the Germans, he responded with characteristic bluntness: "I remember they were bastards."

EPILOGUE

IT'S DIFFICULT TO calculate how many people are alive today because of the actions of the brothers Bielski. Many of the twelve hundred people who walked out of the woods in the summer of 1944 have since died. But their children have borne children, who themselves have borne children. Thousands of people residing in the United States, Israel, Great Britain, France, Germany, Australia, and Russia owe their existence to the brothers' decision, at Tuvia's insistence, to shelter every Jew who arrived at the forest encampment.

The Talmud says, "Whoever saves one life saves the world entire." Yet the brothers' daring deed never gave them in their lifetime the sort of recognition that today we regularly bestow on far lesser men. It quietly pained Tuvia, as he sat behind the wheel of a truck delivering plastic supplies to companies in Queens and Brooklyn, that he was never honored by the world beyond the group of forest survivors and their children. He was ideally suited to lead desperate people through the forests of Belarus, but he lacked a gift for self-promotion, for pithy sound bites or fluid prose. Whenever he spoke before groups of American students—

in the English language that he never mastered as well as Yiddish, Hebrew, Polish, and Russian—he would inevitably break down in tears, overcome by the thought of the sufferings of his people. He often couldn't continue.

A few months before his death, on December 6, 1986, a dinner sponsored by Touro College and several forest survivors was held in his honor in the New York Hilton, and it's easy to see on the videotape how moved he was to be the center of attention. Dressed in a tuxedo, with a rose in the lapel, he walked with a slight stoop as he found his spot on the dais. After his name was announced by the emcee, six hundred people rose to their feet and filled the room with a storm of applause. Raising his right hand, Tuvia Bielski acknowledged the crowd by swiveling his wrist in a manner reminiscent of a proud monarch.

Speaker after speaker ascended the podium over the next few hours to deliver rousing testimonials in praise of the guest of honor, who nervously pushed around the crumbs on his plate, fingered his nameplate, and smoked a succession of cigarettes. His tears were impossible to stanch, and he cried at least once during every speech, barely visible to anyone but his protective wife, Lilka. The old lion was receiving a small measure of what he deserved.

Near the end of the night, after the ballroom guests sang happy-birthday greetings, he took the microphone to say a few words. In the forest, his emotional speeches, given after a raid or before a long march to a new location, often gave his people their only measure of reassurance. But on this occasion, he conveyed little of the charisma that made him one of the great natural leaders of World War II. Instead, he offered simple gratitude in thickly accented English.

"I am very happy this night to hear from everybody, the best of what they understand to say," he said. He mentioned his joy at seeing all the descendants of people who lived through the war with him. "All together I see people I haven't seen in twenty or thirty years or more. Thank God they are alive, they are living and growing. They're growing bigger and bigger. Here is standing a beautiful family—a mother, a daughter, and two sons. This is four people."

He referred to another family that was in attendance, marveling at the size of the group, before ending his brief talk with a nod. As he put down the microphone, several elderly war survivors rushed to hug him. The physical contact gave him a jolt of rejuvenation, and the troubled look that sat so fixedly on his brow was replaced by brightness. The charge of energy that was carried in his smile suggested in an instant the power he once possessed, the natural charisma and generosity of spirit that made him a man beloved and admired by the hundreds fortunate enough to have made his acquaintance. It was the face of a leader.

NOTES

PROLOGUE

Oskar Schindler is credited by most sources with saving between 1,000 and 1,200 Jews. His gravestone at Mount Zion Cemetery in Jerusalem notes that he saved 1,200 Jews. The fighters of the Warsaw ghetto uprising killed 16 enemy soldiers and wounded 85, according to the official German tally cited in *The Destruction of the European Jews: Revised and Definitive Edition* by Raul Hilberg (1985, Holmes and Meier), p. 513. Some Polish sources put the figure higher, with as many as seven hundred enemies dead, according to *The Warsaw Ghetto Revolt* by Reuben Ainsztein (1979, Holocaust Library), pp. 167–171.

The Bielski brothers' Kalinin and Ordzhonikidze units included a total of 1,140 members when they were disbanded in July 1944, according to files in the archive of the Belorussian Staff to the Partisan Movement at the National Archive of the Republic of Belarus in Minsk (Fond 3500; Opus 4; File 241/2; pp. 287–288). The files are also available at the Yad Vashem archives in Jerusalem (M.41/124, pp. 28–29). Bielski fighters from both units killed, according to partisan documentation, a total of 381 enemy fighters, sometimes during joint actions with Soviet bands. The numbers are cited in the partisan histories of Ordzhonikidze (Fond 3618; Opus 1; File 23) and Kalinin (Fond 3500; Opus 4; File 272) in the Minsk archives. The Kalinin history is also available at Yad Vashem (M.41/120).

The most prominent book to highlight the brothers' accomplishments is *Defiance: The Bielski Partisans* by sociologist Nechama Tec (1993, Oxford University Press). Much space is also devoted to the brothers in *Fugitives of the Forest: The Heroic Story of Jewish Resistance and Survival during the Second World War* by Allan Levine (1998, Stoddart) and *The Jewish Resistance: The History of the Jewish Partisans in Lithuania and White Russia during the Nazi Occupation 1940–1945* by Lester Eckman and Chaim Lazar (1977, Shengold).

CHAPTER ONE: FROM THE TSAR TO THE FÜHRER

The author has relied primarily on three sources for the words, thoughts, and actions of Tuvia Bielski. The first source is Tuvia's own unpublished memoir, *Yerushalayim in Vald (Jerusalem in the Forest: Memoirs of the Stormy Days of the Partisan in the Forests of Western White Russia during World War II)*, written in 1955 (YIVO Institute for Jewish Research, #RG 104, Eyewitness Accounts, Series III [Partisaner 2]), and translated from the Yiddish for the author by David Goldman and James Loeffler. The second source is Tuvia's 1970 interview with Yitzhak Alperovitz (Yad Vashem archives, Jerusalem, 03/3607), translated from the Yiddish for the author by Tina Lunson. The third source is Bielski's oral history testimony in *Yehudai Yaar (Jews of the Forest): The Recollections of Tuvia and Zusya Bielski, Sonia and Lilka Bielski and Abraham Weiner as Recorded by Y. Ben-Dor* (1946, Om Oved), translated from the Hebrew for the author by Charles Ronen.

Other sources include the transcript of a 1986 interview of Mr. Bielski by Tuvia's son Michael Bielski, loaned to the author by Michael Bielski, and a video-taped interview conducted by Drs. Lester Eckman and Monty Noam Penkower of Touro College on May 19, 1987, loaned to the author by Dr. Eckman.

The author has used three major sources for the words, thoughts, and actions of Zus Bielski. They are his oral history testimony in *Yehudai Yaar*, his 1980 interview with Yitzhak Alperovitz (Yad Vashem archives, Jerusalem, 03/4165), translated from the Yiddish for the author by Judie Ostroff-Goldstein, and his 1988 interview with Iris Berlitzki (Yad Vashem archives, Jerusalem, 03/4165), translated from the Hebrew for the author by Charles Ronen. Other sources include a video-taped interview conducted by Drs. Lester Eckman and Monty Noam Penkower of Touro College on June 25, 1987, loaned to the author by Dr. Eckman.

The material on the early history of the Bielski family comes from interviews with Estelle (Bielski) Hershthal (Pompano Beach, Florida, January 9, 2000), Aron (Bielski) Bell (several interviews in New York City and Palm Beach, Florida), Haya (Bielski) Dziencielski (May 5 and May 12, 2001, in Haifa, Israel, and several exchanges of correspondence, translated by her daughter, Assi Weinstein), and Lilka Bielski (several interviews in Brooklyn, New York, and Hallandale, Florida). Interviews with Belorussians Maria Nestor (June 26, 2001, Kaminke, Belarus) and Yulia Tishuk (July 10, 2001, in Big Izvah, Belarus) were also helpful.

The material on the history of the Novogrudek area of current-day Belarus comes from several sources, including *Belarus: At a Crossroads in History* by Jan Zaprudnik (1993, Westview Press), *A History of Twentieth Century Russia* by Robert Service (1997, Harvard University Press), *Belorussia: The Making of a Nation* by Nicholas P. Vakar (1956, Harvard University Press), and *Byelorussian Statehood: Reader and Bibliography* edited by Vitaut Kipel and Zora Kipel (1988, Byelorussian Institute of Arts and Sciences). Also helpful were talks with Tamara Vershitskaya, director of the Museum of Regional Studies, Novogrudek, Belarus.

Material on the Musar Movement and Rabbi Joseph Yozel Horowitz comes primarily from the essay "The Musar Movement in Interwar Poland" by David E. Fishman, collected in *The Jews of Poland Between the Two World Wars* edited by Yisrael Gutman, Ezra Mendelsohn, Yehuda Reinharz, and Chone Smeruk (1989, University Press of New England), pp. 248–251. A description of Jewish political and educational institutions in interwar Poland is provided by *God's Playground: A History of Poland Volume II: 1795 to Present* by Norman Davies (1984, Columbia University Press), pp. 407–409. The hardships of Jews in interwar Poland are described in *A People Apart: A Political History of the Jews in Europe, 1789–1939* by David Vital (1999, Oxford University Press), pp. 769–774.

The material on the Jewish history of Novogrudek and surrounding towns comes from several articles contained within *Pinkas Navaredok* (Memorial Book of Novogrudek) edited by E. Yerushalmi (1963, Alexander Harkavy Navareder Relief Committee in the USA and Israel), including "Old Navaredok" by Shimon Yosefon, "The History of the Jews of Navaredok" by Yaakov Goldberg, and "The History of Navaredok" by an anonymous author. The articles were translated from the Yiddish and Hebrew for the author by David Goldman. The author also learned about interwar Novogrudek during interviews with natives of the city, including Sonya Oshman (several interviews in Hillside, New Jersey), Jack Kagan (several interviews in New York City and London, England, and an extensive e-mail correspondence), Raya (Kaplinski) Kalmonovitz (May 3 and 7, 2001, in Kfar Saba, Israel), and Morris Schuster (telephone interview, August 16, 2001). Also helpful was the book Mr. Kagan coauthored with his cousin Dov Cohen, *Surviving the Holocaust with Russian Jewish Partisans* (1998, Vallentine Mitchell and Co.).

Information on the Soviet occupation of 1939–1941 was learned during interviews with several witnesses, including Charles Bedzow (January 11, 2001, in Miami Beach, Florida) and Bella Goldfischer (October 14, 2001, in Queens, New York). Helpful texts included *Revolution from Abroad: The Soviet Conquest of Poland's Western Ukraine and Western Belorussia* by Jan T. Gross (1988, Princeton University Press), pp. 17–70, and *Collaboration in the Holocaust: Crimes of the Local Police in Belorussia and Ukraine, 1941–44* by Martin Dean (2000, St. Martin's Press), pp. 1–16. The quote from author Alan Clark regarding the German invasion appears in *Barbarossa: The Russian-German Conflict, 1941–45* (1965, Quill), pp. 44–46.

CHAPTER TWO: JUNE 1941–DECEMBER 1941

Asael Bielski's actions following the invasion are described by Tuvia and Zus in *Yehudai Yaar (Jews of the Forest): The Recollections of Tuvia and Zusya Bielski, Sonia and Lilka Bielski and Abraham Weiner as Recorded by Y. Ben-Dor* (1946, Om Oved), translated from the Hebrew for the author by Charles Ronen, and discussed with the author by Asael's widow Haya (Bielski) Dziencielski and brother Aron (Bell) Bielski.

Joseph Stalin's radio address of July 3, 1941, is reprinted in part in *The Soviet Partisan Movement, 1941–1944* by Leonid Grenkevich (1999, Frank Cass and Co.), p. 75.

Material on the early days of the Nazi occupation in Novogrudek comes from several sources, including interviews with survivors Jack Kagan, Raya (Kaplinski) Kalmanovitz, and Sonia Bielski (several interviews in New York City and Hallandale, Florida). Also helpful were transcripts of interviews with survivors Pesach Friedberg (Yad Vashem archives, Jerusalem, 03/3780) and Eliahu Berkowitz (Yad Vashem archives, Jerusalem, 03/2774), both conducted by Yitzhak Alperovitz. They were translated from the Yiddish for the author by Judie Ostroff-Goldstein. Also helpful was an interview with survivor Rae Kushner conducted by the Kean College of New Jersey Holocaust Resource Center and available in the United States Holocaust Memorial Museum archives in Washington, D.C. (RG-50.002*0015). Published sources include *Partizanim (Partisans: The Story of a Jewish Partisan Brigade in the Forests of White Russia)* by Yehoshua Yaffe (1952, N. Tabarsky Books Inc.), ch. 1. It was translated from the Hebrew for the author by Charles Ronen.

The description of the killing of 52 Jews in Novogrudek's central marketplace comes from several sources, including *Surviving the Holocaust with Russian Jewish Partisans* by Jack Kagan and Dov Cohen (1998, Vallentine Mitchell and Co.), p. 140; Rae Kushner's USHMM testimony; and Zus Bielski's comments in *Yehudai Yaar. No Greater Love*, a book written by Rev. Aleksander Zienkiewicz), a Polish Catholic priest who spent the war years in Novogrudek, also describes the massacre (1968, Franciscan Publishers), p. 18.

The details about the July killings in Mir and Slonim were found in *Collaboration in the Holocaust* by Martin Dean (2000, St. Martin's Press), pp. 28–29. The details about the November killings in Mir and Slonim were also found in *Collaboration in the Holocaust*, pp. 46–50 (Mir) and pp. 50–51 (Slonim).

The details on the July 5, 1941, killing in Lida come from a war crimes indictment filed in West Germany against Kurt Schulz-Isenbeck on June 30, 1970, by the director of the Central Office in North Rhine-Westphalia for the Investigation of National Socialist Mass Crimes (document 45 Js 15/62, held at Zentrale Stelle der Landesjustizverwaltungen, Ludwigsburg, Germany), translated from the German by Irene Newhouse. The translation is available at Ms. Newhouse's Web site at *www.shtetlinks.jewishgen.org/Lida-District/si-toc.htm*.

Information on the Novogrudek Regional Commissar Wilhelm Traub comes from several sources, including interviews with survivors Murray Kasten (February 6 and October 9, 2001, in Hollywood, Florida), Sonya Oshman (several interviews in Hillside, New Jersey), and Boris Ragula, a Belorussian translator for Traub (June 23, 2002, in London, Ontario, Canada). Information was also gleaned from Mr. Ragula's unpublished memoir, *Reflections from My Past*, a copy of which he provided to the author. The personal details about Traub come from documents he filled out for the "Race and Settlement Head Office of the SS" in June 1940, which are on file under his name at the Berlin Document Center, Berlin, Germany.

The quote regarding the guidelines for RC officials was taken from the war crimes indictment against Leopold Windisch and Rudolf Werner handed down at Landericht Mainz, West Germany, on December 15, 1966 (Yad Vashem archives, Jerusalem, TR-10/646), translated from the German by Irene Newhouse. The translation is available at Ms. Newhouse's Web site at *www.shtetlinks.jewishgen.org/Lida-District/winwer-tit.htm*.

The December 8, 1941, killing in Novogrudek was described to the author by survivors Raya (Kaplinski) Kalmanovitz, Jack Kagan, Sonya Oshman, Sulia Rubin (December 6, 2000, in Fort Lee, New Jersey), and others. The figure of 4,500 dead comes from a document written on March 20, 1942, by three prominent members of the Jewish community and given to a non-Jew for safekeeping. It is kept in the Museum of Regional Studies in Novogrudek, Belarus. Also used was the January 11, 1966, verdict in the war crimes trial against Johann Artmann, a Wehrmacht first lieutenant (document 202 AR-Z 94C/59, Zentrale Stelle der Landesjustizverwaltungen Ludwigsburg, Germany). Portions of it are reprinted in *Surviving the Holocaust with Russian Jewish Partisans* by Jack Kagan and Dov Cohen (1998, Vallentine Mitchell and Co.) pp. 142–147. The response of the gentile population to massacre and the creation of the ghetto were detailed in Sulia Rubin's book *Against the Tide: The Story of an Unknown Partisan* (1980, Posner and Sons Ltd.), p. 74.

CHAPTER THREE: DECEMBER 1941–JUNE 1942

Information on the state of the Russian-German war in winter of 1941 comes from *Russia's War* by Richard Overy (1997, Penguin), pp. 114–118, and the *Penguin History of the Second World War* by Peter Calvocoressi, Guy Wint, and John Pritchard (1972, Penguin), pp. 479–512. The gassing at Chelmno is described in *The Holocaust: A History of the Jews of Europe during the Second World War* by Martin Gilbert (1985, Henry Holt and Co.), pp. 239–240 The boasting of Karl Jager and Himmler's attendance at the Minsk killing are described in *Masters of Death: The SS-Einsatzgruppen and the Invention of the Holocaust* by Richard Rhodes (2002, Knopf), pp. 152 and 215. French MacLean's quote appears in his book *The Field Men: The SS Officers Who Led the Einsatzkommandos—the Nazi Mobile Killing Units* (1999, Schiffer Publishing Co.), pp. 19–20.

The information on the Jewish history of Lida comes primarily from articles appearing in *Sefer Lida (Book of Lida)* edited by Alexander Manor, Yitzhak Ganuscovitz, and Aba Lando (1970, Former Residents of Lida in Israel and the Committee of Lida Jews in USA), including "Jewish Business Life Before World War II" by Abraham Gelman, "Memories" by Yakov Ilitowitz, and "The Lida Rabbi

Aron Rabinowitz" by Henia Rabinowitz. Details about the Nazi civil administration of Lida (led by Nazi officials Hermann Hanweg, Leopold Windisch, and
Rudolf Werner) and the events of May 8–12, 1942, were taken from the war
crimes indictment leveled against Leopold Windisch and Rudolf Werner. It was
handed down at Landericht Mainz, West Germany, on December 15, 1966 (Yad
Vashem archives, Jerusalem, TR-10/646), translated from the German by Irene
Newhouse and available at her Web site at *www.shtetlinks.jewishgen.org/lida-
district/winwer-tit.htm.*

The partisan referred to as Gromov was identified as Vladimir Ugriumov
by Tamara Vershitskaya of the Museum of Regional Studies in Novogrudek,
Belarus. Gromov's reputation is discussed in *Partizanim (Partisans: The Story of a Jewish Partisan Brigade in the Forests of White Russia)* by Yehoshua Yaffe (1952, N. Tabarsky
Books Inc.), ch. 1. According to Ms. Vershitskaya, Ugriumov was killed in June
1942 along with many of his men, which led to the dissolution of his detachment.

The Nazi occupation of Lida and the killings of the spring were described to
the author by survivors Lilka Bielski, Charles Bedzow, Bella Goldfischer, Mike
Stoll (January 12, 2001, in Fort Lauderdale, Florida), Ann Monka (January 10,
2001, in Fort Lauderdale, Florida), Fay Druck (January 27, 2001, in Toronto,
Ontario, Canada), and several others. Another important source was the writings
of Shmuel Amarant collected in *Sefer Lida*, including the article "Dafilda—Before
the Slaughter," which described the events leading up to May 8. The articles were
translated from the Hebrew for the author by David Goldman.

The poster outlining Nazi efforts to track down rural Jews is reprinted in,
Surviving the Holocaust with Russian Jewish Partisans by Jack Kagan and Dov Cohen
(1998, Vallentine Mitchell and Co.), pp. 156–158. The early days of the forest life
were described to the author by survivors Haya (Bielski) Dziencielski, Aron
(Bielski) Bell, Lilka Bielski, and Pinchas Boldo (May 3, 2001, in Haifa, Israel).

CHAPTER FOUR: JUNE 1942–OCTOBER 1942

The personal information on Konstantin Koslovsky and his family comes
from the author's interviews with Konstantin's daughter, Taisija Dorozhkina
(July 5, 2001, in Grodno, Belarus), his granddaughter Svetlana Koslovsky (July 5,
2001, in Grodno, Belarus), and his niece Irina Koslovsky (July 2 and July 7, 2001,
in Makrets, Belarus). Svetlana Koslovsky provided the author with a memoir of
Konstantin's war activities, written with the assistance of her father, Vladimir
Koslovsky, Konstantin's son. Information about the relationship between the
Koslovsky family and the Bielski family was detailed in both of Zus Bielski's Yad
Vashem testimonies, all of Tuvia's writing and testimonies, and the author's
interviews with Aron (Bielski) Bell.

The Bielski brothers' first meeting with Konstantin Koslovsky, and the contents of the letter that Tuvia wrote to Yehuda Bielski, are described in Tuvia Bielski's *Yerushalayim in Vald* (*Jerusalem in the Forest: Memoirs of the Stormy Days of the Partisan in the Forests of Western White Russia during World War II*), written in 1955 (YIVO Institute for Jewish Research, #RG 104, Eyewitness Accounts, Series III [Partisaner 2]), p. 96. The author has edited the letter slightly for clarity.

Among those who provided the author with information about the second Novogrudek killings were survivors Lea (Berkovsky) Friedberg (several interviews in Flushing, New York), Jack Kagan, Sonya Oshman, and Raya (Kaplinski) Kalmanovitz.

Information about the ghetto breakout of Yehuda Bielski and Pesach Friedberg was gathered from Yehuda Bielski's oral history testimony in *Partizanim (Partisans: The Story of a Jewish Partisan Brigade in the Forests of White Russia)* by Yehoshua Yaffe (1952, N. Tabarsky Books Inc.), ch. 1, and from Pesach Friedberg's Yad Vashem interview (Yad Vashem archives, Jerusalem, 03/2774).

Details about the feelings of Zus and Asael Bielski regarding the expansion of the Jewish group were learned during interviews with eyewitnesses Aron (Bielski) Bell and Pinchas Boldo. Said Mr. Bell, "Asael and Zus would never have had the old people and women. They would have their wives and girlfriends, but no way in hell would they take all those people." In his 1970 Yad Vashem interview, Tuvia mentions his brothers' opposition to increasing the size of the group (Yad Vashem archives, Jerusalem, 03/3607). "They could not imagine it either," he said. "How could we live in the forest with a big group of people?" The details about the organizational meeting come from Pesach Friedberg's Yad Vashem interview, Yehuda Bielski's testimony in chapter one of *Partizanim,* and, principally, from Tuvia Bielski's *Yerushalayim in Vald,* ch. 25.

The information about the ghetto escapes was provided to the author during interviews with survivors Lea (Berkovsky) Friedberg, Sonia (Boldo) Bielski, Michael Lebowitz (several interviews in Sunrise, Florida), and Ike Bernstein (several telephone interviews from his home in Winnipeg, Alberta, Canada). Raya (Kaplinski) Kalmonovitz's escape is detailed in her 1970 interview with Yitzhak Alperovitz (Yad Vashem archives, Jerusalem, 03/4055), translated for the author by Judie Ostroff-Goldstein.

The rumors about escapees needing to pay money to enter the Bielski camp are described in *Defiance: The Bielski Partisans* by Nechama Tec (1993, Oxford University Press), pp. 181–182. Ms. Tec suggests that some Bielski fighters who entered the ghetto may have sought money from escapees against Tuvia's wishes. She also notes that the vast majority of arrivals at the Bielski camp were penniless.

The personal information about Viktor Panchenkov (who is often called Panchenko by Bielski survivors) comes from the author's interviews with Mr. Panchenkov's widow, Nadezhda Panchenkov (July 6, 2001, in Lida, Belarus), and his sister Tatiana Panchenkov (June 30, 2001, in Novogrudek, Belarus). Mr. Panchenkov's widow provided the author with several pieces of her husband's writings, including his article "October Detachment," included in the book *V prinemanskikh lesakh (In the Forests Along the Neman River): Memoirs of Partisans and the Underground* (1975, Belarus Publishing), and his untitled and undated memoir of his years as a partisan.

The document in which the partisan leadership speaks of the double standard involving Jewish partisans can be found in the Yad Vashem archives in Jerusalem (file M. 41/250).

The joint actions undertaken by the Bielski and Panchenkov units were detailed in all of Tuvia's writings and in Mr. Panchenkov's article in *V prinemanskikh lesakh*. Information was also gleaned during interviews with survivors Michael Lebowitz and Pinchas Boldo.

Alter Tiktin's attempt to celebrate Rosh Hashanah was described in the article "Rosh Hashanah in the Woods" by Israel Yankelevich, included in *Lubtsch ve-Delatitsh; Sefer Zikaron (Lubtsch and Delatich; In Memory of the Jewish Community)*, edited by K. Hilel (1971, Former Residents of Lubtsch-Delatitsh in Israel), translated for the author by David Goldman.

Tuvia's quote that ends the chapter comes from his memoir *Yerushalayim in Vald*, ch. 31.

CHAPTER FIVE: OCTOBER 1942–FEBRUARY 1943

The quote from Martin Gilbert comes from *The Holocaust: A History of the Jews of Europe During the Second World War* (1985, Henry Holt and Co.), p. 389. Mr. Gilbert also describes the death count at the Belzec death camp on page 417. Details on the battle for Stalingrad come primarily from Richard Overy's *Russia's War* (1997, Penguin), ch. 6. Information on the Pacific War was gleaned from the *Penguin History of the Second World War* by Peter Calvocoressi, Guy Wint, and John Pritchard (1972, Penguin), pp. 1030–1072.

Personal information on Layzer Malbin comes from his interview with Yitzhak Alperovitz (Vad Yashem archives, Jerusalem, 03/3549), translated for the author by Judie Ostroff-Goldstein, and his oral history testimony printed in the *Publication of the Museum of the Combatants and Partisans* (v. 9, December 1989).

The status of women in the Bielski camp is discussed in great detail in *Defiance: The Bielski Partisans*, by Nechama Tec (1993, Oxford University Press), particularly in ch. 12.

Details about constructing an earthen dugout—called a *ziemlanka* in Russian—were provided to the author by survivor Meyer Bronicki (January 15, 2001, in Marco Island, Florida, and several phone interviews from his home in Indianapolis, Indiana). He was one of the workers who helped build the structures.

Information about the German attack on the Lipichanska Puscha was found in *Jewish Resistance in Nazi-Occupied Eastern Europe* by Reuben Ainsztein (1974, Paul Elek), pp. 321–325. Additional information about partisans from the Dzatlovo (also called Zhetel) ghetto was supplied by Jack Kagan. He provided the author with a translation of the article "The Partisans of Zhetel" by Avram Alpert, Lipa Glickman, Avrom Magid, and Yichiel Yoselevitz from the *Book of Zhetel* (1957, Zhetel Association of Israel).

The details about the Hanukkah celebration and the singing around the campfire come from *Partizanim (Partisans: The Story of a Jewish Partisan Brigade in the Forests of White Russia)* by Yehoshua Yaffe (1952, N. Tabarsky Books Inc.), ch. 3.

The details about the confrontation with the Lubchansky brothers are described in detail by Tuvia Bielski in both *Yehudai Yaar (Jews of the Forest): The Recollections of Tuvia and Zusya Bielski, Sonia and Lilka Bielski and Abraham Weiner as Recorded by Y. Ben-Dor* (1946, Om Oved), ch. 10, translated from the Hebrew for the author by Charles Ronen, and *Yerushalayim in Vald (Jerusalem in the Forest: Memoirs of the Stormy Days of the Partisan in the Forests of Western White Russia during World War II)*, written in 1955 (YIVO Institute for Jewish Research, #RG 104, Eyewitness Accounts, Series III [Partisaner 2]), chs. 38, 39. Zus Bielski also discussed it in his Yad Vashem interviews. Sonia (Boldo) Bielski also provided memories of the incident.

Information about the January 5, 1943, attack was gathered during interviews with Sonia (Boldo) Bielski, Haya (Bielski) Dziencielski, Ike Bernstein (whose brother was killed during the incident), and a Belorussian resident of the hamlet, Ivan Koreniuk (July 2, 2001, in Chrapinyevo, Belarus).

Details about the discovery of the Kessler group and the killing of the Belorussian informers were learned during interviews with witnesses Michael Lebowitz, Isak (Nowogrudsky) Nowog (August 26, 2001, in Los Angeles, California), and Israel Kessler's widow, Rachel (Reiff) Zyskind (phone interview on July 26, 2001, from her home in Israel; Daphne Algom served as translator). Mr. Nowog also writes in detail about the incident in his unpublished memoir, *Experiences of a Jewish Partisan: My Journal 1941–1945,* a copy of which he provided to the author. Pesach Friedberg and Zus Bielski spoke in detail about the experience in their Yad Vashem interviews. Tuvia Bielski describes the experiences in each of his writings and interviews.

The personal information about Fyodor Sinitchkin comes from *Navyechno v syerdtse narodnom (Forever in the Heart of the People)* (1984, Belorussian Soviet Encyclopedia), p. 474. This book lists biographical information on those honored by the Hero of the Soviet Union award.

Stalin's quote about including all "honorable male and female citizens" in the fight against the Germans comes from the article "The Soviet Partisan Movement and the Holocaust" by Kenneth Slepyan in the journal *Holocaust and Genocide Studies,* v. 14, no. 1, Spring 2000, p. 11.

CHAPTER SIX: FEBRUARY 1943–APRIL 1943

The German leaflet offering a reward for the capture of Tuvia Bielski is mentioned in Eliahu Damesek's article "The German Occupation" in *Sefer Lida (Book of Lida)* edited by Alexander Manor, Yitzhak Ganuscovitz, and Aba Lando (1970, Former Residents of Lida in Israel and the Committee of Lida Jews in USA), p. viii. Details about ghetto leaders Altman and Alperstein are discussed in Shmuel Amarant's "Our Life in the Ghetto" from *Sefer Lida*, p. 288, translated for the author by David Goldman. The escape attempts are discussed in *The Jews of Belorussia during World War II* by Shalom Cholawsky (1998, Harwood Academic Pub.), pp. 120–121, 129–130.

Details about the Bobrovsky family come from interviews with survivors Jack Kagan and Sulia Rubin and a stepdaughter of one of the Bobrovsky children, Anya Voronovich (July 4, 2001, in Novogrudek, Belarus). Information about the death of Ivan Koslovsky comes from interviews with Irina Koslovsky, his niece.

Himmler's quote about needing more trains for the deportation of Jews appeared in *The Holocaust: A History of the Jews of Europe during the Second World War* by Martin Gilbert (1985, Henry Holt and Co.), p. 526. The detail about 80 percent of the Holocaust victims having been killed by the early months of 1943 is mentioned in *Ordinary Men: Reserve Police Battalion 101 and the Final Solution in Poland* by Christopher Browning (1992, HarperCollins), p. xv.

The executions of Vatya Kushel and Aloysha Stishok are discussed in detail in Tuvia Bielski's *Yerushalayim in Vald (Jerusalem in the Forest: Memoirs of the Stormy Days of the Partisan in the Forests of Western White Russia during World War II)*, written in 1955 (YIVO Institute for Jewish Research, #RG 104, Eyewitness Accounts, Series III [Partisaner 2]), ch. 33. They were also described for the author by witnesses Aron (Bielski) Bell and Haya (Bielski) Dziencielski.

Several survivors of the Bielski group described the February 15, 1943, attack, including Sulia Rubin, Ike Bernstein, and Raya (Kaplinski) Kalmonovitz. It is also described in detail in *Partizanim (Partisans: The Story of a Jewish Partisan Brigade in the Forests of White Russia)* by Yehoshua Yaffe (1952, N. Tabarsky Books Inc.), ch. 3, and in all of Tuvia Bielski's writings and testimonies. The injuries to Shmuel Oppenheim were described to the author by Miriam Stepel, Oppenheim's daughter (phone interview on May 20, 2001). The animal that bled onto the snow is described by survivors variously as a pig, a cow, an ox, and a chicken.

Stalin's feelings about partisans are described in several sources, including Richard Overy's *Russia's War* (1997, Penguin), pp. 142–150. The conflict with the Komsomol members is detailed in Tuvia Bielski's testimony in *Yehudai Yaar (Jews of the Forest): The Recollections of Tuvia and Zusya Bielski, Sonia and Lilka Bielski and Abraham Weiner as Recorded by Y. Ben-Dor* (1946, Om Oved), ch. 10, translated from the Hebrew for the author by Charles Ronen, and in his Yad Vashem interview (Yad Vashem archives, Jerusalem, 03/3607).

The personal history of Solomon Wolkowyski was gathered during an interview with Mr. Wolkowyski's sister, Genia Pinski (June 30, 2002, in the Bronx,
New York).

The details about the massacre at Dobreya Pole committed by the Belous
brothers were gathered during several interviews with former gentile residents of
the hamlet. The author spoke with Anna and Vladimir Oleshkevich, Yevgeny
and Ivan Shulak, and Vladimir Karavajski, all of whom lived in Dobreya Pole at
the time of the incident and now live in surrounding villages.

The establishment of the camp in the Stara-Huta Forest is described in several places, including *Partizanim* by Yaffe, ch. 5. Eliahu Damesek's escape from the
ghetto into the forest is described in his article "The German Occupation" in
Sefer Lída, p. viii. The revenge attack on Dobreya Pole was described for the author
by the gentile residents of the hamlet; also by Michael Lebowitz and Isak Nowog.
It is also discussed in every interview and memoir of Tuvia and Zus Bielski.

CHAPTER SEVEN: MAY 1943–JULY 1943

Details about the Lida ghetto were learned during interviews with survivors
Willy Moll (December 3, 2000, in Toronto, Ontario, Canada), Charles Bedzow,
Fay Druck, and others. Information was also obtained from the unpublished
memoir *From the Lida Ghetto to the Bielski Partisans* by Liza Ettinger, held in the United
States Holocaust Memorial Museum archives (RG-02.133, 1984). Hermann
Hanweg's quote comes from *The Jews of Belorussia during World War II* by Shalom
Cholawsky (1998, Narwood Academic Pub.), p. 129.

Details of the May 7, 1943, killing in Novogrudek come from several sources,
including interviews with survivors Jack Kagan and Sonya Oshman. Information
was also learned from the anonymous testimony—given in 1945 at a displaced
persons' camp in Germany—of a Novogrudek ghetto survivor and included in
Jewish Responses to Nazi Persecution by Isaiah Trunk (1979, Stein and Day), pp.
252–253. Also helpful were witness statements entered into evidence in 1964 in
the war crimes trial against Wehrmacht lieutenant Johann Artmann (document
202 AR-Z 94C/59, Zentrale Stelle der Landesjustizverwaltungen Ludwigsburg,
Germany), translated for the author by Rita Falbel.

The manner of discipline administered by Viktor Panchenkov was described
to the author by three partisans who served in his detachment—Nikolai
Kostriminov (June 30, 2001, in Novogrudek, Belarus), Valentina Nerovnaya
(June 26, 2001, in Novogrudek, Belarus), and Sergei Zhigalo (July 2, 2001, in
Butskevich, Belarus). Tuvia's disciplinary style was discussed by several interviewees,
including survivor Peretz Shorshaty (May 15, 2001, in Eliat, Israel).

Partisan punishment is described in *Soviet Partisans in World War II* edited by
John A. Armstrong (1964, University of Wisconsin), pp. 191–194.

The speech Tuvia gave before the move from Stara-Huta was described to the author by survivor Leah Kotler (November 14, 2000, in Brooklyn, New York). Stara-Huta is sometimes referred to by Bielski survivors as Huta-Sklana, the Polish name for the forest.

The Yasinovo attack was described to the author by several witnesses, including Michael Lebowitz and his wife, Naomi Lebowitz. The most complete account is included in *Yehudai Yaar (Jews of the Forest): The Recollections of Tuvia and Zusya Bielski, Sonia and Lilka Bielski and Abraham Weiner as Recorded by Y. Ben-Dor* (1946, Om Oved), ch. 12, translated from Hebrew for the author by Charles Ronen. Yasinovo is sometimes referred to as Zuravelnik by Bielski survivors. The two forests are close to each other.

Personal information about General Platon comes from the book *Navyechno v syerdtse narodnom (Forever in the Heart of the People)* (1984, Belorussian Soviet Encyclopedia), p. 568. This book lists biographical information on those honored by the Hero of the Soviet Union award. The size and scope of his command is detailed in Viktor Panchenkov's unpublished memoir of the war, p. 19, provided to the author by Mr. Panchenkov's widow, Nadezhda. It is also discussed in an article written by Yefim Gapayev (Sokolov) and included in the book *V prineman-skikh lesakh (In the Forests Along the Neman River): Memoirs of Partisans and the Underground* (1975, Belarus Publishing), pp. 63–73.

The author spoke with Russians who worked with General Platon, including a close friend, Gregori Shevela (June 21, 2001, in Minsk, Belarus). It was Shevela who detailed Platon's banishment to the eastern lands of the Soviet Union in 1937.

CHAPTER EIGHT: JULY 1943–SEPTEMBER 1943

Information about Oskar Dirlewanger comes from *The Cruel Hunters: SS-Sonderkommando Dirlewanger, Hitler's Most Notorious Anti-Partisan Unit* by French L. MacLean (1998, Schiffer Military History). The German orders for Operation Hermann are available at the Bundesarchiv, Berlin, Germany (document group R70 SU/14). Selected documents from the collection were translated for the author by Irene Newhouse.

The attack on the unit in the Naliboki Puscha and the subsequent flight to Krasnaya Gorka were described to the author by several survivors, including Murray Kasten, Lilka Bielski, Sonia Bielski, Meyer Bronicki, Isak Nowog, Leah Johnson (January 10, 2001, in Hallandale, Florida), and Frieda Feit (November 28, 2000, in Brooklyn, New York). Additional information was gathered from *Yehudai Yaar (Jews of the Forest): The Recollections of Tuvia and Zusya Bielski, Sonia and Lilka Bielski and Abraham Weiner as Recorded by Y. Ben-Dor* (1946, Om Oved), ch. 13, translated from the Hebrew for the author by Charles Ronen, and Tuvia Bielski's Yad Vashem interview.

The movements of Kessler's unit were detailed by Isak Nowog, a member of the unit, during interviews with the author and in his unpublished memoir. Also helpful was the author's interview with survivor Rachel Rieff, Israel Kessler's widow, and survivor Abraham Weiner's testimony in *Yehudai Yaar,* ch. 16.

Following the split of the Bielski group into Zus Bielski's Ordzhonikidze Detachment and Tuvia Bielski's Kalinin Detachment, both units were required to send reports to the partisan leaderships detailing all of their activities. The author has relied on these records to determine the size of the groups, their fighting activities, and their movements. The files are available at the archive of the Belorussian Staff of the Partisan Movement at the National Archive of the Republic of Belarus. Some of the documents have been also obtained by the Yad Vashem archive in Jerusalem, Israel.

The field reports, logs, and reconnaissance diaries of Zus Bielski's Ordzhonikidze Detachment are available in the Minsk archives (Fond 3618; Opus 1; Files 23, 28, 30, 90, and 91). Zus Bielski's personnel file is available in Minsk (Fond 3500; Opus 1; File 20).

The records of Tuvia Bielski's Kalinin Detachment are also located in the Minsk archive. Included are the comprehensive history of the detachment, submitted by Tuvia Bielski to the partisan leadership on September 15, 1944 (Fond 3500; Opus 4; Files 272), a detailed roster of all the members of the detachment (Fond 3617; Opus 1; File 20), operational reports (Fond 3623; Opus 6; File 6) and personnel files (Fond 3500; Opus 7; Files 300). Each of the preceding documents is also available at Yad Vashem—files M.41/120; M.41/200; M.41/156; and M.41/225, respectively. Additional Bielski files about military activities are available at the Minsk archives (Fond 3500; Opus 4; File 60; and Fond 3500; Opus 4; File 251).

Translations were provided for the author by David Goldman and Tamara and Olga Vershitskaya.

The death of Kaplan is detailed in *Yehudai Yaar,* ch. 14, and in *Partizanim (Partisans: The Story of a Jewish Partisan Brigade in the Forests of White Russia)* by Yehoshua Yaffe (1952, N. Tabarsky Books Inc.), ch. 6. It was also described for the author by Sonia (Boldo) Bielski.

CHAPTER NINE: SEPTEMBER 1943

The author has relied on the account of the Warsaw ghetto uprising told in *The Destruction of the European Jews: Revised and Definitive Edition* by Raul Hilberg (1985, Holmes and Meier), pp. 500–515.

The story of Layzer Stolicki aiding Lida escapees is told in *Judenrat: The Jewish Councils in Eastern Europe Under Nazi Occupation* by Isaiah Trunk (1972, University of Nebraska Press), p. 523.

The document in which a Nazi official states that "more than two thousand" Jews remained in the Lida ghetto is available in the Bundesarchiv, Berlin, Germany (document R70 SU/14, pp. 76–78).

The escapes from the Lida ghetto were detailed during interviews with escapees Willy Moll, Mike Stoll, and Bella Goldfischer. Escapee Liza Ettinger's testimony comes from her unpublished memoir, *From the Lida Ghetto to the Bielski Partisans*, held in the United States Holocaust Memorial Museum archives (RG-02.133, 1984).

The tunnel escape from Novogrudek was described to the author by escapees Jack Kagan, Sonya Oshman, and Aaron Oshman. Kagan also writes extensively about the experience in *Surviving the Holocaust with Russian Jewish Partisans* (1998, Vallentine Mitchell and Co.), pp 172–183. Escapee Rae Kushner speaks of it in her interview, conducted by the Kean College of New Jersey Holocaust Resource Center and available in the United States Holocaust Memorial Museum archives in Washington, D.C. (RG-50.002*0015). Much valuable information was gained from survivor Eliahu Berkowitz's interview with Yitzhak Alperovitz (Yad Vashem archives, Jerusalem, 03/2774). Information was also learned from the anonymous testimony—given in 1945 at a displaced persons' camp in Germany—of a Novogrudek ghetto survivor and printed in *Jewish Responses to Nazi Persecution* by Isaiah Trunk (1979, Stern and Day), pp. 252–253.

The feelings of Wilhelm Traub regarding the possibility of a ghetto breakout are detailed in a German document in the Bundesarchiv, Berlin, Germany (document R70 SU/14, pp. 76–78).

The actions against the Polish nuns and the Polish population are described in *No Greater Love*, by Rev. Aleksander Zienkiewicz, a Polish Catholic priest who spent the war years in Novogrudek (1968, Franciscan Publishers), pp. 23–36. The eleven nuns, said Father Zienkiewicz, prayed to be taken into Nazi custody in place of Polish townspeople. "Oh, God, if sacrifice of life is needed, accept it from us who are free from family obligations and spare those who have wives and children in their care," one of the sisters told the priest. "We are even praying for this." In 1991, a process was begun to declare the women saints of the Catholic Church. On March 5, 2000, Pope John Paul II beatified the eleven women during a celebration in Rome, the penultimate step before canonization.

CHAPTER TEN: OCTOBER 1943–JANUARY 1944
The *puscha* camp was described in Shmuel Amarant's article "The Tuvia Bielski Partisan Company," included in *Pinkas Navaredok* (Memorial Book of Novogrudek) edited by E. Yerushalmi (1963, Alexander Harkavy Navareder Relief Committee in the USA and Israel), p. 333. Translation was provided for the author by Charles Ronen. Also helpful was *Partizanim (Partisans: The Story of a Jewish Partisan Brigade in the Forests of White Russia)* by Yehoshua Yaffe (1952, N. Tabarsky Books Inc.), ch. 8, and *Yehudai Yaar (Jews of the Forest): The Recollections of Tuvia and Zusya Bielski, Sonia and Lilka Bielski and Abraham Weiner as Recorded by Y. Ben-Dor* (1946, Om Oved), chs. 19, 20, translated from the Hebrew for the author by Charles Ronen. Interviews with survivors

Carmela Shamir (May 13, 2001, in Tel Aviv, Israel), Sol Lapidus (January 16, 2001, in Fort Lauderdale, Florida), Moshe and Pesia Beirach (May 13, 2001, in Tel Aviv, Israel), Gregori Chasid (July 10, 2001, by telephone from Grodno, Belarus), and Isak Pitluk (May 18, 2001, in Netanya, Israel) were also helpful.

Details about life in the Ordzhonikidze Detachment are included in *Yehudai Yaar,* ch. 17, and in both of Zus Bielski's Yad Vashem testimonies. Murray Kasten, an Ordzhonikidze fighter, also provided valuable information. The author has also relied on the extensive operational reports cited in the notes for chapter 8.

The detail about a partisan's desertion resulting in reprisals against the missing soldier's family is described in *Soviet Partisans in World War II,* edited by John A. Armstrong (1964, University of Wisconsin), p. 193.

Tuvia Bielski's dealings with the Soviet partisan leadership are described in great detail in *Yehudai Yaar,* chs. 20, 21. Many of his actions are corroborated by the Soviet documents cited in the notes for chapter 8. Platon's feelings about the utility of the Bielski base as a "quartermaster corps" are described in *The Minsk Ghetto: Soviet-Jewish Partisans Against the Nazis* by Hersh Smolar, a Jewish partisan who worked closely with General Platon (1989, Holocaust Library), p. 129.

The January 3, 1944, document signed by Platon is available in the Minsk archives (Fond 3500; Opus 1; File 244). It is also available in the Yad Vashem archives in Jerusalem (document M.41/126).

The attack on the Germans at the village of Vasilevitch was described to the author by several sources, including partisans from Viktor Panchenkov's detachment, Sergei Zhigalo and Nikolai Kostriminov. Viktor Panchenkov writes about the attack in his article "The October Detachment" printed in the book *V prinemanskikh lesakh (In the Forests Along the Neman River): Memoirs of Partisans and the Underground* (1975, Belarus Publishing). The operational report filed with partisan command was also very helpful, particularly in naming the German officer Kurt Fidler whose jacket Zus confiscated. It is in the Minsk archives (Fond 3618; Opus 1; File 30; Page 100). Zus speaks of the incident in *Yehudai Yaar,* ch. 17.

The quote from General Bor-Komorowski comes from *The Holocaust in Historical Perspective* by Yehuda Bauer (1978, University of Washington, Seattle), p. 58. The account of the White Pole serving in Novogrudek can be found in *The Unseen and Silent: Adventures from the Underground Movement Narrated by Paratroops of the Polish Home Army* translated from the Polish by George Iranek-Osmecki (1954, Sheed and Ward), pp. 141–157. The German document that speaks of "our agreements with Polish partisans" is included in the final reports of the Novogrudek Regional Commissar, written on July 27, 1944, and August 3, 1944. They are available in the Bundesarchiv, Berlin, Germany (document R93 13, pp. 138–148).

The Cossack presence in the Novogrudek area is described in *Cossacks in the German Army 1941–1945* by Samuel J. Newland (1991, Frank Cass and Co.), pp. 127–137. The information on Boris Ragula was gathered during an interview with Mr. Ragula and from his unpublished memoir, *Reflections from My Past,* loaned to the author by Mr. Ragula.

Viktor Panchenkov's letter to the Novogrudek Regional Commissar is on file at the Museum of Regional Studies in Novogrudek, Belarus. The translation was provided for the author by David Goldman.

CHAPTER ELEVEN: JANUARY 1944–JULY 1944

The quote from Isaac Mendelson comes from a videotaped interview conducted by Drs. Lester Eckman and Monty Noam Penkower of Touro College. The tape was loaned to the author by Dr. Eckman.

The Kessler killing was described to the author by several forest survivors, including Lilka Bielski, Haya (Bielski) Dziencielski, Beryl Chafetz (October 30, 2000, in Brighton, Massachusetts), Chaim Basist (May 9, 2001, in Tel Aviv, Israel), Meyer Bronicki, Jack Kagan, and Kessler's widow, Rachel (Rieff) Zyskind. Testimony from Kessler supporters is detailed in *Sefer Hapartizanim Hayehudim (The Jewish Partisan Book)* (1958, Sifraith Poalim, Hashomer Hatzair), pp. 457–460, translated from the Hebrew for the author by Rana Samuels. Among those who described the atmosphere in Kessler's camp before and after his death were survivors Isak and Genia Nowog.

The beating of Konstantin Koslovsky's son was described to the author by witnesses Irina Koslovsky and Taisija Dorozhkina.

The partisan document in which Tuvia describes the group as including 941 people is available in the Minsk archives (Fond 3500; Opus 4; File 241/2 and in the Yad Vashem archives in Jerusalem (M.41/124). The May Day celebration in the *puscha* is described in detail by witness Shmuel Amarant in "The Tuvia Bielski Partisan Company," included in *Pinkas Navaredok* (Memorial Book of Novogrudek) edited by E. Yerushalmi (1963, Alexander Harkavy Navareder Relief Committee in the USA and Israel). The idea that Ivan Shematovich was sent to the Bielski base because of Soviet concerns about the Kessler situation is mentioned in *The Minsk Ghetto: Soviet-Jewish Partisans Against the Nazis* by Hersh Smolar (1989, Holocaust Library), p. 129.

The speech of the partisan commander in preparation for the Nazi retreat was detailed by Isak Nowog during interviews with the author and in his unpublished memoir.

The killing of the captured Germans in the Bielski camp was described to the author by several people who observed it, including Genia Pinski, Leah Johnson (January 10, 2001, in Hallandale, Florida), Frieda Feit, Willy Moll, and Meyer Bronicki. Tuvia Bielski's final speech was quoted by Isak Nowog in his unpublished memoir.

Tuvia Bielski's quote regarding the killing on the last day in the forest—"I shot him without hesitation"—appears in *Yehudai Yaar (Jews of the Forest): The Recol-*

lections of Tuvia and Zusya Bielski, Sonia and Lilka Bielski and Abraham Weiner as Recorded by Y. Ben-Dor (1946, Om Oved), ch. 21, translated from Hebrew for the author by Charles Ronen. Shmuel Amarant's quote comes from his article "The Tuvia Bielski Partisan Company" in *Pinkas Navaredok.*

The final tally of survivors of Tuvia's Kalinin Detachment and Zus's Ordzhonikidze Detachment can be found in Soviet documents on file at the Minsk archives (Fond 3500; Opus 4; File 241/2, pp. 287, 288) and in the Yad Vashem archives in Jerusalem (M.41/124, pp. 28, 29).

The details about the life of Lola (Dziencielski) Kline were gleaned during an interview with Ms. Kline (August 6, 2001, in Freehold, New Jersey).

CHAPTER TWELVE: TO ISRAEL AND AMERICA

The history of the Ordzhonikidze Detachment is available in the Minsk archives (Fond 3618; Opus 1; File 23). Zus's personnel file is also located in the archives (Fond 3500; Opus 8; File 20). The history of the Kalinin Detachment (Tuvia's *puscha* group) is available in the Minsk (Fond 3500; Opus 4; File 272) and Yad Vashem archives (M.41/120).

The number of 50 dead during the time in the woods was cited in *Defiance: The Bielski Partisans* by Nechama Tec (1993, Oxford University Press), pp. 207–208.

The postwar lives of the Russian partisan leaders Chernyshev and Sinitchkin are described in the book *Navyechno v syerdtse narodnom (Forever in the Heart of the People)* (1984, Belorussian Soviet Encyclopedia). This book lists biographical information on those honored by the Hero of the Soviet Union award. The postwar lives of Gapayev, Vasilyev, and Panchenkov were described to the author by Viktor Panchenkov's widow, Nadezhda.

The date of Wilhelm Traub's death was provided to the author by Dr. Stefan Klemp, who operates a private archive connected to the Simon Wiesenthal Center of Jerusalem, Israel.

Zus Bielski's oral history interview, conducted on July 11, 1994, is available at the United States Holocaust Memorial Museum archives (RG-50.030*0024).

EPILOGUE

A videotape of the New York Hilton dinner honoring Tuvia Bielski was loaned to the author by Murray Kushner.

ACKNOWLEDGMENTS

During the course of my work on this book, I have relied on the kind assistance of scores of individuals throughout the world.

The widows of Tuvia, Asael, and Zus Bielski—Lilka, Haya, and Sonia—were extraordinarily generous with their time, willing to sit through hours upon hours of my questions. Each helped arrange interviews with other forest survivors and locate documents and photographs relating to their husbands' war experiences. It was a singular honor to have met them and been entrusted with telling their story. I regret that Lilka Bielski, who died in September 2001, was unable to see the publication of this book.

Aron (Bielski) Bell, the only surviving child of David and Beyle Bielski, was tremendously patient and helpful. He was always willing to discuss any aspect of the forest years, including the darkest days of his life—the events leading to the death of his parents. This work was greatly enhanced by his support.

The Bielski family—including the sons and daughters of Tuvia, Zus, Asael, Aron, and Taibe—were always ready to aid in my efforts. I must make particular note of the help of Assi Weinstein of Tel Aviv, Israel, the daughter of Haya and Asael, who translated hundreds of questions that I e-mailed for her mother, and Michael Bielski of Bonita Springs, Florida, the eldest son of Lilka and Tuvia, who opened up his personal archives and offered me everything that pertained to his parents. Also of great assistance were Zvi Bielski, one of Zus's sons, and Robert Bielski, Tuvia's younger son.

I will be forever indebted to the survivors of the Holocaust who shared their memories with me: Carmela Shamir, Moshe and Pesia Beirach, Pinchas Boldo, Luba Segal, Estelle (Bielski) Hershthal, Frieda Feit, Lea Friedberg, Willy Moll, Ike Bernstein, Beryl Chafetz, Meyer Bronicki, Gitel Morrison, Sol and Ruth Lapidus, Mike Stoll, Lola Kline, Sulia Rubin, Ignats Feldon, Ela Zamoschik, Gregori Chasid, Chaim Basist, Raya Kalmanovitz, Peretz Shorshaty, Isak Pitluk, Rachel Zyskind, Rivka Bernstein, Tamara Katz, Miriam Stepel, Genia Pinski, Tamar Amarant, Isak and Genia Nowog, Murray Kasten, Harry Finkelstein, Fay Druck, Rae Kushner, Charles Bedzow, Leah Johnson, Leah Kotler, Bella Goldfischer, Jack Kagan, Ann Monka, Sonya and Aaron Oshman, Michael and Naomi Lebowitz, Yehuda Levin, Esia Shor, Judi Ginsberg, Alexander Garelick, Arkady Teif, Lev Kravets, Sofia Zaleskaya, Michael Treyster, Pavel Rubinchik, and Lubov Abramovich.

Jack Kagan, a survivor of the Novogrudek ghetto and the Bielski *puscha* camp, provided me with a treasure trove of documents and testimonies that he gathered during the writing of his book about the war. A tireless researcher himself, Mr. Kagan was always eager to answer my questions and offer constructive suggestions. His aid was a godsend.

Tamara Vershitskaya of the Museum of Regional Studies in

Novogrudek provided priceless assistance during my travels in Belarus. Without her efforts as a translator, guide, and researcher, the quality of my work in Belarus would've been considerably poorer. Her daughter Olga, who also served as a translator for me, was a great help. As were Ekaterina Nechai, Nikolai Puchilo, and Alexander Tsaruk.

Translators Hilah Ronen, Daphne Algom, and Assi Weinstein were invaluable during my interviews with survivors in Israel.

Charles Ronen, David Goldman, Irene Newhouse, Judie Ostroff-Goldstein, James Loeffler, Tina Lunson, Rita Falbel, and Rana Samuels did exceptional work translating items from the Yiddish, Hebrew, German, and Russian into English.

Barbara Serfozo recovered many useful documents from Nazi archives in Germany. Jill Berry was a transcriber par excellence, Seth Kaufman provided vital computer help, and Jeffrey Cuyubamba offered crucial photo and map support.

Dr. Lester Eckman of Touro College, a longtime friend of Tuvia and Zus Bielski and the author of important works on Jewish resistance, gave indispensable assistance and advice throughout the length of this project. For decades, he has taught the story of the Bielski partisans in his classes on the Holocaust. His dedication to the memory of the brothers was an inspiration to me.

Other scholarly help was provided by Leonid Smilovitsky of the Diaspora Institute of Research of Tel Aviv University, Martin Dean of the United States Holocaust Memorial Museum, and David Meltser, formerly a professor of history at the Belorussian State University. Thanks also to Jerrold Schecter, Zach Levin, Mark Stamey, Janon Fisher, Andrew Page, John Stamey, Patrick Weaver, Frank Flaherty, Miriam Kuperstock, John Driscoll, Jon

Hart, Dennis Heaphy, Joe Fodor, Frank Shattuck, and Alan Goldberg.

This book would not have been written without the encouragement of Connie Rosenblum of the *New York Times*, who edited the article I wrote about the Bielski brothers for the newspaper in May 2000, and without the tireless advocacy of my agent, Mary Evans. My editor at HarperCollins, Dan Conaway, helped bring focus and precision to the finished text. His enthusiasm for the project sustained me through the more than two years that it took to finish the job.

My wife, Laura, has been a constant source of love and support. Without her, none of this would've been worth it.